POLICY GOVERNANCE IN MULTI-LEVEL SYSTEMS

Policy Governance in Multi-level Systems

Economic Development and Policy Implementation in Canada

CHARLES CONTEH

McGill-Queen's University Press
Montreal & Kingston • London • Ithaca

ISBN 978-0-7735-4120-7 (cloth)
ISBN 978-0-7735-4121-4 (paper)

Legal deposit second quarter 2013
Bibliothèque nationale du Québec

Printed in Canada on acid-free paper that is 100% ancient forest free (100% post-consumer recycled), processed chlorine free

This book has been published with the help of a grant from the Canadian Federation for the Humanities and Social Sciences, through the Awards to Scholarly Publications Program, using funds provided by the Social Sciences and Humanities Research Council of Canada. Funding has also been received from Brock University.

McGill-Queen's University Press acknowledges the support of the Canada Council for the Arts for our publishing program. We also acknowledge the financial support of the Government of Canada through the Canada Book Fund for our publishing activities.

Library and Archives Canada Cataloguing in Publication

Conteh, Charles, 1974–

Policy governance in multi-level systems : economic development and policy implementation in Canada / Charles Conteh.

Includes bibliographical references and index.
ISBN 978-0-7735-4120-7 (bound). –
ISBN 978-0-7735-4121-4 (pbk.)

1. Economic development – Government policy – Canada. 2. Canada – Economic policy – 21st century. 3. Canada – Economic conditions – 21st century. 4. Public-private sector cooperation – Canada. I. Title.

HC113.C6559 2013 338.971 C2012-907640-6

Typeset by Jay Tee Graphics Ltd. in 10.5/13 Sabon

Contents

Figures and Tables

FIGURES

TABLES

Foreword

This book, which is about regional economic development in Canada, is comprehensive in its theoretical scope and empirical depth. It analyzes the history of government experiences at trying to stimulate economic development in some of the economically challenged parts of Canada. The major descriptive focus is on detailed case studies of current initiatives for economic development in four areas of Canada: New Brunswick, Manitoba, Northern Ontario, and Southern Ontario. But the book is not just about these regions; the author considers economic development and, even more so, regional economic development to be a "generic challenge worldwide." He takes as a basic assumption that in even the most liberal economies the history of economic development has included state involvement in some major way. But he suggests that the Canadian experience with a long history of policy experimentation in the policy sphere of regional economic development holds valuable lessons for academics and practitioners in other countries.

Three things, in particular, set this book apart from other studies. In the first place it reflects the author's own background. Many studies of regional development are carried out by academics or consultants whose primary frame of reference is a national stage, and in the case of Canada, a background in Canadian politics and political economy. Professor Conteh's early academic training was in international relations and international development. Within the area of public policy and administration, his earliest focus, his PHD dissertation, was a comparative study of the success of state-led, or state-facilitated, development in Singapore and Botswana. Thus, he has been able to apply a wider theoretical context to this study than might be the norm.

Second, in addition to focusing on the theoretical literatures of governance and policy implementation, he has added a third dimension with the application of organization theory, particularly with inter-organizational-complexity and open-systems approaches, which allow him to consider economic development as a multi-actor series of interactions involving participants from a wide range of sectors – public, non-governmental and private, along with various hybrid groups. This approach varies from the more standard one adopted within a federal state of looking at policy from a largely federal-provincial (or national/sub-national) perspective. Finally, he focuses on the field delivery and implementation of development initiatives. A large portion of his interviews were with the field participants actually trying to implement the various initiatives. The emphasis is on the community-driven aspects of development: the needs of the community are a major concern, as is what actually gets done, as opposed to what is planned or what is supposed to be done.

The choice of the case studies is also interesting. Three of the units studied are relatively low in population (Manitoba, New Brunswick, and Northern Ontario), two are self-contained provincial units (Manitoba and New Brunswick), and two are relatively sparsely populated (Manitoba and Northern Ontario). All share the problem of the lack of, or the loss of, well-paying jobs during a period of global restructuring, the need for infrastructure investment and a dependency on outside economic forces for markets, and the necessity of no longer being able to rely only on domestic industries. Only Southern Ontario is not a largely resource-based economy, and the addition of Southern Ontario to the cases broadens the concept of regional development, since it was traditionally the powerhouse of the Canadian economy but has been badly hit by changes in the industrial and manufacturing base of Canada and North America. These cases with their similarities and differences also allow for a more rigorous comparative analysis.

It is too early to tell from statistics the extent to which these initiatives will be successful, and given the nature of the counterfactuals involved, it may never be possible to do so. But as the economics of transportation changes the cost structures of some industries, there is reason to hope that the organizational framework that has been put in place and the existence of raw materials and nearby markets in North America will become a comparative advantage for these regions. There do, however, seem to be some lessons common to the multi-governance implementation models adopted in the four regions, and the extent to which they are adhered to might help to explain the long-term success (or failure) of each region.

The first lesson is to be realistic and somewhat incremental in policy development and implementation, rather than developing grandiose schemes. A second is to focus on local interactive-based approaches that can foster the development of trust ties among the multiple parties, regardless of their formal institutional affiliations. A third is to place a heavy emphasis on coordination and cooperation – not knowing who is doing what and jurisdictional squabbles have always created problems in this field. Finally, there is a need for flexibility. The very fact that each region has used a slightly different institutional framework and a model of organizational interaction reflecting unique needs of the region is encouraging. In some cases there is more emphasis on existing institutions, as with ACOA in New Brunswick. In others, new frameworks have been developed, as in Southern Ontario and in Manitoba, where there is more reliance on contractual solutions.

The intended audience of this book extends beyond Canadian borders. A sample of the targeted audience would include scholars of public policy and public administration in Canada and other advanced industrialized countries; advanced undergraduate and graduate students in public policy, public administration, economic development, and comparative politics; and public servants in Canada and other industrialized systems. Researchers in public policy think tanks and non-governmental agencies will also find the book helpful for understanding the growing complexity of public policy governance in multi-actor settings. And finally, grassroots policy activists wishing to understand the interactions between globalization and local policy ownership will find the book to be an asset.

It has given me great pleasure to write the foreword to this book, which makes a considerable contribution to our understanding both of multi-level and multi-actor governance and of the intricacies of regional economic development in a time of global economic restructuring and change.

Barbara Wake Carroll
Adjunct Professor, Department of Political Science
Editor, *Canadian Public Administration*
Professor Emeritus, McMaster University

Acknowledgments

I would like to acknowledge the support of all those who in various ways have contributed to the successful completion of this book. I wish first and foremost to thank my wife, Sharmila, daughter, Hannah, and son, Jesse, for their immense patience and unconditional love throughout those countless hours of self-imposed solitary confinement in my study and at work away from home conducting research. I am also indebted to the Social Sciences and Humanities Research Council (SSHRC) of Canada for funding this book project. I really could not have done it without SSHRC's financial support, which enabled me to travel to the various provinces and regions to collect the data I needed.

I should also acknowledge the support of some truly great and selfless colleagues, mentors, and friends – Professor B. Carroll (who kindly agreed to write the foreword of this book), Professor D. Siegel, and Professor K. Kernaghan – all of whom invested their precious time in making specific comments on portions of the manuscript. (I should ask for Professor Kernaghan's forgiveness for possibly destroying his Florida vacation by sending him a sizeable copy of my manuscript for his comments within a limited time frame.) I am no less thankful to my graduate research assistant, A. Monteiro, for her diligent research support, and to my editor, J.E. Field, for his candid critique and keen attention to details – he must be relieved finally to be left alone! No less gratitude is reserved for D. Krynicki, who always provides tremendous administrative assistance with her usual great sense of humour and seemingly inexhaustible patience. The same thanks should be extended to my colleagues, Dr I. Roberge and Dr F. Ohemeng, for their comments, support, and friendship during our various meetings at many conferences. In a similar vein,

I should also thank my many fellow panelists at the annual conferences of the International Research Society for Public Management (IRSPM), the Trans-Atlantic Dialogue (TAD), the Institute of Public Administration of Canada (IPAC), and the Canadian Political Science Association (CPSA). I received many comments and much invaluable feedback during my presentations of various chapters of this manuscript at these international and national academic (and practitioner) forums between 2009 and 2011. Cantankerous but well-meaning friends are priceless assets that every serious researcher must pray and endeavour to have – they force you to think twice (sometimes more) about every observation you make. My hope is that I have returned (and will continue to return) the favour.

The most fervent expression of gratitude is reserved for the interviewees in the public sector and in a number of non-governmental and private sector organizations who contributed their valuable experiences and insight to this book. For reasons of respect for confidentiality, their names cannot be mentioned, but they endured my harassment and sometimes erratic schedule with patience and a willingness to avail me of their valuable time. Without their expertise and support, this book would not have been possible.

Acronyms

ABC	Aboriginal Business Canada
ABSN	Aboriginal Business Services Network
ACOA	Atlantic Canada Opportunities Agency
ADM	Association of District Municipalities
Agric-Canada	Agriculture and Agri-Food Canada
AIF	Atlantic Innovation Fund
ANA	Ministry of Aboriginal and Northern Affairs
ARDA	Agricultural and Rural Development Act
ARDI	Agri-Food Research and Development Initiative
ARRG	Agricultural and Rural Restructuring Group
BNB	Business New Brunswick
CAF	Community Adjustment Fund
CBSA	Canada Border Services Agency
CDEM	Conseil de développement économique des municipalités bilingues du Manitoba
CED	Community Economic Development
CFDC	Community Futures Development Corporation
CFP	Community Futures Program
CMA	Census Metropolitan Areas
CME	Canadian Manufacturers and Exporters
CPSA	Canadian Political Science Association
CRA	Canada Revenue Agency
CRRF	Canadian Rural Restructuring Foundation
CTT	Canada's Technology Triangle Inc
DFAIT	Department of Foreign Affairs and International Trade
DMCI	Downtown Moncton Centre-ville Inc
DREE	Department of Regional Economic Expansion

DRIE	Department of Regional Industrial Expansion
EAP	Economic Action Plan
EDC	City of Toronto's Economic Development & Culture Division
EDC	Export Development Canada
EDI	Economic Development Initiative
EDW	Economic Development Winnipeg Inc.
ERDA	Economic and Regional Development Agreement
FCC	Fredericton Chamber of Commerce
FedDev	Federal Economic Development Agency for Southern Ontario
FedNor	Federal Economic Development Initiative for Northern Ontario
FONOM	Federation of Northern Ontario Municipalities
FORD-Q	Not defined specifically in text, other than as the agency for Northern Quebec
FRED	Fund for Rural Economic Development
GDA	General Development Agreement
ICF	Innovative Communities Fund
ICT	Information and Communications Technologies Sector
IMRIS	Innovative Magnetic Resonance Imaging Systems
INAC	Indian and Northern Affairs
MAC	Municipal Advisory Committee
MAFRI	Ministry of Agriculture, Food and Rural Initiatives
MEDT	Ministry of Economic Development and Trade
MEPA	Canada-Manitoba Economic Partnership Agreement
MID	Moncton Industrial Development
MNDM	Ontario Ministry of Northern Development and Mines
MNDMF	Ontario Ministry of Northern Development, Mines, and Forestry
MNR	Ontario Ministry of Natural Resources
MRI	Ministry of Research and Innovation
MSERD	Ministry of State for Regional and Economic Development
MTPG	Moncton Technology Planning Group
NAC	Northern Advisory Committee
NBIF	New Brunswick Innovation Foundation
NDS	Northern Development Strategy
NEDC	Niagara Economic Development Corporation
NEDF	Northern Economic Development Fund

NOACC	Northwestern Ontario Associated Chambers of Commerce
NOCC	Northern Ontario Chambers of Commerce
NODP	Northern Ontario Development Program
NOHFC	Northern Ontario Heritage Fund Corporation
NOMA	Northwestern Municipal Association
OCRIF	Ontario-China Research and Innovation Fund
OECD	Organisation for Economic Co-operation and Development
OLMC	Official Languages Minority Communities
OTR	Ontario Ministry of Transportation
PEAC	Premier's Economic Advisory Council
RDC	Regional Development Corporation
REA	Rural Entrepreneur Assistance Guarantees
REAP	Rural Entrepreneur Assistance Program
REDI	Rural Economic Development Initiatives
REDO	Regional Economic Development Organization
RInC	Recreational Infrastructure Canada
SME	Small and medium-sized enterprises
WD	Western Economic Diversification Agency
WEPA	Western Economic partnership Agreement

POLICY GOVERNANCE IN MULTI-LEVEL SYSTEMS

1

Introduction

This book analyzes the transitions in the governance of public policy in multi-level systems within the context of increasing global socioeconomic restructuring over the past two decades. The implications of these transitions are examined with a focus on major changes in Canada's controversial but resilient regional economic development policy. The problem of economic development presents a generic challenge worldwide. Even resource-rich regions in developed and developing countries struggle to adapt to seismic global economic perturbations, as well as to reach or maintain a sustainable level of economic growth. Canada has had a long tradition of seeking to alleviate the socioeconomic disadvantages of less-developed regions through various mechanisms of economic development policy intervention. The critical difference over the past two decades has been that regional economies around the world have been part of a globally integrated system of continual transformation as new markets, new technologies, and new opportunities constantly emerge. Within this context of a rapidly changing world, regions and communities are under immense pressure to position themselves for success and, sometimes, survival by making better use of their existing potential competitive advantages.

In this regard, past and present trends in the research on and practice of public administration and policy partly reflect global trends and a country's political culture. Through mirroring current trends, some of the emergent themes in public administration research and practice focus on issues such as partnership, networks, collaboration, and horizontal management. In the current age of increasing complexity and profoundly dynamic change, the practice of public administration in Canada and around the world is characterized by processes of mutual adjustment between public and non-governmental agencies bound by shared rules and norms that constrain behaviour, as well as provide incentives for collective policy action. This means that the implicit assumptions of conventional public administration, which view public agencies as passive, "objective" cogs in a bureaucratic machine must be rejected. Public servants from various echelons of the civil service are often active policy entrepreneurs, moral agents, conveyors of contestable value frames, and engaged citizens with subjective perceptions and vested interests in preferred policy outcomes. Public organizations (including ministries, departments, agencies, and corporations) leverage and even exploit shared rules and norms, rather than mindlessly accepting subjugation to the dictates of institutions.

A key objective of this volume is to answer some questions about public administration implementation that reflect the complexities of the operating environment of policy implementation. Although public management should be best understood as inextricably bound to and influenced by the institutional conditions, it is equally, if not more, influenced by the nature of social interactions within a given operating environment. Public management scholarship and practice should thus be viewed through the lens of dynamic interactions, iterations, and the subjective value frames of policy actors within and outside the public sector, rather than through purely legalistic or technical assumptions about administrative structures and institutions.

Public policy governance in complex multi-level policy systems is increasingly concerned with strategic partnerships and network models of service-delivery innovation and reform. In economic development policy governance, for instance, the emphasis is on strategic partnerships that facilitate inter-jurisdictional and inter-organizational co-operation through which governments solve socioeconomic problems or commission innovation aimed at productivity and economic development. While such network models of policy governance are becoming ubiquitous, the critical objective of research becomes partly an appreciation for the "politics" of these partnerships and partly an understanding of the requisites of effective management of these dynamic inter-organizational relationships.

The discussion focuses mainly, therefore, on the complexities of public policy implementation in multi-level systems. One of the key characteristics that sets this book apart from other works on this subject is that it uses the multi-actor implementation framework as its tool for the analysis of regional economic development. The multi-actor implementation framework advanced in this book draws insights from public policy, inter-organizational theory, network analysis, and governance literature. The value of an integrated approach is that pulling together these theoretical traditions can connect the missing link between politics, institutions, and administration. It is concerned with understanding the nature of the interaction and exchange between organized policy stakeholders from various levels of government, as well as from the private sector and from society more generally. Policy implementation research is undergoing a conceptual transformation in favour of focusing on concerted action across institutional boundaries. In this way, one notices a broadening of perspective on implementation to a multi-disciplinary, multi-level, and multi-foci exercise (by looking at a multiplicity of actors, loci, and levels) (Lindquist 2006; O'Toole 2000). This book intentionally integrates these insights into a holistic framework of policy implementation in multi-level systems, which entails drawing from the strengths of apparently divergent theoretical perspectives and reframing the discourse into an integrated concern about public policy governance in complex systems.

Three considerations are factored into the present analysis. First, it pays attention to vertical and horizontal inter-jurisdictional cooperation in joint policy action. Second, it recognizes the multiplicity of interpretive lenses among agents, including the perceptions and values of non-governmental stakeholders and the strategic outreach of public agencies to these groups. And third, it traces the various stages of evolving networks, noting the changes and adaptations characterizing the processes involved in joint policy actions, such as the emergent governance of modern regional economic systems. This book, therefore, views collaborative governance arrangements as complex mechanisms of policy implementation operating within and across layers of government, as well as between the public and non-governmental sectors, and as mechanisms that are constantly evolving over time.

CONTEXT

Global trends over the past two decades have created apparent contradictions or paradoxes in which a globalized world with integrated markets coexists with a greater desire on the part of sub-national jurisdictions, including local communities, to find their own niche as the classical tools of the central state are proving inadequate to foster economic competitiveness and performance. Regional development policy has been reflecting these trends as discussions have metamorphosed into preoccupations with local development in which communities and regions strive to become dynamic clusters of learning and innovation linked to global value chains. A significant corollary of these trends, therefore, is the shift in the focus of regional development towards what is generally referred to as "innovation" policy (OECD 2009).

But regional economic development as a policy domain is not new. For example, the economic history of Canada, which is based on a staples system, means that the Canadian state has tended to maintain strong elements of interventionism in its approach to national development (Nelles 2005). In social policy, such interventionism has crystallized into a gradual transition to collectivism: its most recent manifestation over the past five decades has been a developed welfare state (Brooks and Miljan 2003). In economic development policy, a key example of active policy intervention in society has been the government's effort to correct structural imbalances in industrial diversity and growth among Canada's regions (Careless 1977). From its humble beginnings in the creation of a number of uncoordinated boards and agencies in the early 1960s, regional development policy has become an enduring feature of public policy and governance in Canada.

Some of the major theoretical considerations surrounding regional economic development date back to the "growth pole" concept of the 1960s (Economic Council of Canada 1977). Over the decades since the 1960s, Canada (like other OECD countries) has experimented with various models, such as the "development approach of the 1970s" (Savoie 1986; OECD 1997). Although regional economic development in the industrialized world dates back to the 1960s, the present institutional configuration of regional economic development policy governance in Canada came into existence through a major restructuring in 1987 in which the federal government created three regional development agencies for Western Canada, Atlantic Canada, and Northern Ontario, namely, the Western Economic Diversification Agency (WD), the Atlantic Canada Opportunities Agency (ACOA) and the Federal Economic Initiative for Northern Ontario (FedNor), respectively. The agency FORD-Q was eventually created in 1991 for Northern Quebec. In 2009 the Federal Economic Development Agency for Southern Ontario (FedDev) was established.

The 1987 restructuring was considered to be a response in part to the administrative and political discontent expressed by the provinces with respect to the centralized administration of regional development. The rationale was that decentralization of regional development to agencies whose mandates focus directly on particular regions (and provinces) could enhance the capacity for closer federal-provincial cooperation, thereby resulting in greater responsiveness to local economic development initiatives. Over the past two decades, however, regional development policy governance in Canada has undergone some noticeable changes that coincided with movements toward a highly integrated global economy; a new focus on emerging priority economic sectors such as advanced manufacturing, the digital economy, and renewable energy; and the decentralization of governance institutions as the best mechanism for managing the "new economy."

Since the 1987 restructuring, a few scholars have examined the activities of these specially mandated federal agencies for industrial assistance and business support programs in "socioeconomically disadvantaged regions." However, no systematic effort has been made to analyze the changing instruments and strategies of policy intervention in light of the structural transformations in the Canadian and global economy over the past two decades. It would seem, therefore, that the modern institutional and policy configuration of regional economic development in Canada needs a proper re-examination.

Regional economic development policy is an intrinsically multidimensional or inter-disciplinary field of study. Comprehensive research would include certain political, economic, and administrative considerations. Although this book highlights and examines the political and administrative dimensions of regional development policy implementation, such a discussion would be incomplete without a basic understanding of the underlying theories of economic development. The theoretical framework that guides the analysis here, therefore, covers both the substantive policy of regional economic development as well as theories of public policy implementation in multi-level systems.

This book analyzes the transitions in regional economic development policy in Canada and focuses on changes in the provinces of New Brunswick, Manitoba, Northern Ontario, and Southern Ontario. (Northern Ontario and Southern Ontario are each given distinct chapters because of the fundamentally different characters of the two regions). Although initially formulated as a policy framework for correcting economic disparities among Canada's disparate regions, the present context of regional economic development in the four regions can be referred to as moving towards collaborative governance of innovation policy as the focus shifts towards promoting emerging priority economic sectors. Increasingly, this approach involves the various orders of government, along with the inclusion of non-state actors such as business, industry, and community groups. The four cases illustrate how policy governance within such a context can be viewed as increasingly strategic, rather than merely operational.

In particular, economic development policy governance within a globally integrated market system has come to reflect the new context of regional development (OECD 2007). This new focus distinguishes between what are called the "old" and the "new" paradigms of economic development in terms of the policy rationale, the strategy and tools of policy intervention, and the key actors involved (OECD 2009). While the old paradigm focused on providing advantages for domestic industries, the new paradigm tends to be nondiscriminatory as attention shifts towards enhancing regional global competitiveness. Moreover, the strategy of the old paradigm focused on a sectoral or, even, individual-firm approach, whereas the new paradigm is more integrated and cross-sectoral, focusing on the innovative capacities of regions within the global economy.

Innovations leading to economic growth and development thrive in systems where high levels of interaction and collaboration take place among economic and community stakeholders. At the centre of such a policy environment are social clusters of knowledge production, dissemination, and utilization facilitated by interaction through local networks and relationships. Thus, the shift in emphasis towards innovation means more decentralized governance frameworks as the most conducive mechanisms of public management. The aforementioned ideational and structural changes mean that economic development policy governance is becoming more diverse and complex.

Current policy discussions about regional economic development in Canada and other OECD countries draw extensively from the emergent discourse on regional clusters of knowledge economies (OECD 2009). The knowledge economy suggests that with the right mix of strategic intervention and market rationality, any region has the potential to become a productive centre, cluster, or node within the globally integrated economy (Ministry of Finance, Canada 2006). The proposed strategies for consideration usually focus on creating a "networked regional economy" by capitalizing on certain physical and human capital strengths, among other things. This emergent framework is referred to as the "new regionalism" (OECD 2009; Public Policy Forum 2007).

Regional economic development policy in Canada is currently influenced and guided by the above ideas of "networked regional economies." This book, therefore, analyzes Canada's experimentation with various models of regional economic development, paying particular attention to the policy and institutional implications of the most recent paradigm of regional economic development in an age of increasingly knowledge-based economic systems and unprecedented international competition. The evidence suggests that more and more the role of government is to serve as a facilitator or enabler of community-driven processes of economic adaptation. Within this context, regional economic development is no longer merely about redistribution or equalization among regions, but about a strategic vision focused on investing in the globally oriented, innovation-related assets of each region in Canada. For instance, this is the rationale behind the recent creation of FedDev (Government of Canada 2009c).

As the rest of the discussion illustrates, the imperatives of the new economy require a reconceptualization of regional economic development policy governance in Canada and in other multi-level governance systems. First, it calls for policy alignment across levels of government through the development of frameworks of policy governance giving a central importance to "place," not only as a geographical construct but also as an institutional construct. Second, it requires horizontal collaborative governance between the public, private, and community sectors where the private sector in particular regions can be seen less as comprised of objects of economic development and more as comprised of agents of adaptation to global and local changes. In this emerging context of economic development policy, this book analyzes the capacity and legitimacy of Canada's federalist architecture of public policy management in light of the increasingly complex dimensions of economic development policy governance.

IMPLICATIONS OF THE DISCUSSION

While the discussion focuses on Canada, the cases illustrate similar processes of public policy governance in multi-level systems beyond Canada's borders. The complexity of modern political and economic environments means that public policy governance could be better viewed as a process of navigating institutional boundaries rather than simply optimizing program output. The effectiveness of policy governance in such settings requires the ability of managers to make connections across levels of government and outside government and to share ideas, resources, and power with public and non-state actors.

The implications of this discussion for public policy and management theory are threefold. First, the present approach views concepts such as strategic planning and performance management as instruments of feedback and self-regulation. They serve strategic purposes often geared towards organizational learning and adaptation in complex environments. Second, the discussion emphasizes the importance of building coalitions of strategic alliances in successfully managing the many dependencies that are a natural and necessary component of delivering services or implementing policies operating in highly politicized and dynamic environments. Third, this book argues that public policy governance intrinsically consists of finding and sustaining a good fit between public agencies' mission and strategies, internal systems and structures, and the forces in their external environment that create opportunities and threats.

The practical implications of the discussion for policy actors and public managers operating within complex inter-jurisdictional and inter-organizational policy environments are as follows. First, policy governance entails a proactive rather than reactive approach to an agency's interaction with its external environment. Second, the public manager or policy actor needs to continuously discover trends and identify opportunities, as well as anticipate future problems. Third, public agencies tend to use systematic approaches in identifying issues and establishing organizational priorities. Fourth, public agencies build the requisite expertise in forecasting, strategy development, and constant evaluation. Fifth, policy governance involves expanding the range of interaction between public agencies and stakeholders, and sixth, operating in complex network systems requires the active involvement of top management in close interaction with front line staff for the development and implementation of successful response strategies. Such a close interaction between top management and front line staff allows for more accurate and precise boundary-scanning and boundary-spanning strategies, thereby allowing agencies to systematically monitor environmental forces and identify issues and trends.

In a nutshell, this book examines the extent to which the complexity of modern public policy environments means that public policy governance should be viewed as navigating institutional boundaries, rather than as simply optimizing program output. Moreover, it assesses the value of the proposition that the effectiveness of policy governance in such settings requires the ability of public managers to make connections across levels of government and outside government and to share ideas, resources, and power with public and non-state actors. Furthermore, it examines the critical factors that influence the success of adaptive regions, such as the presence of local champions, institutional intermediaries, equitable participation, a dynamic and creative civic culture, and the availability of financial and technical resources. Finally, but not least, the book argues that the increasing role of local regions in public policy governance does not necessarily translate into greater adaptive capacity for such regions, since capacities are a function of the institutional structures of inter-jurisdictional and inter-organizational governance in multi-level systems such as Canada.

METHODOLOGY AND SIGNIFICANCE

Methodology

As mentioned, this book analyzes the transitions in regional economic development policy in Canada with a focus on developments in New Brunswick, Manitoba, Northern Ontario, and Southern Ontario. These four cases have been chosen because they are drawn from the generally recognized regions of Canada – namely, Atlantic Canada, Western Canada, and Central Canada, respectively. While each case may not perfectly represent its region, nevertheless, as will be illustrated in subsequent chapters, the cases are microcosmic reflections of broader forces of economic and political change in the regions and in Canada as a whole. Moreover, each region has been assigned a federal regional development agency (each with similar mandates), which provides an interesting context for a comparative analysis of organizational adaptation to environmental complexity and change. Furthermore, as maintained earlier, while the discussion focuses on Canada, the cases illustrate similar processes of public policy governance in multi-level systems beyond Canada's borders. By focusing on Canada, however, the analysis taps into Canada's long, controversial, and rich history of regional economic development policy and contested federalism to illustrate the complexity of public policy governance in multi-level systems in an age of increasing globalization.

Using the analytical framework discussed in the previous section, this book employs a number of data collection methods to analyze the transitions in regional economic development policy governance in Canada over the past two decades. The data has been collected over a period of four years (2008–11) by a combination of semi-structured interviews, reviews of primary (mostly government) documents, and process tracing. The semi-structured interviews were conducted with over eighty officials (high-level, mid-level, and front line) drawn primarily from public sector agencies, private sector associations, and relevant community groups in the four regions. Not all the interviews were directly referenced in the discussion, but together they provided considerable insight that enriched the analysis of the cases. Each of the interviews took an average of one hour and consisted of questions relating to the mandate of the interviewee's organization, key programs, critical implementing partners, and how the interviewee's roles and strategies might be changing over time in light of possible changes in their operating environments.

The review of primary documents provides some measure of triangulation with the semi-structured interviews through an examination of policy and program documents of the agencies for evidence or indications of changes in their policy implementation goals and strategies over time. The primary government documents include annual departmental "Performance Reports" as well as "Reports on Plans and Priorities" to the Treasury Board Secretariat of Canada. Other policy documents reviewed for this book include departmental "Strategic Outcomes" and "Corporate Business Plans." Weaving these documents together provides significant "footprints" of the agencies' changing program priorities and operational strategies over the years. They also contain useful information about the agencies' perceptions of their operating environments, including economic and market trends, emerging sectors, and potential partners, as well as opportunities and risks. Moreover, the main websites of each of the agencies contain fact sheets about key program activities, targeted sectors and groups, links to funded studies and reports, and names of important partners.

The method of process tracing is often used to complement comparative case study methods, such as the one used in this book (Checkel 2005; Ford et al. 1989; Schulte-Mecklenbeck et al. 2011). In the present case, the two methods of data collection are combined to apply and further develop the integrated framework postulated in this book. Through process tracing, I extracted all the observable implications of the analytical framework based on the large body of insights and anecdotes provided by the interviews and policy document reviews. This process enabled the construction of a narrative and analysis of the strategic adaptation of public agencies to the imperatives of their operating environments.

Significance

This book raises critical issues about our understanding of policy implementation in multi-level systems. Understanding and appreciating the changing contours of policy implementation in multi-level systems is particularly relevant for policy actors and scholars in federal systems. But more than that, this understanding also applies to regional contexts such as the European Union, where the institutions of policy governance (including economic, social, and environmental policies) are increasingly approximating a federalist infrastructure. Even in unitary systems, such as Britain, the increasing decentralization of policy implementation is leading to stronger sub-national jurisdictions, which are creating contexts of intergovernmental complexity unseen in previous years.

Moreover, this book draws attention to the fact that global economic integration is creating both new opportunities and new threats for multi-level governance for nations – federal or unitary. There is an inextricable link between localized policy governance and global complexity. The issues of public policy governance in globally integrated societies and economies primarily involve addressing the perennial challenges of coordination among agencies and navigation of institutional boundaries between the public and the private, and domestically and internationally. Public policy governance in the complexity of a highly integrated global economy, therefore, is not only technical but also political and institutional. Policy governance and public management are, more than ever, about synchronizing the activities of public agencies within the same level of government and with other levels of government, as well as with international and domestic non-state actors.

Finally, the book draws attention to the fact that while Canada's ability to fully exploit the opportunities of integrated global economic systems requires national political and policy oversight, it does not presuppose top-down directives, as has been the tendency in Canada (Roy 2007). As I illustrate in the context of regional economic development, the endogenous nature of dynamic clusters of innovation in emerging priority economic sectors (clusters consisting of knowledge production, dissemination, application, and commercialization) is more conducive to locally driven adaptation to bottom-up processes of policy governance in identifying and pursuing new opportunities and confronting the challenges of economic change in a fast-changing world. The lessons drawn from regional economic development policy implementation in Canada, therefore, serve as an empirical basis for further improving our understanding of the complexities surrounding the world-wide challenges of public policy governance in globally integrated multi-level systems.

UNIQUENESS AND STRUCTURE

Uniqueness

This book is distinct from the works of several scholars who have attempted to analyze regional development policy in Canada. For instance, the most widely referenced Canadian authority in the field is Donald Savoie (1986, 1992, 1997, 2003). His work has covered the history of federal-provincial collaboration in regional economic development but generally focuses on the pre-2000 era, with a greater emphasis on the 1960s to the mid-1990s. The present book argues that significant trends toward globalization accelerated around the mid-1990s and that these transitions have fundamentally altered the character of regional economic development in Canada and around the world.

Other notable scholars in the field include Anthony Careless (1977), Harley McGee (1995), Raymond Blake (2003), and Frances Abele (2006). While their works have shed considerable light on our understanding of regional economic development in Canada, they tend to be focused on particular regions, mostly Atlantic Canada (or the Northern Territories, in the case of Frances Abele). For this book I purposefully selected four regional agencies, covering provinces from Central Canada, Western Canada, and Atlantic Canada. Moreover, the analyses and conclusions of the above-mentioned scholars tend to have a domestic orientation and make little or no effort to project Canada's lessons to a wider international audience. This book undertakes a thorough policy and institutional analysis of regional economic development in Canada, but it also uses the Canadian case to illustrate emergent trends of public policy governance in globally integrated multi-level systems. It therefore projects Canada's changing experience with regional economic development onto the international debates about the value propositions and tensions of the new regionalism in an age of global economic integration.

The book is also distinct in its analytical framework. Other scholars in the field have either focused on econometric analysis (see Mario Polese 1999; Mintz and Smart 2003; Desjardin 2002) or statistical analysis of demographic and structural trends in Canada's disadvantaged regions (see Southcott 2006; Bollman et al. 2006). The present book is interdisciplinary, combining analytical frameworks drawn from economics, political science, organization theory, and the emergent subfield of public policy. Moreover, the book draws from analytical frameworks in international relations about the phenomenon of globalization and its interaction with domestic policy processes and institutions. It also draws from the literature on federalism and the emerging framework of multi-level governance (especially the European Union's model).

Structure of the Book

This book is structured according to the following format: the next two chapters provide the analytical framework. Chapter 2 provides an analytical framework of public policy governance in multi-level systems, integrating insights drawn from policy implementation research, organization theory, and the new governance literature. This chapter also explains the relevance of this framework – referred to here as the multi-actor implementation framework – for understanding the challenges and prospects of public policy governance in complex and dynamic systems. Chapter 3 provides an overview of economic development theories and approaches, with a particular focus on what is referred to as the new regionalism in knowledge-driven economies. Chapter 4 contains a brief historical sketch of regional economic development in Canada. Since much work on the history of this controversial but resilient policy has already been done by other scholars, the purpose of this chapter is to provide the historical context for the present discussion about the emerging prospects of economic development policy intervention in highly dynamic knowledge-based and globally integrated economies.

The next four chapters (5 through 8) then examine each of the four federal economic development agencies selected for this book by analyzing the adaptation of their mandates, strategies, instruments, and processes of policy implementation in Canada's complex federal system over the past two decades. Chapter 5 focuses on the Atlantic Canada Opportunities Agency (ACOA) in New Brunswick. This case study forms the longest of the four chapters because, in addition to introducing most of the programs used by the agencies, it also provides the context and rationale for these programs. In order to avoid unnecessary repetition, therefore, chapters 6 through 8 exclude some of the descriptive details found in chapter 5. In a similar vein, the reader will observe that each of the chapters presenting case studies becomes progressively shorter than the preceding one.

Chapter 6 analyzes the Western Economic Diversification Agency's (WD) experience in Manitoba, and chapter 7 discusses the Federal Economic Development Initiative for Northern Ontario (FedNor). Chapter 8 looks at the Federal Economic Development Agency for Southern Ontario (FedDev), created in 2009. Since FedDev is a new agency, the discussion assesses the prospects and challenges it is likely to confront in light of the experience of the older "sister" agencies in other regions of the country. Chapter 9 – the concluding chapter – makes a thorough comparative assessment of the four regional development agencies, extrapolating lessons for policy implementation in multi-level systems around the world. This chapter also highlights some of the theoretical and conceptual contributions that the discussion makes to the improvement of practice and the advancement of research on public policy implementation, public administration, and multi-level governance.

2

Policy Implementation in Multi-level Systems

INTRODUCTION

This chapter provides the analytical framework that explains the institutional and political parameters of public policy governance in multi-level and multi-actor systems. Within the field of public policy and public management research, the past decade has witnessed a transition in the analytical framing of policy implementation processes from "management" to "governance" (Osborne 2010). This transition reflects broader transformations in both government and society, especially in industrialized democracies (Pal 2006; O'Toole 2007). As a result of such transformations, public policies are increasingly being implemented in concert with organized non-state actors in inter-organizational, collaborative, or partnership arrangements (Pierre and Peters 2005). These new inter-organizational partnerships are not merely a passing fancy but are likely to become permanent features on the landscape of policy implementation or public administration (Kernaghan, Marson, and Borins 2000).

Indeed, the twenty-first century is proving to be an increasingly complex and unpredictable environment for public management in particular and public policy governance in general as the traditional relationship between the state and its citizens continues to rapidly change. Citizens are increasingly becoming value creators in every public policy issue, seeking either to take more direct ownership of their own welfare or, at least, to be co-producers of public services that affect them directly (Lewis, Considine, and Alexander 2011). This means that the public policy space has expanded a bit more than before while the boundaries of the public sector are being redrawn. These factors present an expanded range of opportunities as well as challenges with respect to the roles, relationships, and tools that the public agencies have at their disposal. In such environments, the key difference separating public agencies (and even governments) exists between those who will "muddle through" complexity and those who will harness complexity to create competitive advantage (Bourgon 2007). This trend calls for creative public sector leadership, the reinvention of "citizen" or "service user" relationships, and the building of operational dexterity in ways that constitute new approaches to thinking about, and practising, public management.

Among the core competencies critical for public sector leadership under the environmental conditions described above, one of the most important is collaborative management (Lewis, Considine, and Alexander 2011), which is central to proactive initiatives geared towards building and developing leadership capacity within public agencies for meeting current and future challenges and opportunities for public management in complex and dynamic environments. Collaborative management has become a ubiquitous concept transcending disciplines and research traditions. Its presence suggests that in the face of the centrifugal forces of national and global socio-economic transformation, public agencies from all levels are required to cooperatively generate creative solutions to ensure coherence and effectiveness in the delivery of public services required by the citizens.

For example, in complex multi-level governance systems such as Canada, the United States, Australia, and the European Union, authority tends to be dispersed between orders of government (local, regional, provincial, national and supra-national) as well as across loci and sectors, which include market actors and civil society. While there is a growing appreciation for the imperatives of coordination of policy governance across these multiple levels and loci, not enough attention is given to how different political systems actually adapt their institutional and policy designs to operate effectively in the emergent complexity of multilevel governance systems design.

To take the example of Canada further, although the Constitution grants de jure responsibility for economic development policy to provincial governments, in practice, this responsibility is shared between the federal centre (in Ottawa) and its constituent units in the various provincial capitals (Simeon 2006). Moreover, although municipalities are "creatures" of the provinces in Canada, in reality, they have been assuming greater policy responsibility and attendant policy autonomy and discretion, including governance over local economic development (Sancton 2009). Finally, even though public agencies are granted the official mandate and responsibility for policy domains such as economic development, these mandates are increasingly shared with non-governmental organizations and active citizen groups. Each of these nodes of governance suggests different and increasingly assertive manifestations of policy engagement outside the traditional boundaries of economic development policy intervention. Understanding the imperatives of joint policy action across these multiple levels and loci within the specific context of a given political system is absolutely necessary.

Some of the questions addressed in subsequent chapters include, What institutions and mechanisms facilitate or deter collaborative engagement, and how do these contribute to, or undermine policy innovation and problem-solving in multi-level and multi-actor systems? Is authority in public policy governance moving downwards or upwards? What are the patterns of mutual adjustment among public and non-state agencies, and how effective is overall coordination? How does shared governance affect outcomes in specific policy domains such as economic development policy? The theoretical framework most conducive to answering these questions is the multi-actor implementation framework, which weaves together insights drawn from implementation theory, organization theory, and the governance literature. Such a framework is concerned with understanding the nature of interaction and exchange among organized policy stakeholders in the public sector, as well as between public agencies and non-governmental organizations and the private sector.

Public policy governance has historically been an interdisciplinary field that has enjoyed cross-fertilization with other research traditions such as organization theory, political science, public administration, and sociology. An integrated analytical framework is particularly consistent with the mission of policy implementation research to identify and connect the "missing link" between politics and administration (Hjern 1982). The present discussion leverages this almost lost tradition and undertakes an interdisciplinary analytical approach that weaves together insights from organization theory, policy implementation, and the new public governance to enrich our understanding of joint policy action in complex environments. Indeed, one of the future prospects of public policy theorizing is to break existing disciplinary silos and establish conceptual links between various analytical lenses sharing similar interests in phenomena.

THE MULTI-ACTOR IMPLEMENTATION FRAMEWORK

The goal of this section is to combine the analytical strengths of three distinct but parallel research traditions to contribute to the understanding of policy implementation processes in complex, diverse, and dynamic societies. To that end, the next three sub-sections will briefly introduce the ways in which implementation research, organization theory, and the governance literature have each addressed policy implementation involving multiple partners. The fourth subsection seeks to integrate these perspectives into a single framework.

Policy Implementation

The history of policy implementation research has been turbulent but productive since its inception in the early 1970s. Over the past two decades, the search for theories of implementation has focused on concerted action across institutional boundaries (O'Toole 2000; Lindquist 2006). Analytical perspectives on implementation are taking a broader scope to account for policy intervention across multiple jurisdictions involving large numbers of actors, loci, and layers.

The term "implementation" became popular among scholars of public policy through the work of Pressman and Wildavsky (1973) in the early 1970s. Policy implementation research provides the essential link between the political and economic analysis of policy implementation and the organizational or institutional analysis of public administration (Hjern and Hull 1987). Implementation research has been through three major phases of development since its inception – commonly referred to as the first-, second-, and third-generation approaches to policy implementation research (Goggin et al. 1990; Howlett and Ramesh 2003; Pal 2006). Elaborating these approaches in detail is beyond the scope of the present work; a brief overview, however, can serve as a context for advancing our understanding of the multi-actor implementation framework.

When implementation research was originally developed as a field of inquiry, it was marked by the emergence of a "top-down" approach in the scholarly literature (Pressman and Wildavsky 1973; Bardach 1977; Sabatier and Mazmanian 1981). The theoretical and empirical assumptions of this approach were immediately criticized as excessively mechanistic and unable to do justice to the realities of policy delivery in democratic societies. The critics who espoused a "bottom-up" approach were unified by their effort to examine the politics and processes of policy implementation, starting from the front lines of public administration, where street-level public officials often interact with organized societal interests (Elmore 1981; Barrett and Fudge 1981; Klijn 1996; Kickert 1997). The debates on the relative merits of the "top-down" and "bottom-up" approaches were grouped under the label of "first-generation implementation research" (Hill and Hupe 2002).

One consequence of the normative schism between the two traditions was the theoretical impoverishment of first-generation implementation research. A new generation of scholars emerged in the late 1970s and early 1980s, and they produced a "second generation" of implementation research concerned with synthesizing the insights of the top-down and bottom-up approaches and developing conceptual frameworks consisting of a set of theories of implementation (Sabatier 1986; O'Toole 1986; Palumbo and Calista 1990). The synthesis approach, however, has its own problems – especially its tendency to be little more than a combination of variables from the two perspectives, leaving the reader with a long list of variables and complex diagrams of causal chains (Linder and Peters 1987; Sinclair 2001; Exworthy and Powell 2004).

A third generation of researchers eventually emerged in the late 1980s and early 1990s; they took as their goal the distillation of the large number of variables into a manageable framework (Winter 1990). By doing so, they hoped to develop more elegant theories that could lend themselves to broader generalizations and more longitudinal inquiries (Goggin et al. 1990). As Laurence O'Toole (2000) notes, however, this effort has proved too ambitious, since very few scholars have been willing so far to undertake such inquiries. In the 1980s, moreover, policy implementation processes were influenced by structural changes in public administration towards decentralization, the devolution of responsibilities, partnerships, and the restructuring of accountability relationships in service delivery (Pal 2006; Kettl 2000; O'Toole 2007). As a result of such transformations, public policies are increasingly implemented in concert with non-state actors in cooperative or collaborative partnership arrangements. These new inter-organizational partnerships are not merely a passing fancy but are likely to become permanent features on the landscape of policy implementation (Kernaghan, Marson, and Borins 2000).

As a reflection of the transitions towards the complex and multi-actor policy processes noted above, the focus of implementation research shifted from meta-theory building towards explaining concerted action across institutional boundaries (O'Toole 2000; Lindquist 2006). Thus, one notices the broadening of the perspective on implementation into a multi-focus exercise looking at a multiplicity of actors, loci, and levels (Hill and Hupe 2003). In federal systems, for instance, the different levels of policy action consist of federal, provincial, or state and municipal jurisdictions and their agencies. The loci of policy action often consist of constellations of ideational and interest coalitions within and outside the state within a policy subsystem (Sabatier and Jenkins-Smith 1993).

Policy implementation thus connects the politics of public policy and the procedural preoccupation of public administration. While the classical literature on policy implementation in the 1960s and 1970s saw implementation as a top-down process, the recent literature has demonstrated a greater appreciation for the complexity of an operating environment consisting of multiple powers and authorities, organizations and personalities. Modern policy environments have reinforced this premise among recent scholars as trends move towards greater decentralization, devolution of responsibilities, and restructuring of accountability relationships. These shifts are consequently raising concerns about openness, accountability, inclusion, and performance.

Understanding policy implementation, therefore, requires making a distinction between three levels of analysis – the macro-, the meso-, and the micro-levels. The macro-level consists of broader variables like the type of polity – parliamentary or presidential, democratic or autocratic, and so on. Micro-level analyses focus on the internal structure, resources, and culture of a particular organization, often neglecting the environmental contingencies surrounding that organization. The meso- (or sectoral) level involves the analysis or policy "sectors" or "fields" or "domains" – focusing on the functional levels of state activity (Howlett and Ramesh 2003). Focusing analysis on the meso allows for a substantive highlight of the critical roles played by different types of policy actors (public and non-governmental) in policy processes. While departments and agencies within the executive bureaucratic apparatus of government often constitute the core element of sectoral policy governance, processes of policy intervention are increasingly influenced by the nature of the state's interaction with interest groups. For instance, Peter Evans (1990) uses the term "embedded autonomy" to describe variations of state-societal relations in which the state is deeply immersed in and influenced by power relations in society, while still maintaining a degree of independence that serves as an arbiter over the conflicting interests of society . In complex, industrialized, and institutionally fragmented systems, a more precise way to understand the character of public policy governance, therefore, is to direct the analytical focus on empirically examining the capacity, autonomy, and embeddedness of governmental institutions in specific policy subsystems.

A related development in the policy implementation literature has also been marked by a move from linear constructs of policy governance emphasizing the stages and cycles to a focus on policy arena. Rather than tracing the stages of a policy as a linear process marked by problem definition, agenda setting, and policy formulation, implementation, and evaluation, since the 1980s scholars have tended to map the constellations of actors around a given policy field or sector, with the general assumption that power relations among these well-integrated groups of actors explain policy decision making and policy outcomes (Klijn 2008). A wave of research on iron triangles (three-sided relationships between a parliamentary body, a government agency, and a particular interest group), policy subsystems, and, later, policy communities grew out of this understanding. A central thread running through all these frameworks of policy governance is that each policy sector consists of solid and self-conscious actor coalitions that share a common desire to influence the outcome of public policies, while at the same time competing among themselves. Rather than there being one policy actor – usually a government agency – there is instead profound structural diversity in which many actors are bound together by a cognitive unity (though not without contest and conflict) about policy problems and solutions (Sabatier and Jenkins-Smith 1993). Understanding policy implementation, therefore, also requires an understanding of the character of state-society relations, or how the government is linked to the society whose problems it is supposed to resolve.

Over the past decade in particular, policy implementation has increasingly been about strategic partnerships and network models of service delivery. The emphasis is on strategic partnerships that can facilitate inter-jurisdictional and inter-organizational co-operation through which governments can pursue solutions to social problems. While such network models of policy governance are becoming ubiquitous, the critical objective of research is becoming partly an appreciation for the "politics"[1] of these partnerships and partly an understanding of the requisites of effective management of these inter-organizational relationships. In the future, policy implementation research needs to pay more attention to integrating external factors that influence public agencies and to those agencies' capacity for strategic thinking, learning, and adaptation to the changing currents of the environment (or the society) they are supposed to govern. This also means that policy implementation research needs to bridge the connections between public management and politics in democratic systems.

Rather than delivering and directing, the legitimate role of government becomes facilitating and empowering (Pal 2006). Target groups once considered merely beneficiaries or recipients of government programs are increasingly viewed as policy actors in their own right. Policy implementation is, therefore, neither primarily about public agencies on their own undertaking policy implementation nor about shifting such responsibilities completely to non-state actors. The emphasis, rather, is on building synergies for joint action with partners drawn from the private and not-for-profit sectors. Within such a context, governments act as partners and facilitators, providing support and frameworks that empower rather than engaging in direct delivery.

Organization Theory

A brief review of organization theory will also highlight certain axioms that assist in understanding how public agencies manage complexity in their operating environments. For our purposes, a growing emphasis in organization theory on the interaction between organizations and their external environment must be recognized (Thompson 1967; Denhardt and Denhardt 2003). Certain elements of organization theory facilitate explanations of the complexity of implementation processes within policy subsystems by situating organizations as the principal players in the policy process. Policy implementation can thus be understood as a process involving interactions among public agencies, on the one hand, and between public agencies and organized target groups within the community and the private sector, on the other (Schoffield 2004; Sinclair 2001).

Organization theory's long tradition of examining the interactions between organizations and their external environment has given rise to two competing analytical approaches to understanding complex organizations: the closed-systems and the open-systems approaches (Thompson 1967; Denhardt and Denhardt 2003). The classical literature of organization theory, with Max Weber (1964) and Frederick Taylor (1967) as the chief heralds, reveals rational, control-oriented machine-like organizations committed to mechanistic processes of service delivery as a means of minimizing institutional constraints and maximizing opportunities. Subsequent amendments to this model posit permeable organizational boundaries, recognizing that public agencies are not as concrete and fixed as the mechanistic model had supposed. The closed systems tradition posits a bureaucratic or "administrative" model of public management that directs us to view public agencies in constitutional democracies as pyramids with cascading levels of authority that ensure all work activities are properly coordinated, controlled, and accounted for. On the other hand, the open systems perspectives draw our attention to public management as an exercise of collective action within cooperative social systems composed of human beings with complex needs that differ from agency to agency and from one culture to another.

Open-systems analysts, therefore, focus on understanding the relationship between public organizations and their strategic (or external) environment (Wamsley and Zald 1973; Denhardt 2004; Tompkins 2005). As Jreisat (2002) succinctly put it, the open-systems approach broke fundamentally from the machine-models (closed-systems) view of policy implementation, focusing instead on complex relations in the organization and the broader political context within which they operate. Indeed, the assumptions of order and control that preoccupied early organization theory led to analyses of power and conflict in organization behaviour becoming the essence of policy implementation. Organization theory has been grappling with the need to re-examine policy intervention by public agencies as a highly complex process in which public agencies engage other organizations (including community and private sector organizations), often as partners rather than subordinates.

Kettl (2000) provides a compelling summation of the above-mentioned trends in observing that organization theory, in particular, and public administration, in general, are revisiting and adjusting the discipline's analytical approach to allow for the view that agencies are adaptive organisms that respond to political and technical change in their environment in order to survive and be effective. Thus, in attempting to further understand service delivery or policy implementation in complex and dynamic systems, scholars of organization theory are increasingly required to describe and analyze the relationship between public agencies and their political environments in order to generate a complete picture of the implementation process.

The open systems perspective can be considered the crown jewel in the evolution of public management theorization, since it correctly predicted the profound and increasing complexity of modern public policy environments in which public agencies are best seen as living organisms seeking to survive in uncertain environments. This acknowledgment, however, does not imply a supplanting of Weberian or Taylorist (machine-like) models of government institutions as bureaucratic machines. Rather, the goal is to build on and modify them so that a richer and more complete understanding of complex organizations is developed. Public agencies are partly rational, purposeful systems seeking to achieve established objectives. But importantly, they are also partly open systems adapting their goals and structure as needed to function effectively in highly dynamic and uncertain environments.

Public management as a process of policy implementation is thus understood as inextricably bound to, and influenced by, the institutional conditions and social interactions within a given operating environment. The strategic choices of public agencies are therefore based on environmental characteristics (Young-Hyman 2008). The practice of public management is characterized by processes of mutual adjustment among individuals, agencies, interest groups bound by shared rules, and norms that constrain behaviour as well as provide incentives for joint action. The environmental conditions of public management are inter-subjective and man-made, rather than given, and the actions of agencies are constrained by path-dependent processes within these institutions.

To survive, organizations often try to reach out and change or control elements in the environment (Selznick 1984; Thompson 1967).

Two strategies can be adopted: first, establish favourable links with key elements or actors in the environment. The external actors on which agencies depend include funding bodies, suppliers of human and material resources, clients and consumer groups, public interest groups, and oversight bodies. For instance, establishing favourable links, contracts, and joint ventures reduces uncertainty through legal and binding relationships. Such inter-organizational links can range from collaboration to co-optation. A second strategy is to shape the environmental domain by shifting goals, instruments, partners, or even clientele. For example, as we will see in subsequent chapters, Canada's federal agencies have often entered into "marriages of convenience" with similar provincial and municipal agencies to reduce the degree of contestation that comes from operating in provincial and local jurisdictions.

From the discussion above, it can be seen that organization theory thus entails the task of public management research in making empirical assessments about the management of a particular policy issue or outcome and in mapping out the complex interdependence not only between an agency's components but also between an agency and its operating environments, which consis of numerous agencies and actors. Within such environments, the rationalistic underpinnings of public management as a process of planned change are bound to be confronted with unanticipated consequences and new problems, some of which, ironically, are created by the ambitions of those seeking to control organizational activities in a deliberate fashion. Public management is thus best viewed through the lens of behavioural, rather than purely legalistic or technical, assumptions (Merton 1949; Selznick 1984). Public agencies must respond appropriately to external opportunities and threats, including changes in mandates, markets, and technologies, if they are to maintain a steady state. This paradox can be further elucidated: rather than being merely bureaucratic machines, public agencies are dynamic and sometimes aggressive entities that are willing to transform themselves completely if necessary and to alter environmental conditions whenever possible (Selznick 1984). Public agencies are adaptive structures governed by the instincts of self-preservation and survival. Their actions are thus moulded or influenced by forces tangential to their rationally ordered structures and stated goals.

Organization theory reminds us that public policy subsystems are shifting coalitions of public and non-state agencies, each undertaking sometimes aggressive efforts to adjust the environment to their organizational needs. Successful policy governance is about coping in an operating environment by finding an optimal fit between the agencies' goals, environmental forces, and the legitimate instruments available. Therefore, change and stability are not dichotomous, since to remain viable, organizations must maintain stability in the face of change and change their structure and behaviour for the sake of stability. Instruments for strategic planning and performance measurement provide methods that may be used for purposes of feedback and self-regulation. Performance measurement in this sense is not merely used to make categorical statements (concerning, for example, success or failure) about outputs or outcomes; instead, it serves the more strategic purpose of learning and adaptation.

The significance of these considerations for public managers is that they underscore the importance of building coalitions of political support and successfully managing the many dependencies that are a natural and necessary component of operating in highly politicized environments. Similarly, public managers need to learn to think and plan strategically. Through deliberate and thoughtful strategic planning, public managers can engage members of a network, subsystem, or environment in finding and sustaining a good fit between its mission and strategies, its internal systems and structures, and the forces in its external environment that create both opportunities and threats.

Governance

Since the present study conceptualizes policy implementation as involving institutionalized policy subsystems centred on a number of organizations with diverse sources, an equally important element in the analysis is the consideration of the governance literature's concern with the dialectics of horizontal engagement between public agencies and non-state organizations. For instance, insights from governance theory have accounted for the actions of organized target groups and other societal interests in less hierarchical policy settings (Agranoff and McMguire 1998; Kooiman 2000; Rhodes 2000; Peters and Pierre 2000, 2003). Although the concept of governance has escaped a clear definition, in the context of advanced democracies it generally refers to a wide variety of self-sustaining networks through which the state engages in sharing power and administrative responsibility with non-state policy actors (Frederickson 2007). The concept has also been widely used in the development literature to address issues of state capacity and legitimacy in developing countries, but this usage is beyond the scope of the present discussion (Conteh 2009; World Bank 2009). The governance literature embraces a broad range of perspectives, from those that identify a dominant public sector constrained by a constellation of organized societal actors within a relatively complicated policy subsystem (Peters 2001) to those that perceive highly complex systems in which adaptive abilities are required of all members within a network (including public agencies). This adaptive process has been described as "co-evolution" (Teisman and Klijn 2008).

Some of the major analytical frameworks in the governance literature include network governance (Keast, Mandell, Brown, and Woolcock 2004), governance networks (Kooiman 2003; Pierre and Peters 2005), and collaborative management (Agranoff and McGuire 2003). These broad analytical frameworks overlap in many ways and have been further grouped under themes such as multi-level governance (Hill and Hupe 2002), transition management (Kooiman 2006; Loorback 2007), and complex adaptive systems (Tesiman et al. 2009; Klijn and Teisman 2008). Pierre and Peters (2005), for instance, identify various types of state-society relations that can exist, providing a typology of governance settings along a continuum from the most statist (state-dominant) to what reads like near anarchy (a society-dominated system). Three major challenges to the traditional conception of the state are communitarianism, deliberative democracy, and direct democracy. Communitarianism seeks to replace large-scale government with smaller units of governing with an appropriate basis in the "community." Variants of this model can be found in the literature on governance networks (Kickert 1993; Koppenjan and Klijn 2004). Deliberative democracy is a more process-oriented initiative calling for reform in the decision-making institutions that privileges citizen-driven deliberation over technocratic policy outcomes (Pierre and Peters 2005). Direct democracy is the most radical, calling for a supplanting of existing representative institutions in favour of the public making its own decisions through mechanisms such as initiatives and referendums.

The main contention of the society-centric versions is that the monopoly of governance capacity that liberal-democratic theory accords the state is no longer a valid account. Using concepts like "associative self-governance" (Hirst 1994), these perspectives reject any attempt to impose objective assessments of efficiency or effectiveness that are suggestive of policy control by public agencies (Rhodes 2000). Governance should be thought of simply as a process, since there are multiple ways of steering policy directions and outcomes in the political context (Stoker 2000; Rothstein 2007). Some scholars, who are concerned about what they consider the excesses of society-centric approaches, are providing a counterweight to the prevalent disdain for government in some of the governance literature (Pierre and Peters 2005). They call for caution regarding the enthusiasm of the recent governance literature's rather sanguine portrayal of societal arrangements of self-governance. The ideals of democracy, they argue, necessitate some form of public authority (wielded by the state) to maintain the goals of accountability, coherence, steering, and a common set of priorities for the collective good of society. The significance of such a counterweight to society-centric perspectives is that the emergence of governance does not necessarily presuppose the decline of the state but rather presents an analytical framework for assessing the state's ability to adapt to changes in the external policy environment as the twenty-first century unfolds (Treib, Bahr, and Falkner 2007; Newman 2006).

The governance perspectives thus generally share a concern for the relationship between state intervention and societal autonomy, with different facets of this continuum (as noted above) emphasized or highlighted by different orientations in the literature. Governance as a new framework of authoritative intervention poses some opportunities and some challenges for our understanding of policy implementation. The most significant implication of the governance discourse for understanding policy implementation is the need to revisit the visions of the role of government, the feasible tools at its disposal for dealing with public problems, and how best to organize the administrative machinery of government to achieve those ends. The new governance literature in general stresses networks, bargaining, and interaction, rather than hierarchies, as the best way to govern and understand public policy action (Drache 2006). Whether conceptualized as self-governance or "co"-governance, the task of government (which is no longer supreme) is to enable socio-political interactions among the multiple societal actors, to encourage many and varied arrangements for coping with problems, and to distribute services among several actors (Kooiman 2000, 2003).

For the purpose of the present discussion, governance refers to policy implementation processes that are inter-jurisdictional (involving several levels of government) and inter-organizational (involving policy engagement between the state and non-state actors). Governance is thus about inter-jurisdictional cooperation and network management (Frederickson 2007; O'Toole 2000). It is also characterized by variations of state-society relations, which consist of societal groups mobilized by principles of self-governance in various forms of joint action (or co-production) with public organizations (Agranoff and McMguire 2003; Kooiman 2000; Rhodes 2000; Peters and Pierre 2000). A key question for policy implementation in the multi-actor governance framework, then, is not so much about what specific formal areas of control the state has retained as it is about what types of adaptive instruments and capabilities it possesses. While coordination and coherence are central to the discourse of a multi-actor governance framework, policy implementation still depends on the capacity and legitimacy of the state to enforce decisions in some ways – something that implies the power of the public sector and its legitimate authority to provide policy leadership and direction. The governance approach, at a minimum, suggests a conceptual or theoretical representation of cooperation, coordination, and collaboration as central features of policy implementation. But it should not necessarily imply the demise of the state in that process. The multi-actor governance framework, therefore, is concerned with how governments interact with their external environment to make and implement decisions agreeable to all parties. In economic development policy implementation, for instance, success at coordination transforms potentially conflicting, short-term, and fragmentary sets of development projects offered by similar agencies in silos into complementary and coherent programs with a more strategic, sectorally comprehensive, and longer-term orientation leading to the structural transformation of a given economy. The governance literature, therefore, can be seen as reflecting a keen awareness of the realities of politics as an intrinsic element of policy implementation or public administration. As such, it seeks to identify the nature of the interaction between public organizations (as necessary agents of policy implementation) and other organized entities outside the state, often focusing on the front lines of service delivery.

Integrating the Three Perspectives

From this review, we see that there has been a gradual shift in analytical focus over the past two decades in the separate subfields of policy implementation, organization theory, and governance towards explaining public management or policy implementation in complex multi-level and multi-actor systems. The central concern shared by policy implementation research, organization theory, and the governance literature is about how government organizations interact with their external environments in the delivery of policies. A common thread flowing from this shared concern is the need to re-conceptualize power and authority among public and non-state organizations in the policy environment.

In attempting to integrate the insights from the aforementioned analytical traditions, identifying the distinct element of each perspective is important. Implementation research has long sought to synthesize top-down and bottom-up approaches to policy implementation, which has resulted in the accumulation of insights into the relationships between various levels of government. The tensions between front-line agencies and their head offices have posed a constant challenge in this regard. In Canada's federal systems, for instance, these tensions are particularly poignantly illustrated in intergovernmental jurisdictional rivalries and frustrated efforts at joint action (Simeon 2006). Organization theory adds to this by suggesting that the success of policy implementation is a function not merely of the government's intra-organizational integrity, expertise, and coherence but also of its adaptation to the imperatives of its external environment. This perspective calls our attention to the willingness or ability of organizations to reorganize their culture, operations, and, even, structural features in ways that may involve sharing authority and power, as well as developing a learning culture. How public agencies adjust their mission to reflect the changing values and interests of the local environment thus becomes an important consideration in understanding policy implementation (Lewis, Considine, and Alexander 2011).

The governance literature calls our attention to the emergent phenomenon of third-sector engagement in co-production, since the institutional and ideational forces underlying the shift in policy implementation can be understood as causing a transition from simply delivering and directing to facilitation, coordination, and empowerment. The expectations and demands of organized actors outside the public sector imply that the external environment is not simply a set of variables to be manipulated by public agencies. Building legitimacy for effective policy intervention requires public agencies to identify the main actors within the field and their specific demands, and then to seek ways to coordinate the various bases of power. The structure of support and the established feedback loops that public agencies maintain with local organized actors are, therefore, crucial factors for the success of implementation.

Through the lens of an integrated framework, two interrelated propositions emerge: first, the political legitimacy and coordinating capacity of public agencies are indispensable elements of policy implementation. In this regard, the success of public policy governance depends more on the strength of strategic leadership than on organizational type. Second, policy implementation is a complex mix of hierarchy and collaboration. Policy intervention generally operates under the directive of a larger governing authority (such as a provincial or a federal government in Canada). Within the context of economic development policy intervention, for instance, this enables the larger governing authority to determine the service area. Public agencies help to facilitate the development of a shared vision and provide supportive services (i.e., planning, research, resource referral, funding) and the logistics for coordination within the policy domain (McSweeney 2011). However, since programs and activities are often largely driven by local interests, local champions must be *on board* – which requires engagement with local leaders from the outset. Inter-organizational interactions in this context are based in both cooperation and conflict as public agencies navigate various levels of constitutional and policy jurisdictions, while also striving to gain legitimacy and positive feedback from non-state policy stakeholders. Structured hierarchies are thus confronted with the need to adjust their processes to environmental imperatives of horizontal management in order to maintain system stability, manage change, and deepen the impact of their policy intervention (Brown et al. 2010). Flexible strategic planning, for example, can thus be a useful instrument of policy governance in inter-jurisdictional and inter-organizational policy subsystems as agencies constantly find an appropriate fit between their task environments and their own strategies and structures.

The complexity of modern political and economic environments necessitates viewing regional development policy implementation as a process of inter-organizational and inter-jurisdictional cooperation, rather than one of simply optimizing an organization's program output (Rosenbaum 2006; O'Toole 2007; Kettl 2000). Mechanisms for building synergies among a number of public agencies and non-governmental organizations are therefore increasingly important. The present discussion focuses on the inter-organizational and inter-jurisdictional context of collaborative policy implementation. "Collaboration" refers to different agencies committing to work together over more than the short term with the aim of securing benefits delivery or added value that could not have been provided by any single agency acting alone (Lewis, Considine, and Alexander 2011). It also often includes a formal articulation of a purpose and plan to bind partners together (Kernaghan et al. 2000; Agranoff 2007). As will be seen in subsequent chapters, the effectiveness of economic development policy implementation requires that managers make connections across organizations and share ideas, resources, and power with state and non-state actors. The present discussion, therefore, views collaborative governance arrangements as complex mechanisms of policy implementation constantly evolving over time and operating within and across layers of government, as well as between the public and the non-governmental sectors. In particular, economic development agencies' strategic choices are based on the specific environmental and institutional characteristics of a given region.

Four considerations are factored into the present analysis: first, vertical and horizontal inter-jurisdictional cooperation. Here, attention is given to the various levels of jurisdiction in the public sector involved in joint policy action. Second, the extension of the state to non-state actors or third parties is considered, recognizing the potentially influential ideas and resources of non-governmental agencies. Third, the discussion traces the various stages of evolving governance arrangements, noting the constant changes and adaptations characterizing the processes involved in joint policy actions. Finally, the synthesis of the aforementioned analytical perspectives entails conceiving of collaborative governance contexts as learning networks. The effectiveness of policy implementation in such settings requires that managers make connections across organizations, bridge diverse cultures across levels of government and outside government, and share ideas, resources, and power with state and non-state actors.

In conclusion, the multi-actor implementation framework provides this type of integrated perspective. This framework, as subsequent chapters demonstrate, fits well with the emergent complexity of regional economic development, especially modern knowledge-based economies. The multi-actor implementation framework views policy implementation as encompassing diverse expressions of inter-jurisdictional cooperation among public agencies, on the one hand, and the complex relation between state agencies and organized interests within the market and society, on the other. These inter-jurisdictional and inter-organizational co-operative efforts are strategic networks of complex relationships involving cooperation among agencies with similar mandates from different levels of government and state-society partnerships that incorporate community development organizations and business groups.

3

Old and New Theories of Economic Development

INTRODUCTION

In chapter 1, I presented economic development policy as an intrinsically multidimensional, or inter-disciplinary field of study. A comprehensive analysis of this policy field would therefore be incomplete without including a basic understanding of the underlying theories and assumptions that have influenced various approaches to regional economic development policy in OECD countries. This chapter provides a broad historical and panoramic overview of the major debates between the influential schools of thought in the field of economic development. The goal in this section is to provide background understanding of early discussions about the intersections (including tensions, contradictions, and complements) between the economy as a space of free enterprise and public policy as an authoritative action.

The next section then relates the discussion to the specific context of regional economic development since the postwar period (especially from the late 1950s). This section illustrates how competing visions of the intersection between public policy and economic development filter into debates over the legitimacy and limitations of various instruments of regional economic development. The final section of the chapter then traces the emergence and key characteristics of the "new regionalism." This emergent framework makes certain assumptions about global economic restructuring and their implications for the changing roles and imperatives of public policy engagement in the adaptation of regions (distinct from nations) as competitive nodes in the still rapidly unfolding global economy.

THE CLASSICS AND THE MODERNS OF ECONOMIC DEVELOPMENT THEORIES

A survey of theories of economic development can be traced to medieval times with the emergence of formal economic-development trade practices referred to as mercantilism (Mitchell 1967). Mercantilism was one of the first theories of systematic policy intervention to emerge during the medieval age, as superstition gave way to reason and as the state embarked on more ambitious domestic policy undertakings (beyond the traditional provision of defence and internal security). "Mercantilism" refers to a set of protectionist and discriminatory policy instruments used by governments to boost economic activity for the purpose of maximizing aggregate national wealth (North et al. 1975). Since mercantilists believed that resources were limited and growth physically limited, the goal was to advance a nation's economic power at the expense of its neighbours or competitors. The emphasis, however, was on increasing gross national wealth (as opposed to individual welfare), and the focus was on securing maximum imports of raw materials and exports of manufactured products.

Members of another school of thought, referred to as the physiocrats, were contemporaries of the golden age of mercantilism (Brenner 1966). Physiocrats, however, rejected the intervention of the state in the market for the purpose of advancing international trade and national wealth. They believed in the natural order of things – including a free market – and the superiority of agriculture over other sectors of the economy (North et al. 1975). They were not concerned with foreign markets, because their primary interest was in trade flows within the domestic economy. The classical economists who are more widely recognized in modern discourse followed on the insights of the above two early theories and ushered in what became the modern discipline of economics as a scientific field of study (Galbraith 1987). Adam Smith ([1776] 1937), considered the father of modern economics, championed the theoretical advancement of classical economics. Like the physiocrats, classical economists developed formal models and arguments that emphasized the liberty of property as the keystone of every rational economic order (Gide, Rist, and Richards 1948). They shared the physiocrats' belief in a free market society rather than state intervention and resource distribution (although Adam Smith and his colleagues rejected the idea that agriculture was the only source of productive employment in the economy). Classical economists, including influential scholars such as David Ricardo, Thomas Robert Malthus, and John Stuart Mill, also argued that the economy is governed by certain "natural laws" that can be studied with the rigorous methodology of the natural sciences – hence advancing the evolution of modern economics as a scientific discipline (Stirati 1994; Galbraith 1987). To summarize the fundamental principle of the then-emergent science of economics: economic growth depends on the growth of capital and population (labour), scientific and technical progress, and comparative advantage in international trade, allowing for the importation of limited or unavailable materials or inputs.

Other competing schools in the era of classical economics, such as dialectical materialism, challenged what they described as the sanguine or naïve claims of the "free market" notions of the classical economic thought. The chief contention of its leading proponents, such as Karl Marx and Friedrich Engels (1848; 1867), was that the "free market" assumptions of classical economics tend to be narrowly focused on capital without a proper treatment of the full nature of its effect on, or interaction with, labour and the attendant human condition (Hirshman 1965). Dialectical materialism, in its various branches, insisted that every economic order has within it (as with all of objective reality) inherent tensions and contradictions leading to constant change, including occasional revolutionary perturbations. Thus, the dialectical materialists claimed that within capitalism the contradictions and tensions in the logic of capital accumulation through labour exploitation would produce certain dialectics that would resolve themselves in an ultimate revolution leading to a higher order of economic organization – a non-capitalist order. In short, dialectical materialists were mostly concerned with the destructive forms of "pure market-ism," which they claimed, undermined the fabric of social cohesion and nation-building (Hutchison 1981).

The debates between classical economic thinkers and the discourse within this era constitute the intellectual canopy under which subsequent discussions about the nature and working of the economy and its relationship with human development have been held (Skousen 2007). For our present discussion of regional economic development, for instance, the various approaches and experiments of the past six decades draw implicitly or explicitly from the fundamental (and competing) assumptions of the classical era. For instance, scholars who share the assumptions just mentioned about the free market tend to be critical of economic development policy intervention, viewing it as a perversion of the natural order of the market in a nation's economy. On the other hand, supporters of forms of active economic development policy tend to see a more complex set of processes at work and seek to negotiate the contradictions between the market, geographical and other physical constraints, and human development (Hutchison 1981). The economic policy debates that defined the broad intellectual contours of the classical era largely set the parameters for the emergence of what became known as neoclassical economic theory around the late nineteenth and early twentieth centuries.

Influential neoclassical economic theorists such as William Stanley Jevons ([1871] 1970), Carl Menger ([1871] 1950), and Leon Walras ([1874] 1954) built on the premises of the classical free-market thesis, advancing our scientific understanding (largely through econometrics) of the "natural laws" of the market that govern prices, outputs, and income distributions in a nation's economy.[1] The dominance of neoclassical economic thought and the influence of some of its most widely known proponents, including Alfred Marshall,[2] remained generally undisputed throughout much of the early twentieth century (and arguably until the emergence of what became known as Keynesianism) (King 2002). An in-depth discussion of the merits and demerits of neoclassical economic theory is beyond the scope of the present discussion, but it is worth noting that several criticisms have been levelled against what is perceived as its overly unrealistic assumptions about the rationality of human behaviour or the self-correcting properties of free-market systems. Most of these criticisms have emerged from a wide range of heterodox approaches to economics, most notably institutional economics, neo-Marxism (a variant of classical dialectical materialism), and a number of other historical schools of economics. Even though the dominance of neoclassical economic theory officially dates back to the late nineteenth and early twentieth centuries, however, it still casts a long "shadow" over current debates about the economic development policy. As we will see later in this chapter, for instance, the somewhat radical anti-statist neoliberal economic thinking of the 1970s and 1980s has strong conceptual links with some of the key premises of neoclassical economic theory. An example relevant to our present purpose is that modern scholars who are strongly influenced by some of the neoclassical assumptions about the intrinsic merits and self-correcting properties of free markets tend to be critical of industrial policy interventions aimed at assisting disadvantaged regional economies (Coulombe 1999; Mintz and Smart 2003).

The emergence of what became known as Keynesianism constituted a paradigm shift in economic thinking, drawing our attention to understanding aggregate laws that govern the behaviour and trajectories of national economies. In particular, Keynesianism shifted the focus from microeconomic laws to the macroeconomic variables of a nation's general economic welfare. It became the dominant postwar macroeconomic paradigm and provided an overarching justification for active economic-development management in industrialized countries (King 2002). The Keynesian approach espouses the use of certain instruments of policy intervention in the economy to achieve full employment, with the general assumption that government intervention is required to reduce the severity and duration of downturns in business cycles. Such responses by governments to economic fluctuations became known as either discretionary stabilizers or automatic stabilizers. Discretionary stabilizers are a set of instruments like taxation policies, subsidies, and the like aimed at increasing the rate of capital returns. Automatic stabilizers are established measures such as income-maintenance programs aimed at correcting cyclical fluctuations in the business cycle.

Keynesianism, therefore, legitimized the "activist" state of the postwar years, which became dedicated to maintaining high levels of employment and economic growth by, first, identifying trends in the economy and, second, by using fiscal, monetary, and other policies to correct market failures. In Canada and other industrialized countries, Keynesianism also provided the intellectual bedrock for the emergence of policy instruments designed to promote the development of strategic industries intended to serve as engines of economic growth for regional or national economies. Keynesianism, at least as understood in the mainstream of economic theorization, did not prescribe central government planning in the socialist sense of the term but was, rather, consistent with more selective government intervention in the economy. Beyond macroeconomic management, for instance, governments can assist strategic sectors of the economy, helping to create a positive environment for business and employment growth (Hale 2009; Simeon and Robinson 1990) Keynesian policy advocates in most industrialized countries stressed the failure of the markets, pointing to the depressing perversions of the financial and manufacturing sectors during the interwar years and other major postwar recessions as their most poignant examples. Within the Canadian context, for instance, the Keynesian economic paradigm provided a basis for the postwar emphasis on promoting Canada's national and regional economic development (Science Council of Canada 1967). In particular, strategic government intervention was viewed as necessary to stem the tide of what were seen as the pernicious forces of American economic penetration, especially the inefficiencies of branch plants organized primarily to serve the Canadian markets rather than project the country into the global economy.

Strategic industrial policy was thus seen in Canada as a proactive antidote to the structural weaknesses of an economy that is regionally fragmented, geographically dispersed, sparsely populated, and generally vulnerable to the economic might of its sometimes aggressive southern neighbour and a generally volatile world (Science Council of Canada 1978). For instance, discussions about regional economic development during this period centred partly on providing the incentive structures to address the tendency of Canadian resource industries to export much of their production rather than processing and manufacturing higher value-added products capable of generating higher incomes for Canadians (Hale 2009; Bradford 1998). Thus, the Keynesian school of thought is significant for our present discussion of regional economic development because it provided a compelling justification for government policy intervention to stimulate the natural laws of the market for the advancement of socio-economic welfare. Governments became increasingly willing to use various macroeconomic and microeconomic policy instruments to try to correct structural weaknesses or adverse cyclical trends in their regional and national economies.

The thread weaving through the various approaches going back a few hundred years to the classical era is the concern over the possible integration or balancing of the imperatives of economic growth, wealth creation, human welfare, and a just society (Mair and Miller 1991). And it is the search for this integration of somewhat competing values or aims that has characterized regional economic development in Canada and other industrialized countries since the 1960s. Regional economic development in OECD countries over the past five decades represents a complex and rather schizophrenic set of compromises between respect for the laws of market efficiency and the need for some form of intervention to correct structural disadvantages within certain geographic regions in order to provide equal opportunity for all citizens and regions to maximize their full potential – whatever that happens to be. The underlying assumption is that economic development depends not only on finding the optimal combinations of a given set of tangible resources and factors of production but also on mobilizing intangible resources and abilities that are hidden, scattered, or badly utilized in certain regions (Hirshman 1965; Meier 1994). Based on this assumption, the problem of economic development, therefore, is the challenge of organization – the "binding agent" of social and political coordination for the factors of production, including entrepreneurship and access to capital.

Central to these ideas are assumptions about the role of the state in creating certain institutional mechanisms to support the economies of disadvantaged regions (Mackenzie et al. 2010; Bastian and Ulrich 2003). For example, the state can serve as a "binding agent" through systematically using policy instruments to leverage productive capital to disadvantaged and under-exploited regions, encourage entrepreneurship, support skills development and facilitate the interaction between talents, entrepreneurship, capital, and commodity markets (Kurz 2011). How these assumptions feature in the various approaches to regional economic development is the subject of the next section.

THE EMERGENCE OF POSTWAR REGIONAL ECONOMIC DEVELOPMENT

A wide range of theories have framed the field of economic development over the past few decades, including staples theory, dependency theory, the geographical pyramid of control, centre-periphery theory, export-base theory, import substitution, and more recently, community economic development. For the purpose of analytical focus, however, the discussion in this section covers only the major theoretical frameworks that have influenced regional economic development in industrialized countries since the postwar years. These frameworks include the growth-pole concept, the development approach, the trade theory approach, the mixed-economy model, and, by the mid-1990s, the new regionalism. The new regionalism will be treated in a separate section because it represents the most contemporary and influential approach to regional economic development in industrialized countries.

The growth-pole concept (later known as the growth-centre approach) as developed and advanced by Francois Perroux (1961) proved to be one of the most influential theories of regional economic development in Canada and other industrialized countries in the 1960s and early 1970s (Economic Council of Canada 1977; Bradfield 1988). This approach calls for a number of interventionist measures designed to stimulate growth within a particular geographical space. This geographical space, often a particular city chosen for its location and/or size, will act as the engine of growth and development for the rest of the surrounding regions. The measures of intervention often include encouragement of capital accumulation; assistance in creating adequate industrial infrastructure; promotion and application of new technology; and assistance in modernizing agricultural methods – all with the aim of creating new geographical centres of economic growth in what were considered under-developed regions. The growth pole concept eventually fell into disuse as students of regional economic development in OECD countries joined a wider international school of thinking on economic development known as the "development approach" in the 1970s (Benedetti and Lamarche 1994; Savoie 1986).

The development approach briefly influenced earlier formulations of Canadian regional development programs in the mid- to late 1970s. Theories within this approach include the "growth stages" model, championed by economic historians such as Simon Kuznets and Walt Rostow (Meier 1994; Todaro 2001). Other perspectives within the development approach include dependency theory – which provides critical insight into the organic complexity of world economic systems regarding the governing conditions of under-developed economies or regions. The adaptation of this approach to Canada not only pointed to the potential widening of disparity in growth and development between urban and rural areas but also acted as a reinforcement of peripheral economies in Canada's less populated provinces and regions (Savoie 1986). Thus, left to the dictates of market forces, peripheral communities face the risk of entering a phase of sustained economic stagnation and population decline resulting from out-migration of the young and educated as they seek better career opportunities elsewhere.

One major limitation of the dependency school is that it tends to provide an overly critical and cynical account of the prospects of economic development in certain underdeveloped regions of the world, especially the periphery, but often lacks any practical solution for how these regions can move past the socio-structural barriers. More broadly, the "development approach" was limited inasmuch as it was inspired by the study of underdeveloped countries and thus made certain theoretical assumptions about institutional and societal capacity that did not fit advanced, industrialized countries like Canada (Anderson 1988; Melvin 1987). Even though provinces in Atlantic Canada were considered "underdeveloped" and "peripheral" relative to the rest of the country (Savoie 1997), the fact was clearly not overlooked that such descriptions were based on comparisons of provinces in Canada and did not refer simply to the dismal realities of extreme poverty and under-development in most developing countries. Nevertheless, dependency theory provided powerful rhetorical ammunition in the politics of regionalism in Canada, especially during the 1970s and 1980s (Polese 1999; Savoie 2003; Southcott and McBride 2003).

Underlying the apparent consolidation of regional economic development as a fixture of public policy in Canada, however, were internal contradictions and tensions, as well as exogenous shocks that eventually sparked a new debate about its relevance. The debate shook the foundation and eroded the fabric of the high status that regional economic development was enjoying by the late 1970s (Mintz and Smart 2003). The exogenous shocks consisted of a set of factors linked to the integration of global trade and investment and the rise of new markets and growth-spurts in developing regions of the world, which coincided with the rise of multinational corporations and the movement of manufacturing firms, including many Canadian companies, "southwards" (OECD 2009). Greater global connectivity has meant more off-shoring of key industries away from OECD countries, increasing competition, and growing interdependence of the world's economies (Wilkins 2011), which has resulted in major downturns and structural changes in OECD economies. With the frequency and increasing severity of exogenous shock brought on by the seismic shifts in the global economy, the internal contradictions of an uneasy policy compromise in regional economic development finally gave way to the weight of global economic pressures. The world's economy was in transition, and the prevalent instruments of regional economic development were found to be of limited value in facilitating the required adjustments in Canada's struggling regions (Mintz and Smart 2003).

Moreover, the pervasive macroeconomic doctrine of active economic management supported by Keynesianism was gradually and quietly replaced by the emergence of neoliberalism during the late 1970s and early 1980s (Henry 2011). Neoliberalism has some conceptual links with the neoclassical economic thinking of the late nineteenth and early twentieth centuries in the sense that both analytical traditions are essentially a restatement of the central axioms of classical free-market economics. Neoliberalism is generally suspicious of the role of government in supporting the economy, preferring the wisdom of the marketplace over the judgments of economic policy technocrats. Neoliberalism of the 1980s enjoyed such global dominance that the term "Washington Consensus" became synonymous with the standard macroeconomic doctrines of most major international financial and monetary institutions. The theoretical preferences of the Washington Consensus place greater emphasis on fiscal discipline and the centrality of market forces over any strategic attempt by governments to promote their economy (Stiglitz 2006).

Neoliberal conceptions of economic growth are thus fundamentally opposed to most forms of state intervention to foster economic growth and development and instead insist on the invisible hand of economic restructuring and market adjustments; any attempt by the state to support less competitive regions and sectors, for instance, is regarded as intrinsically inefficient (Peet and Hartwick 2009; Mintz and Smart 2003). The key assumption is that the market is inherently self-adjusting and that government intervention leads to distortion or adverse economic conditions (Henry 2011). For example, the explanation for Canada's higher than "normal" unemployment rate, relative to other OECD countries, is often attributed to rigidities in the country's labour market resulting from regional transfer payments and other related social policies (Mintz and Smart 2003). Regional economic development aimed at easing disparities is viewed as bound to distort natural market forces and as potentially damaging to full economic growth (Coulombe 1999). In short, in the face of seismic global economic restructurings, regional development as conceptualized and designed within the Keynesian edifice of the postwar Canadian state was considered no longer credible (Savoie 1997; Bradford 2010). Moreover, globalization and economic (trade and investment) liberalization further undermined the fiscal and institutional capacity of most industrialized countries to fully intervene in economic sectors as they had previously. Furthermore, in the face of the perceived failures of regional economic development after four decades of experimentation, critics, including some researchers at the influential C.D. Howe Institute, found enough "evidence" to point to the institutional limitations of centrally designed regional development in the Canadian economy (Coulombe 1999; Savoie 2003; Blake 2003; Mintz and Smart 2003).

But ironically, proponents of regional economic development also saw a window of opportunity in emergent global economic liberalization. For them, globalization meant that the edifice of the central state was less relevant and that sub-national and local communities could take care of their own economic destinies (Roy 2007; Holbrook and Wolfe 2002; Loxley and Silver 2007). Shifts in thinking about the governance of regional economies were changing policy perspectives on regional development in Canada and around the world (Di Matteo 2006). By the close of the 1990s, global trends had moved towards an almost complete integration of economies around the world (OECD 2009).

The continuous economic revolution that the economic historian, Joseph Schumpeter (1947) once called the "creative destruction" of capitalism has taken on an accelerated pace, and the successful players must counter the creative destruction of capitalism with ongoing "creative reinvention." For example, by the late 1980s, globalization was rapidly becoming a buzzword used to explain perplexing economic challenges in Canada's rural and northern regions, including those emerging for agriculture, forestry, mining, and fishing (MacNeil1994; Rounds 1994). The problems of rural and northern regions result from a vicious combination of factors, such as resource depletion, the substitution of synthetics for natural commodities, the substitution of capital for labour in production (the irony of technological productivity), the relocation of natural resource industries to low-cost jurisdictions in the developing world, and the fact that low real prices on global markets are no longer mitigated by subsidies, trade protection, and business incentives (Bollman 1997; OECD 2007). These long-term structural trends have continued to plague the efforts to diversify Canada's rural economy over many years. The data confirm the relative decline of the natural-resource-based economy in rural Canada as the problems of sustaining employment in rural-based manufacturing and increasing regional disparity and rural impoverishment persist, despite large income-equalization payments (Bollman 1992; Industry Canada 2008). These trends reinforce certain apparent contradictions or paradoxes, wherein a globalized world with integrated markets witnesses the emergence of a greater desire from sub-national governments and local communities to exercise more control over their socio-economic destinies. Proponents of regional development policy in Canada and abroad have been quick to capitalize on these trends and ideas as discussions metamorphose into preoccupation with local development (Goldenberg 2008). As we will see in subsequent chapters, provincial governments, municipalities, and local communities (including private sector groups) have begun to experiment with their own economic development strategies – resulting in a de facto decentralization of the governing institutions of regional economic development in Canada.

However, although the ideological consensus among OECD countries under the influence of neoliberalism since the late 1980s has been to adopt industrial policies that favour minimal state intrusion, the rhetoric has far out-distanced the reality and actual practice of economic management (Atkinson and Coleman 1989). The policy rhetoric of this era indicates that idea of the sanctity of the market and the autonomy of the firm describes the values and discourse of industrial policy in the international community. But as Atkinson and Coleman observe, in spite of the relatively open or liberal character of the OECD economies, some forms of industrial policy have always been in evidence. All countries in the OECD have been preoccupied with positioning their industries to carve a niche in the global economy and make considerable investments targeting particular sectors. In short, regardless of the rhetoric of market liberalization, all industrialized countries have pursued some variant of interventionist industrial policies. All have sought to influence the investment decisions of private capital, even if countries have had different policies and strategies. Just as governments in OECD countries have often assumed responsibility for stabilizing their economies (most recently evident in the Stimulus Plan in Canada and in other industrialized countries), they are increasingly willing to acknowledge that the structure of the economy and the performance of economic sectors and regions are matters of public policy concern.

Interestingly, by the latter part of the 1990s the assumptions of the now predominant neoliberalism were increasingly questioned as seismic shifts in the balance of trade brought on by the emerging global economy lent credibility to more "developmental" or "mixed-economy" approaches employed by countries like China and India (Sun 1997; Broome 2007). What is needed, it is generally agreed, is a mix of economic policy instruments that could mobilize human capital in unlimited ways, while still building on natural comparative advantages. Along with these shifts in thinking has come a focus on the strategic means by which governments could help nurture sectoral and regional competitiveness in their domestic economies (Goldenberg 2008; Di Matteo 2006). Governments are thus increasingly faced with considerable political and economic pressures coming both from domestic actors (including the private sector) and from the dictates of international competition, leading them to find the means of funding and encouraging certain industries through strategic policy intervention in the market. The concept of free markets as advanced in the neoliberal literature has been widely dismissed as idealistic and naïve, based as it is on abstract assumptions of market behaviour that do not always occur in practice (Sun 1997; Leiva 2008). However, the dichotomy between free and interventionist systems is also considered false. While the new model of economic development values free trade and the validity of market forces of efficiency, it rejects the wholesale embrace of comparative advantage in neoclassical trade theory and considers, therefore, that with the right mix of strategic intervention and market rationality, any region could become a productive centre, cluster, or node within the global economy. Regions will no longer be restricted by their geographical isolation or other structural determinants of comparative advantage. Regional economic development has come full circle since the emergence of the growth-pole concept in the 1960s (Polese 1999). The spatial logic of once-discredited approaches, such as the growth-pole concept, is being resurrected, except with an emphasis on new imperatives and rationales (Di Matteo 2006; Florida 1995). Although there are many overlaps and continuities between what is referred to as the "old" economy and the "new" economy, certain dichotomies can be drawn (Holst 2011). In the old economy, markets were relatively more stable, whereas in the new economy they tend to be dynamic and fluid. Moreover, the scope of competition in the older economy was mostly national but now is fundamentally global. Furthermore, the production systems in the older economy were based in mass production (for example, in the golden age of industrial capitalism in the postwar period), whereas the new economy is characterized by flexible production processes. Finally, while key factors of production in the old economy were capital and labour, the new economy tends to be driven by innovation and ideas.

There are other critical differences between what the OECD (2009) calls the "old" and the "new" paradigms of regional development. While the old paradigm focused on providing advantages for domestic industries, the new paradigm tends to be non-discriminatory as attention shifts towards enhancing regional global competitiveness. Furthermore, under the new paradigm, the focus has shifted toward leveraging the capital, technology, and competitiveness of all companies, local- or foreign-owned, to improve the global competitiveness of a particular region. Moreover, the strategies of the old paradigm tended to focus on sectoral or, even, individual firm approaches, whereas the new paradigm is integrated and cross-sectoral, seeking to position regions as niches within the global economy. For example, rather than focusing on the auto sector or the pulp and paper industry in isolation, the new paradigm builds a complex and intricate fabric of regional clusters of inter-sectoral innovation, production, and exchange systems. These cross-sectoral systems of cooperation even extend beyond industries within the private sector. Thus, the system of co-production among a network of actors constitutes a key element of the new paradigm of regional development.

Notwithstanding the distinguishing characteristics of the new economy, especially the centrality of knowledge creation and knowledge industries, they must be placed alongside traditional "old-economy" economic determinants such as costs of production, tax policy, interest rates, resource availability, and labour-force skills. The strategies proposed for consideration require embarking on strategies designed to create a "networked regional economy" by capitalizing on certain human capital strengths. Knowledge-sector economies generate products and services in a region that can lead to both internally driven and export-led growth. The main difference, therefore, is that the current focus of economic development policy intervention is on promoting the intangible assets of a region – knowledge creation, dissemination, application, and commercialization (Porter 1990; Krugman 1994; Florida 1995). For example, current policy discussions about regional economic development in Canada and Europe draw extensively from the emergent discourse on regional clusters of knowledge economies (OECD 2007, 2009). Knowledge-sector activities create nodes and clusters of high value-added activity that will serve as sources of both demand- and supply-side economic growth and attract additional development. The next section elaborates on this emergent model of regional economic development.

THE NEW REGIONALISM

Since the 1990s there has been a resurgence of scholarship on the spatial dimensions of economic growth and development (Krugman 1990, 1991, 1994; Porter 1990; Scott 2001). For example, there has been an increasing recognition of the positive synergies between the competitiveness of firms and the spatial and institutional characteristics of regions as "organic units of economic reality" (Scott and Storper 2003). This emerging analytical endeavour draws from a solid body of research that combines the insights of new-growth theory (Krugman 1991; Lucas 1988; Romer 1986), the cluster approach (Enright 2003; Porter 1990, 1998; Steiner 1998), the knowledge economy (Nonaka and Takeuchi 1995) and the literature on knowledge spillovers (Anselin et al. 1997; Audretsch and Feldman 1996). And as noted earlier, these new ideas about economic development through networked regional economies became conventional wisdom by the turn of the millennium (OECD 2009; Council of Canadian Academies 2009). The rest of the discussion in this section traces the analytical contours of this new regionalism.

The underlying premise of the growing literature on the new regionalism is that the global economy is in continual transformation as new markets, technologies, and opportunities emerge. Within this context of a rapidly changing world, regions and communities are positioning themselves for success by making better use of their existing potential competitive advantages. Central to these ideas are assumptions about the role of the state in creating new structures, organizations, and institutions, as well as the augmentation of existing ones to support the networked regional economy (Bradford 2010; Bastian and Ulrich 2003). The state is expected to systematically use policy instruments to encourage the development and application of knowledge that leads to the adaptation or improvements of products, processes, and services. The emergent threads of regional economic development policy governance in Canada and around the industrialized world thus weave through a wider fabric of innovation policy discourse (OECD 2009; Holbrook and Wolfe 2002; Cooke and Schwartz 2007). "Innovation" refers to an economic process rather than mere science and engineering activities; it refers to new or better ways of doing things that create or add value (Council of Canadian Academies 2009), and it extends beyond products to include improved processes and novel forms of business organization. Innovation has been defined as "the successful development and application of knowledge, which leads to the development, adaptation or improvements of products, process, services, markets, governments, institutions and ideas" (Manitoba Innovation Framework 2009).

Innovation is considered the bedrock of economic development in a knowledge-based economy, or a new economy (OECD 2007). Shifting trends towards the new economy are underpinned by structural and institutional changes brought about by the phenomena of globalization. As the capacity of the state to actively intervene and regulate the economy decreases, it is viewed less as a regulator of markets and more as a facilitator of market processes led by private corporations (Mackenzie et al. 2010). Nevertheless, the state is actively involved in the promotion and development of the new economy, while the private sector and research institutions take the lead in effecting the transformation. Several emergent changes have driven home the urgency of innovation policy (Ministry of Finance, Canada 2006): first, the intensification of global competition, especially with the rapid rise of the BRIC countries (Brazil, Russia, India and China), creating both growing challenges and opportunities for industrialized countries; second, the shift towards less resource-intensive and more ecologically sound production methods to allow for continued economic growth and development; third, the demographic time-bomb of Canada's and other OECD countries' aging population, which also threatens productivity growth as the proportion of the working age population plateaus and begins to decline; fourth, unfolding and outstanding developments in the transformative technologies of information and communications, life sciences, and advanced materials, which are providing new and immeasurable opportunities (Council of Canadian Academies 2009).

Innovation has been considered to be the key driver of labour productivity growth (increased output per hour worked) and thus the main source of a nation's economic success and socio-economic prosperity (Howitt 2007; Industry Canada 2008, 2009). Productivity growth is strongly related to the international competitiveness and commercial dynamism on which high employment and good jobs ultimately depend. Factors influencing the choice of innovation as a business strategy transcend the firm, sectoral (meso-), and national (macro-) levels. Key factors include the following: the structural characteristics of private firms; the competitive intensity of the various economic sectors (particularly those where technology or customer tastes change rapidly); the climate for new ventures (involving a range of early-stage venture financing, the presence of research institutions, and an ecosystem of supplier firms that help nurture an innovation from concept to commercialization); public policies that encourage or inhibit innovation (such as taxation, regulations, targeted assistance programs, and public procurement favourable to innovation); and business ambition such as entrepreneurial aggressiveness and growth orientation (often reflected in the dedication of businesses to market expansion and taking sectoral control), which can also be referred to as the entrepreneurial ethos. For example, new ventures are the "green shoots" of the innovation system; they are essential to the nurturing and commercialization of new ideas to market and to the creation of new competition. The most significant enabling conditions can be grouped into three broad categories: first, venture financing and the acquisition of commercial skills, which are the sources of risk capital and mentorship supporting the development of new firms from concept to sustainable business. A second category is technology transfer: research and intellectual property developed within universities and government laboratories require institutional and public policy mechanisms for their dissemination, application, and commercial realization (Industry Canada 2008; OECD 2009).

Another significant characteristic of innovation systems or clusters is that they tend to be geographically concentrated and locally driven ecosystems or networks that need not be restricted to metropolitan areas or technology-intensive sectors and economies, but may also be processes resulting in the rejuvenation and growth of traditional economic activities in sectors such as those producing resource-based products (Holbrook and Wolfe 2002). The concept of innovation, therefore, has a broader application than simply to the activities of highly developed metropolitan regions. It applies to the diverse range of knowledge-generating activities, from multimedia and biotechnology activities in large metropolitan areas to activities in more traditional sectors, such as sectors located in non-metropolitan settings manufacturing wood products. For example, the forestry and the minerals sectors tend to be vital to the economies in the socio-economically peripheral regions of Canada's provincial norths (New Brunswick Northern Development Strategy 2010; Northern Ontario Growth Plan 2011). Value-added products and services and sustainable resource-management practices constitute the major challenge of innovation systems in these non-metropolitan regions because these primary sectors still serve as the economic foundation of those regions and will continue to drive their economies well into the future. However, other opportunities exist for these regions to carve niches in the emerging bio-economy, such as forest-based biomass, bio-plastics, agri-fuels, and biopharmaceuticals. Moreover, these regions' natural assets can potentially generate opportunities in renewable-energy, water, and other environmental technologies. And the digital economy is creating new opportunities for regions traditionally isolated from the global value chains because of distance. For example, regions that were once geographically peripheral are expanding their access to health, education, and other services (Northern Ontario Growth Plan 2011).

A key feature of the governance of such an economic development policy environment is developing frameworks for policy intervention that encourage and facilitate collaboration among the orders of government, as well as non-governmental actors. Non-governmental actors in this context often include industry, businesses, labour organizations, community organizations, and education and research institutions, all of which need to work together over the long term. Within such an inter-governmental and inter-organizational collaborative framework, the goals of policy intervention may include joint efforts in seeking to attract new investment, facilitating the growth and retention of existing competitive businesses (including export-development activities and diversification into value-added business opportunities), responding to labour market needs and opportunities through education, supporting training and entrepreneurship, and supporting research tailored to a region's context to inform business development and infrastructure planning. In the advanced manufacturing sector, for instance, this will involve joint policy mechanisms for supporting innovation, research and the commercialization of value-added products and services in the existing and emerging priority economic sectors, and working with prospective investors to identify opportunities in a given region. Similarly, in the agriculture and forestry sectors of non-metropolitan regions, such activities may involve identifying opportunities for developing the bio-economy within these sectors, including innovative uses of agriculture and food processing, the biomass, and collaboration among producers, processors, the forest industry, bio-refineries and the biopharmaceutical industry, and the chemical, energy, plastics, and automotive industries (Manitoba Innovation Framework 2003; Northern Ontario Growth Plan 2011).

As noted in the previous section, a significant consequence of the seismic global economic restructuring over the past two decades has been the rise of sub-national jurisdictions as the centres of economic policy intervention (OECD 2009). Sub-national market governance and innovation policy seem to complement each other. Innovations leading to economic growth and development are considered to thrive in systems where high levels of interaction and collaboration take place among economic and community stakeholders (Krugman 1994; Porter 1990; Scott 2001). At the centre of such a policy environment are social clusters of knowledge production, dissemination, and utilization that are facilitated by interaction through knowledge networks and relationships at the local level. The shift in emphasis towards innovation thus means that more decentralized governance frameworks are the mechanisms most conducive to economic success.

Large and small communities are now positioning themselves to function as the economic and service hubs of particular regions (OECD 2007, 2009) Some of these communities act as points of convergence for major infrastructure, including transportation, energy, and information and communications technology. For example, more than half of northerners live in the cities of Greater Sudbury, North Bay, Sault Ste Marie, Timmins, and Thunder Bay. These cities, which are economic hubs for all of Northern Ontario (Government of Ontario 2009), possess the critical mass of skilled people, as well as regional assets like colleges and universities, innovation centres, media centres, and commerce and cultural facilities that can anchor many of the region's existing and emerging priority economic sectors. They are optimal locations for infrastructure investments that can help to expand this potential and serve citizens across the region, and they also have great potential to leverage investments and growth in order to develop vibrant, mixed-use core areas with a range of employment and housing opportunities, higher density development, and public transit. Moreover, competitive advantage is not limited to the acquisition of codified knowledge and capital that are available worldwide. Rather, it reflects the social and institutional capital that fosters the acquisition and utilization of codified and tacit knowledge, and these institutional and social variables are increasingly found at certain centres within a region or locality. A set of economic, political, and institutional structures existing within a geographical area generates a collective learning process leading to the rapid dissemination of knowledge (Holbrook and Wolfe 2002).

For this reason, the research and practice of innovation systems management has been gradually shifting from the national to the regional level (Mackenzie, Silver, and Sheldrick 2010; OECD 1997). Governance of the new economy is characterized by the building of a complex and intricate fabric of regional innovation systems (RIS), which focus on location and presuppose a geographical concentration of linkages and dynamic interactions among key actors within an innovation ecosystem (Porter 1990, 1998; Cooke and Morgan 1998; Holbrook and Wolfe 2000). Some of the major institutional players in this governance infrastructure are private and public research-intensive firms, research universities, and government labs. This trend has given rise to the growing importance of "places" (metropolitan and non-metropolitan alike) as distinct jurisdictions in their own right, with governance systems involving networks of government, business, community, and civic actors. Regional innovation systems are thus consistent with the concept of strategic policy initiatives aimed at facilitating regional economic adaptation.

These ideational and structural changes mean that regional economic development policy governance is becoming more diverse and complex. Such transformations have implications for state restructuring (Doornbos 2006; Timonen 2003). Management of the new economy is characterized by the building of a complex and intricate fabric of regional innovation systems that transcend several jurisdictions and mobilized interests, including the private sector and research institutions. This means a deepening of the complexities of federalism in countries like Canada, the United States, and Australia, as well as the multi-level governance systems of most European countries (Anderson 2010; Bosch and Durán 2008; Krasnick 1986). The imperatives of the new economy, therefore, require a rethinking of the institutional infrastructure of economic development policy implementation, or public management. The governance of innovation systems requires a governance architecture that transcends and integrates the various levels of government, as well as institutionalizes a network governance framework incorporating and legitimizing the nexus between proximity, innovation, and economic growth and development. The organic clusters among market actors, knowledge producers, and civic interests that emanate from their identification with their immediate surrounding communities can be leveraged into formal mechanisms of engagement and collaborative forms of governance (Cooke and Schwartz 2007).

In a country like Canada, where federal agencies are mandated to support economic adjustment in sub-national regions, economic development policy governance within a multi-layered institutional system reflects the new context of regional development. As discussed in the previous chapter, structured hierarchies in multi-level systems are confronted with the need to adjust their policy-delivery processes to environmental conditions that reflect the imperatives of increasing complexity. The complexity of the modern economic environment, in particular, necessitates viewing regional development policy implementation as a process of inter-organizational and inter-jurisdictional cooperation. Mechanisms for building synergies among a number of actors both in the public and in the private sector are increasingly important. Networked regional economies require collaborative approaches to market governance in which public managers make connections across organizations and share ideas, resources, and power with state and non-state actors. This means that regional development agencies' strategic choices of policy intervention are based on the specific environmental and institutional characteristics of a given region.

The integration of insights from the preceding and present chapters indicates that the imperatives of the new economy require a rethinking of regional economic development policy governance in Canada and other multi-level governance systems. First, it calls for policy alignment across levels of government through the development of frameworks of policy governance that give a central importance to "place," not only as a geographical but also as an institutional construct. Second, it requires horizontal collaborative governance between the public, private, and community sectors in which the private sector in particular regions can be seen less as an object of economic development and more as an agent of adaptation to global and local changes. Third, public policy governance mechanisms need to emphasize building coalitions of strategic alliances in order to successfully manage the many dependencies that are a natural and necessary component of delivering services or implementing policies in highly politicized environments. Finally, economic development policy governance can be understood as finding and sustaining a good fit between federal economic development agencies' missions and strategies and the forces in their external environment that create both opportunities and threats.

The next chapter (chapter 4) situates the discussion within the Canadian context by providing a brief history of regional economic development in the country over the past five decades. This discussion sets the stage for the subsequent chapters, which verify the relevance of the multi-actor framework developed in chapter 2. Chapter 4 will also briefly highlight the institutional and policy changes over the past five decades as Canada experimented with the various approaches to regional economic development discussed in chapter 3. Chapters 5 to 8 analyze four federal agencies in four distinct regions in Canada and the complexities and challenges of their institutional and policy adaptation to the imperatives of the new regionalism. Lessons are drawn from the Canadian experience to enrich our understanding of multi-level governance around the world. While the discussion focuses on Canada, the cases illustrate similar processes of public policy governance in multi-level systems beyond Canada's borders. The complexity of modern political and economic environments means public policy governance should be seen as a process of navigating institutional boundaries, rather than simply optimizing program output. The discussion in subsequent chapters illustrates how public policy governance in modern systems entails a proactive rather than reactive approach to public agencies' interaction with their external environments.

4

Historical Overview of Regional Economic Development Policy in Canada

INTRODUCTION

This chapter briefly outlines the ideational and institutional metamorphosis of regional economic development in Canada over the past five decades. The economic history of Canada has been based on a staples system, which means that the Canadian state has shown a tendency towards strong elements of interventionism in its approach to national development (Innis 1956; Norrie and Owram 1996; Nelles 2005). In social policy, such interventionism crystallized into a gradual transition to collectivism, with its most recent manifestation over the past five decades in a developed welfare state (Brooks and Miljan 2003). In economic development policy, a key example of active policy intervention has been the government's effort to correct structural imbalances in industrial diversity and growth among the regions (Careless 1977).

Regional economic development policy can be traced back to the 1957 Gordon Commission, which urged Ottawa to shift to a more systematic approach for correcting regional disparities. The report noted the need to develop the economics of the regions rather than merely compensating provinces for lower rates of economic growth than those achieved by the country as a whole (Canada Royal Commission 1957). The Gordon Commission's recommendations reflect the political desire (at least in economically disadvantaged regions) for a more deliberate focus on regional development issues aimed at a systematic easing of "disparities" (Savoie 1990). The commission maintains that the socio-economic realities of Canada's geographically remote and structurally fragile regions, such as Atlantic Canada, justify and, indeed, necessitate the "visible hand" of the state as a key agent of resource mobilization and allocation in pursuing economic development.

The newly elected Diefenbaker government pledged in 1957 to move away from what it considered the previous governments' passive, or *laissez faire*, approach to economic development, which was seen as to have overlooked major pockets of Canadian society (Norrie and Owram 1996). All successive federal governments have pledged to "alleviate regional disparities" and introduced their own schemes (Bakvis and Skogstad 2002), which have ranged from the establishment of the Funds for Rural Economic Development (FRED) under the Pearson administration to the establishment of the Department of Regional Economic Expansion (DREE) under Trudeau, to the creation in 1987 of special federal regional development agencies for each of the major regions under the Mulroney government (Savoie 2001).

Regional development policy had a rather humble origin in the tax incentives programs designed to induce firms to locate in slow-growth and high unemployment regions. But over the years, regional economic development policy has created an ideal theatre for dramatizing the cleavages between nation and province building in Canadian public policy governance. Most of the theoretical approaches to regional development discussed in the previous chapter have featured in the Canadian policy discussion and program development since the 1960s.

The thread that binds these experiments together is a belief in the spatial or geographic determinants of economic development (Colgan and Tomblin 2004). Regional economic development is a testament to its proponents' belief that sufficient public and private investment can force slow-growth regions to catch up with the rest of the country. Another central premise underlying the policy rationale is that national governments (in Canada, Ottawa) can fashion the spatial structure of the economy and significantly affect the economic fortunes of lagging regions (Polese 1999). As we shall see in the next section, however, most of these experiments over the past five decades were informed by conflicting political pressures and disparate sets of often competing assumptions or theories of economic development (McGee 1995).

THE HISTORICAL INTERSECTION OF IDEAS AND POLITICS: THE 1960S TO 1987

Regional economic development policy has seen its share of controversy. The period between the early 1960s and the late 1980s in

Canada was characterized by the steady rise, demise, and rebirth of regional economic development policy, often based on the vacillations of politics, economic crises, and the emergence of ideas supporting or contesting the logic of regional development (Polese 1999; Savoie 1992). This section examines the intersection of ideas, politics, and the institutional evolution of Canadian regional economic development between 1960 and 1987.

Our appreciation for, and understanding of, the complex ideational, political, and institutional challenges of regional economic development policy in Canada between the 1960s and mid-1990s has been enriched by the works of Anthony Careless (1977), Donald Savoie (1981, 1992, 1997, 2003), Harley McGee (1995), Guy Beaumier (1997), and Peter Aucoin and Herman Bakvis (1984), among others. A central thread running through the history of regional economic development in Canada is the fraught nature of the political controversy of regionalism and federalism, which largely explains the constant organizational change noticed between the early 1960s and the late 1980s.

Powerful ideas in the form of "scientific" understandings about the nature of regional economies formed the undercurrents of regional economic development policies. In general, regional economic development policy in industrialized democracies can be traced to the postwar optimism of development economists and public managers and their strong belief that deliberate and systematic policy intervention can drive the engine of regional economic development (Polese 1999). As shown in the previous chapter, in Canada, just as in most other OECD countries, the prominence by the late 1960s of regional development as an area of policy concern was a natural consequence of the rise of postwar Keynesianism and the attendant belief in various forms of economic policy activism designed to correct the cyclical fluctuations of the market and address the structural causes of regional disparities in wealth distribution. Keynesian assumptions about the role of the state in promoting industrial development and economic growth created a powerful and highly influential consensus among Canadian scholars and practitioners of regional economic development policy. Thus, the spatial and regional ordering of society became an important policy concern in Canada, as in most industrialized nations.

Regional development policy in Canada is a reflection of the structural feature of the country's physical, cultural, and institutional fragmentation and the projection of attendant tensions and contradictions into politics and public policy. As Richard Simeon (2006) has observed, the concept of regions and regionalism, despite the surrounding debates, have enduring features and salience as permanent as the realities of Canadian regionalism and federalism. Owing to Canada's vast geographical size, it is considered one of most fragmented developed market economies of the world (Watkins 2010). Part of the high policy profile that regional economic development enjoyed in the country, therefore, is attributable to this reality and the consequent desire to improve the living standards of lagging or peripheral regions. The disadvantages generally associated with certain peripheral regions in Canada are well known, including their physical remoteness from central markets and underdeveloped transportation and communication modes, their sparsely distributed population and small domestic markets, their statistically lower education and skills levels relative to the rest of the country, the loss of technical and managerial expertise from these regions, their lagging adoption of new technologies, their lack of marketing opportunities, and insufficient supporting infrastructure to overcome these deficiencies (McGee 1995).

Several factors that indicate socio-economic disadvantage in Canada's peripheral, or "hinterland," regions (Southcott 2006) include a declining population, increasing youth out-migration, rapidly aging communities, and declining industrial-resource sector employment. A particularly poignant example of these enduring regional disparities and tensions in Canada exists in the province of Ontario. Northern Ontario has been referred to by some commentators as the "hinterland" of Southern Ontario, echoing sentiments of dependency theory (see chapter 3) in this characterization (Southcott 2006; Nelles 2005). As Chris Southcott (2006) points out, industrial stagnation and decline gives the impression of developing-country conditions in the North, conditions exemplified by socio-economic underdevelopment by most indicators, except that these realities are hidden by Canada's redistributive mechanisms through a range of social policies. The history and structure of industry in the region confirms a trend of persistent decline in the mainstays of its economies (mostly primary-resource industries) with a gradual shift towards service industries, but with a general decline in industrial activity and a traditional weakness in secondary manufacturing and service industries. For example, from 1996 to 2001 the population of the region (786,000) decreased by 4.8 percent (Southcott

2006). Meanwhile, Ontario's overall population grew by 6.1 percent and Canada's by 4 percent. Between 1996 and 2001, the number of people employed in Northern Ontario decreased by 0.4 percent, whereas in Ontario that number increased by 12.5 percent. The number of people actively looking for work in Ontario increased by 8.9 percent, but decreased by 3.3 percent in Northern Ontario (indicative of a larger number of people giving up the job search in Northern Ontario). The most glaring fact is that the communities in Northern Ontario with the highest rate of unemployment were Aboriginal communities (Di Matteo 2006; Southcott 2006).

Furthermore, seismic shifts in the global economy since the 1970s have further rattled the fragile foundations of the peripheral resource-dependent economies in Canada. The vagaries of international trade and investment have subjected the region to profound socio-economic insecurity. The economic challenges associated with peripheral resource-dependent communities are related to a variety of domestic and international factors, including resource depletion, vulnerability to world commodity prices, vulnerability to corporate policy changes, the cyclical nature of the resource industries, fluctuations in the Canadian exchange rate, changes in the interest rate and cost of capital, and changes in government policies regarding Northern Ontario (Di Matteo 2006). Single-resource communities have seen the worst of these vagaries – some towns have disappeared altogether. Their dependence on external markets has made them vulnerable to global fluctuations in the price of natural-resource commodities – which over the past two decades have experienced a downward trend. Moreover, new technologies have displaced workers in the resources sector.

A key part of the underlying resilience of regional economic development in Canada over the decades between the 1960s and the late 1980s was persistence in the belief that these problems could be rectified through policy and institutional mechanisms. For proponents of regional economic development policy intervention, the solution appears to lie in how assets are used, how different stakeholders interact, and how synergies are exploited in different types of regions. The market, they claim, does not always achieve this alone. Various ideas competed for attention in the policy subsystem of regional economic development, including the highly influential growth-pole concept discussed in the previous chapter. The development approach was also widely referenced, but primarily as a rhetorical tool to underscore the urgency of policy intervention on behalf of socio-economically disadvantaged regions. Moreover, the neoclassical, or trade-theory, approach saw its day under the Canadian sun as skeptics of regional economic development drew from this paradigm to attack the legitimacy of such policies. The "mixed-economy models" also penetrated the debates surrounding regional economic development, which set the context for the eventual emergence of the new regionalism. Each of these approaches (with the exception of the neoclassical paradigm) used various rationales or frameworks to justify a similar set of interventionist measures to stimulate growth within particular socio-economically disadvantaged or peripheral regions in Canada. The measures of intervention often included encouragement of capital accumulation, assistance in creating adequate industrial infrastructure, the promotion and application of new technology, and assistance in modernizing agricultural methods, especially for rural regions.

In addition to fostering the plethora of ideas that sustained the resilience and contradictions of regional economic development policy in Canada, politics also left indelible imprints on the character of this policy. A particular example of the influence of politics on Canadian regional economic development is how the struggle for policy control between federal and provincial governments between the 1960s and 1980s caused considerable inconsistencies in regional development policy instruments and organizations (McGee 1995). The frequent organizational and program changes marking this period led some observers to describe the institutional features of regional development in Canada as an "alphabet soup" of agencies and programs (Desjardins, Hobson, and Savoie 2000). Several distinct stages mark the evolution of regional economic development policy in Canada since the early 1960s (Aucoin and Bakvis 1984; Dupre 1985). A brief overview of this evolution is in order.

One of the foundational institutional configurations of regional economic development in Canada was the creation of the Agricultural and Rural Development Act (ARDA) in 1961. Operated with the provinces on a shared-cost basis, ARDA involved intergovernmental transactions conducted on a bilateral basis by the federal Department of Agriculture and its provincial counterparts (Dupre 1985). ARDA's main program focus was to improve the average incomes of rural regions through the provision of assistance to create work opportunities. Its operation was extended in 1966 to nonagricultural projects in rural regions, with the aim of diversifying the regional economies away from agricultural dependence. Also in 1966, a special Fund for Rural Development (FRED) was established with a focus on supporting the economic adjustment of depressed rural regions (Savoie 1997, 2001). The five regions designated under FRED's program were the Mactaquac of New Brunswic, the northeastern regions of New Brunswick, the Interlake region of Manitoba, Prince Edward Island, and the Gaspé Peninsula in Quebec (Watkins 2010). With the arrival of the government of Prime Minister Trudeau in 1968, the ARDA-FRED mechanism gave way in 1969 to the creation of the Department of Regional Economic Expansion (DREE). The creation of DREE was a result of the perceived need for a centralized federal agency to coordinate all federal regional development efforts and to enter into more cooperative agreements with the provinces. DREE merged all existing regional development programs under one governance umbrella, the regions designated for its economic development programs included all the Atlantic provinces, Eastern and Northern Quebec, parts of Northern Ontario, and the northernmost regions of the four Western provinces.

Also, influenced by the prevailing growth-pole concept, DREE shifted the focus of regional development away from rural poverty and towards industrial and urban growth. In particular, two programs were developed under the influence of the growth-pole concept: a "special-areas" program and a "regional-industrial incentives" program (Careless 1977). The special-areas program focused on infrastructural projects like industrial parks, sewer systems, schools, highways, and water systems. The regional-incentives program offered financial capital in the form of grants and low-interest loans to firms in order to create new jobs in specially designated regions. The period of DREE proved to be one of the most controversial ones in the history of regional economic development in Canada. The department faced numerous criticisms from various quarters (Savoie 1986; Aucoin and Bakvis 1984). Western provinces criticized it for focusing too much on the Atlantic provinces, but the Atlantic provinces criticized it as being too centralized. Moreover, an ideational attack came from the then resurgent theorists in the neoclassical school. Their main contention was that after four years in operation, this otherwise very powerful and ubiquitous department could show no convincing evidence of having accomplished its goals of reducing regional inequality in Canada (McGee 1995).

The straw that eventually broke DREE's "back" was a 1972 review that found several problems within the department (Canada 1972). In particular, the review questioned the wisdom of using nationally designed programs to address the complexities of each region's problems. More importantly, the analysis shifted from a focus on regional disparity to one on regional economic and social development. The rationale of policy intervention became less about "catching up" with more prosperous regions and more about providing opportunities for each region to realize its own potentials. Equity of opportunity, rather than equality among regions, became the leitmotif.

DREE also attempted to reformulate its relationship with the provinces. However, given the swell of discontent from various quarters, it was decentralized and the General Development Agreements (GDAs) between the federal and provincial governments were created (Savoie 1997, 2003). In principle, the GDAs were designed to provide opportunities for provincial governments to take the initiative in proposing projects that the federal government could support or reject. Operating under the umbrella of a ministerial General Development Agreement with a ten-year lifespan, a provincially based DREE general director was designated the prime negotiator of subsidiary agreements with the provinces. Between 1974 and 1982, 130 agreements were made under these programs throughout Canada, with a financial commitment of close to $6 billion (Watkins 2010). The costs were shared, but 80 to 90 percent of the funding for these projects was federal. However, regional economic development suffered another major crisis of credibility during this period as virtually every conceivable project was labelled regional economic development. Ironically, the lack of theoretical coherence in regional economic development coincided with the resurgence of a virulent strain of neoclassical thinking that showed little tolerance for any policy instruments that smacked of market intervention. By early 1982, DREE's GDAs scheme was discredited and the department was dismantled, but regional economic development proved itself the cat with seven lives. In the end, the politics of Canadian regionalism prevailed over the ideology of pure market-ism. A new Ministry of State for Regional and Economic Development (MSERD) was established to succeed DREE. MSERD has a special department – the Department of Regional Industrial Expansion (DRIE), dedicated to regional economic development, and the GDAs that used to exist under the disbanded DREE were replaced with Economic and Regional Development Agreements (ERDAs). Though disbanded, the GDAs were allowed to die a natural death at the expiration of the ten-year lifespan and were then replaced by the new ERDAs.

MSERD was also quickly abolished in 1984, and the responsibility for regional development was given to a new minister of state for regional development, a portfolio under the aegis of DRIE. DRIE was designed to combine both regional and industrial perspectives. The claim was that the new initiative called the Industrial and Regional Development Program would end regional favouritism and would apply everywhere in the country. It was not long before complaints began to surface that regional economic development was under control that was too centralized in Ottawa and that provincial governments were not given enough autonomy over the design and implementation of programs affecting their own provinces. Moreover, complaints surfaced from the Atlantic and Western regions that private sector firms in central Canada were being given preferential treatment (McGee 1995; Savoie 1997). In 1987, there was major restructuring leading to the amalgamation of DRIE with the former Ministry of Science and Technology as the Ministry of Industry, Science and Technology and the creation of decentralized regional agencies. DRIE was eventually disbanded in 1988 after the establishment of separate departments and agencies for each of the regions.

As is evident in this kaleidoscope of institutional restructuring between 1961 and 1987, regional economic development in Canada has been a roller-coaster ride of experimentation infused with the vicissitudes of political theatrics, theoretical fads, and ideological pendulum swings. It is the quintessential manifestation of regional and federal politics in a highly fragmented and controversial institutional system such as Canada. Viewed through the lens of regional economic development policy, it is difficult to overstate the complexity of Canadian federalism and its supporting policy institutions in such a large and diverse country, with provinces and territories of starkly different fiscal, population, and land characteristics. The present institutional configuration of regional economic development policy implementation in Canada dates back to the 1987 restructuring, which created the three regional development agencies for Western Canada, Atlantic Canada, and Northern Ontario, namely, the Western Economic Diversification (WD), the Atlantic Canada Opportunities Agency (ACOA) and the Federal Economic

Initiative for Northern Ontario (FedNor), respectively. The agency, FORD-Q was eventually created in 1991 for Northern Quebec. The mission of the four agencies is to promote economic growth, diversification, job creation, and sustainable, self-reliant communities by working with community partners and other organizations (Goldenberg 2008). The agencies' programs and services have the goal of addressing some of the structural, sectoral, and community economic development challenges facing Canada's socio-economically disadvantaged regions.

The principal feature of the 1987 restructuring was the decentralization of administrative and policy functions away from Ottawa and towards the regions. Each of the agencies is located outside Ottawa and headed by deputy ministers, and each agency reports directly to a minister (Savoie 1990). Programs and measures were to be developed according to the needs of the region they were intended to assist and would no longer be expected to apply throughout the country. This new approach, in principle, would allow for more direct interaction between decentralized federal agencies and various policy actors in their operating environments in the design and implementation of programs. These institutional features, as we will see in subsequent chapters, set the stage for the rather remarkable adaptation and transition of regional economic development over the past two decades. In particular, the 1987 restructuring granted sufficient autonomy for the federal government's regional development agencies to accommodate the emergence of a new wave of assertive provincialism marked by increasingly strong, willful provincial governments and local interests bent on pursuing locally defined economic strategies. The institutional flexibility built into the 1987 restructuring set the template for the relatively successful navigation of the virulent strains and sometimes murky waters of intergovernmental rivalry and contestation that plagued and bedevilled previous federal agencies. After 1987, regional development policy governance in Canada became increasingly intertwined and achieved varying degrees of success with the navigation of institutional boundaries between levels of government as well as with non-state actors and community groups.

The next four chapters examine the transitions of regional economic development policy governance over the past two decades, with a focus on the federal government's regional development agencies' policy engagement in the provinces of New Brunswick,

Manitoba, and Ontario. The examination of four federal agencies in these three cases illustrates how these agencies adapted to the shifts towards collaborative governance, while seeking to preserve organizational mandates and distinct identities as federal agencies. The next four chapters, therefore, explain how the peculiar characteristics of specific regions in Canada interacted with the broader features of policy governance in increasingly complex multi-level and multi-actor institutions over the past two decades. Policy governance in such systems has the potential for cooperation or conflict as public agencies navigate various levels of constitutional and policy jurisdictions, while at the same time striving to maintain their identity and legitimacy. As this discussion reveals, federal agencies created with structured hierarchies are confronted with the need to adjust processes to the environmental imperatives of horizontal management in order to maintain system stability, manage change, and deepen the impact of their policy intervention.

5

Regional Development Policy Governance in New Brunswick

INTRODUCTION

This chapter analyzes the transitions in regional economic development policy governance in the Canadian province of New Brunswick under the mandate of a federal agency, the Atlantic Canada Opportunities Agency (ACOA). Although general trends in New Brunswick are highlighted, the focus of discussion is on the implications of these trends for the mandate and strategies of ACOA as a federal agency operating within a sub-national jurisdiction. As maintained in preceding chapters, certain shifts that occurred in the regional development policies and practices in Canada and other OECD countries have necessitated a growing emphasis on collaborative governance mechanisms of policy delivery. This chapter illustrates how regional development policy implementation tasks in such complex policy subsystems are best viewed as strategic and not merely operational. These requisite governance mechanisms are distinguished from traditional administrative processes in that policy implementation or program delivery primarily involves building partnerships with various agents across different levels of government and with non-state actors in other institutions and the private sector. Acknowledging the importance of collaborative governance, therefore, entails seeing the boundaries of the public sector as more porous than ever, and it also entails seeing that policy implementation must frequently involve multiple agencies and groups working in concert (Bourgon 2007).

New Brunswick is one of the smaller provinces of Canada, with a population of approximately 750,000. The majority of the province's residents are English-speaking, and a large Francophone minority

Table 5.1
Demographic and Economic Characteristics of New Brunswick

Capital	Fredericton
Largest city	Saint John
Largest metropolitan area	Greater Moncton
Total area	72,908 km^2 (28,150 sq mi)
Population (2010)	751,273
Total GDP (2009)	C$27.497 billion
GDP per capita	C$33,664

Source: Courtesy of Statistics Canada.

(mostly of Acadian origin) makes up about 33 percent of the population. The provincial capital is Fredericton, while Saint John, the most populous city, is the industrial capital. Moncton is the commercial capital as well as the largest census metropolitan area. (Table 5.1 summarizes the province's key characteristics, and figure 5.1 provides a map of the province.) Since the formal inception of regional economic development policy in Canada in the 1960s, New Brunswick, like the rest of the provinces in Atlantic Canada, has been considered a "slow growth" or "lagging" region in the country (Government of New Brunswick 1989; Atlantic Provinces Economic Council 2006). Some of the province's main economic challenges include declining employment opportunities in primary industries, lower population and labour force increases owing to higher rates of out-migration, labour participation rates lower than the rest of Canada, high levels of unemployment, the relative absence of significant manufacturing activities, and average incomes lower than the national average.

Significant weaknesses in New Brunswick's economy during the late 1980s could be seen in private sector activities such as lower business capital investment relative to the national average, lower R&D investment, poor utilization of the provincial supply of scientific and technical human capital, the skewed nature of industrial distribution (such as the limited role of manufacturing and the lack of creation of high-tech industries), and a relatively lower productivity level compared to the Canadian average (Atlantic Provinces Economic Council 2002) As Pierre-Marcel Desjardins (2005) notes, the seasonal nature of employment in peripheral resource-dependent regions is an example of the factors that undermine the economic stability of the province. Rural-urban out-migration and the seasonal nature of the labour force present two examples of the major challenges to economic development in New Brunswick. In addition

Figure 5.1 Map of New Brunswick. Courtesy of Natural Resources Canada

to, or because of, the structural weaknesses of its economy, New Brunswick, like the other Atlantic provinces, has long suffered from perceptions among Canadians that it is a province of "federal largesse" (Maritimes Union Study 1989). Against this backdrop, one can appreciate the driving force of public policy in the province to change perceptions about New Brunswick by projecting an image of an organized, driven, and visionary province rather than a fractious, parochial economic backwater.

Against this background, New Brunswick has made considerable economic progress over the past two decades. The province's standard of living has been steadily rising (Government of New Brunswick 2011; ACOA's Five-Year Report to Parliament 2003–2008). Over the past decade alone, the New Brunswick economy grew by an average 2.0 percent per year, and investment in emerging (knowledge-intensive) sectors was one of the principal drivers of growth. Personal income is higher, dependence on federal transfers has dropped, employment has increased, and participation in the labour force is up. New Brunswick has also been undergoing a transition from a primarily resource-dependent economy to an increasingly knowledge-based one, driven by innovation, technology, and growth in non-resource sectors. Increasingly, as we will see later in the chapter, the focus is on creating a "new" knowledge-driven economy in the province with an emphasis on innovation generating growth, jobs, and development. The strong employment recorded in management and administrative services (call centres); professional, scientific, and technical services (IT); and information, culture, and recreation (software publishing, telecommunications, tourism, and so on) points to this trend (Canadian Institute for Research on Regional Development 2001, 2003). Moreover, New Brunswick has several strengths to tap into: first, the province's workforce is bilingual; second, the smaller size of the province enables greater networking capability and potential – factors critical for knowledge-based economies; third, the geographic location of the province is well suited for the major markets in Central Canada, the Northeastern United States and Europe; and fourth, there is a wide variety of knowledge-based companies with world-class capabilities that are willing to create partnerships with other companies already existing in the province (Government of New Brunswick 2011).

ACOA IN NEW BRUNSWICK

As noted in chapter 4, the federal government's economic development policy intervention in Atlantic Canada (including New Brunswick) beginning in the 1960s emphasized a national framework of policy development and management (McGee 1995; Aucoin and Bakvis 1984). Although there were periodic vacillations between centralization and decentralization, and for a brief period in the 1970s, the creation of a department with some autonomy for partnering with provinces, the inclination of the federal government in developing and implementing regional programs throughout most of this period was to centralize the management of regional development in the national capital. A major restructuring in 1987, however, led to the creation of relatively autonomous regional development agencies for each of Canada's major regions. The agency responsible for Atlantic Canada was the Atlantic Canada Opportunities Agency (ACOA) (Government of Canada 1987a). The restructuring reflected the discourse in the field of public administration at the time about certain advantages associated with decentralized administration. The prominent arguments were that programs would be delivered more quickly, with fewer costs, and that they could be modified to reflect local circumstances (Savoie 1992). Moreover, the restructuring was a response to the dissatisfaction of the provinces with the centralized administration of regional development, whose rationale was that devolution of policy authority to agencies with particular regional mandates could enhance the capacity of provincial and local actors to participate in the management of regional development initiatives. ACOA is thus the successor agency to a long tradition of regional development policy geared towards improving socio-economic conditions in Atlantic Canada, including the province of New Brunswick. The agency's mandate as legislated by a 1987 act of Parliament has been to "support and promote opportunities for the economic development of Atlantic Canada" (Government of Canada 1987a). ACOA is headed by a federal minister with the title Minister of State for the Atlantic Canada Opportunities Agency and has a head office is in Moncton, New Brunswick, with regional offices located in each of the other Atlantic provinces – Nova Scotia, Prince Edward Island, and Newfoundland and Labrador.

Since its creation, ACOA's mission, in principle, has consisted of providing support to small and medium-sized enterprises; engaging in policy, program, and project development and implementation; and advocating for the interests of Atlantic Canada in national economic policy, program, and project development and implementation. ACOA's main program activity areas are Enterprise Development, Community Development, and Policy, Advocacy, and Coordination. Enterprise Development consists of supporting initiatives to improve the climate of business as well as lending a direct hand for individual business start-ups, modernizations, and expansions (ACOA's Five-Year Report to Parliament 2003–2008). Community Development involves working with communities to nurture economic growth, improve local infrastructure, and develop opportunities in the local economy. The third area of operation, Policy, Advocacy, and Coordination mandates the agency to serve as a conduit for presenting Atlantic Canada's interests at the national level. ACOA is expected to represent and cater to the region's general interest through activities like economic policy development, research and analysis, and networking with other departments to ensure coordination of policies and programs affecting the region.

The 1987 restructuring, however, did not lead to a dramatic change in the nature of regional development policy implementation. Between 1987 and 2000, the agency's activities were mostly in Enterprise and Community Development (ACOA's Departmental Performance Report 2000–2001).[1] The instruments of its Enterprise Development program were mostly project-like loans and subsidies aimed at business development. The Community Development program was primarily directed at the vague goal of fostering dynamic and sustainable communities in New Brunswick. Much of the agency's activities under this program consisted of provision of support to community-based regional economic development (planning) organizations and funding for community business development corporations. Viewed through the lens of the policy implementation literature, ACOA's approach was marked by a "top-down" approach. Its model of policy engagement with the region was rather mechanistic, as it focused on disbursing grants, rather than fully engaging the complex structural realities and actors of the region's economy.

Moreover, for much of the first decade of its existence, ACOA's policy development, advocacy, and coordination mandates remained virtually latent (Savoie 2001). The differences between ACOA and a typical line department was only superficial, but it was too small (by federal standards) to influence policies or ongoing activities of other federal departments. In fact, ACOA was operating in the shadow of the federal Department of Industry – a department whose sectoral orientation goes against the concept of ACOA's spatial logic. The agency's policy development mandate would have required it to provide sustained intelligence about market trends and opportunities in New Brunswick and the rest of the Atlantic region, and it would have engaged in global investment and trade forecasting to help project New Brunswick's industrial strategy onto the world stage. In addition, ACOA's advocacy mandate would have required it to serve as the conduit through which the regional concerns and interests of Atlantic Canada were channelled into Canada's national macroeconomic and industrial policies. The agency's mandate required it to act as a lynchpin coordinating the programs of federal departments in New Brunswick and the rest of Atlantic Canada. This mandate also meant that the provincial government would need to rationalize its economic development with the policy vision of ACOA (which had yet to be formulated) (McGee 1995). ACOA's approach during the early years of its existence was thus consistent with the closed-systems perspective in the classical literature of organization theory whereby the tendency of public agencies is to emphasize overly rational, control-oriented, and mechanistic processes of service delivery to minimize institutional constraints and maximize opportunities.

During the early years of its existence ACOA was still breaking out of what was perceived (whether rightly or wrongly) as the institutional inertia and limitations of its predecessor – the Department of Regional Economic Expansion (DREE) (Ruff, Aucoin and Bakvis 1989). As a federal department, ACOA was coping well with the realities of intra-organizational management in the sense that the administrative model of public management in constitutional democracies requires pyramids with cascading levels of authority that ensure that all work activities are properly coordinated, controlled, and accounted for (ACOA's Report on Plans and Priorities 2011–12). But the success of policy implementation is both a function of an agency's organizational expertise and of technical as well as its strategic adaptation to the imperatives of its external environment. Given its mandates, it quickly became evident that ACOA was too small to command the institutional respect or to have the organizational capacity necessary for effective policy advocacy and coordination.[2] It also lacked the organizational and human resource capacity to engage in sustained regional development policy analysis. As we shall see, it took both organizational adaptation and capacity building to reach the agency's current annual budget of well over $300 million (ACOA Report on Plans and Priorities 2011–12).

Thus, despite the 1987 restructuring, the new agency carried on business as usual. The fact was that ACOA was initially designed as a small agency, with a staff of about a hundred (McGee 1995; Savoie 1992). Even more challenging was the fact that as ACOA struggled to find a policy niche within New Brunswick, the provincial government continued with its own economic development program that was separate from ACOA but based on a similar delivery model.[3] Each of the parallel programs basically determined the needs of individual firms based on submitted grant applications and responded with subsidies or loans (Mintz and Smart 2003). Although the provincial government had a broader cross-sectoral strategy than ACOA to create a favourable climate for industrial development, its general approach was intended to be – and was – responsive, short-term, and project-driven (Savoie 1997).

In theory, one of the key advantages of a decentralized policy implementation process is greater coordination of programs among public agencies of different jurisdictional levels, but the relationship between ACOA and the New Brunswick government during this period did not strongly demonstrate such coordination. The relationship could, rather, be described as still broadly influenced by the institutional and policy legacies of four decades of centralized regional economic development. The clash of federal and provincial organizational cultures was an obstacle to ACOA's policy penetration of the province. Organization theory calls our attention to the nature of the interaction between public organizations and their external environment. Policy implementation, from this perspective, should be understood as fundamentally a process involving a series of interactions among public agencies, on the one hand, and between public agencies and organized target-groups within the community and the private sector, on the other. ACOA viewed itself as a federal agency with a set of uniform programs to deliver in the four eastern provinces, including New Brunswick (Savoie 2001). The government of New Brunswick, on the other hand, emphasized adaptation of federal programs at the provincial level.

The merely organizational restructuring of 1987 proved insufficient to transcend the institutional boundaries between levels of government inasmuch as the provincial government merely communicated its responses to federal development activities as they affected the economic interests of New Brunswick. Apart from the province accepting the agency's money, the extent to which the economic development priorities of the province were influenced by ACOA remains unclear.[4] ACOA was struggling to find a niche in New Brunswick. Moreover, in seeking to demonstrate its administrative capacity, ACOA became focused on optimizing program output rather than on coordinating its implementation processes with the provincial government. ACOA thus became vulnerable to the New Brunswick government's ability to use the former's resources for any conceivable provincial scheme that was ostensibly for development. This was, in fact, the general perception in the early 1990s (Savoie 1997).

The earlier chapter on the multi-actor implementation framework suggests that the success of policy implementation is a function not merely of the government's intra-organizational expertise and resources but also of its adaptation to the imperatives of its external environment. This perspective calls our attention to the willingness or ability of organizations to reorganize their culture, operations, and structural features. But by the latter part of the 1990s, the consolidation of emergent ideas about the new regionalism as the rationale for economic development policy intervention slowly began to influence and transform ACOA's engagement in the province. Its strategy of organizational survival and legitimacy became a matter of adapting to the institutional demands of a knowledge-based economy articulated and driven by a number of more assertive policy actors in the province of New Brunswick. The next section sketches the range of key actors and their specific demands and highlights the implications of these trends for economic development policy intervention in the province. The trends in New Brunswick were microcosmic reflections of broader trends in Atlantic Canada, but for the purpose of analytical depth and clarity, the discussion focuses on New Brunswick. The following section then analyzes ACOA's adaptation to these developments over the past decade. These adaptations required certain organizational changes that would eventually position ACOA for greater relevance and engagement in the province.

THE EMERGENCE OF ASSERTIVE SUB-NATIONAL JURISDICTIONS AND ACTORS

The growing challenges confronting ACOA's policy intervention in New Brunswick emerged in the form of a province increasingly willing and eager to more actively decide the course of its economy. This trend dates back to Premier Frank McKenna (1987 to 1997), whose leadership style has left an enduring institutional legacy and political culture of active provincial assertiveness in economic development policy governance (Canadian Institute for Research in Regional Development 2002). Premier McKenna has been described as one of the more ambitious and influential premiers in efforts to transform the economy of New Brunswick (Desjardin 2005). For example, the province aggressively pursued a vision of economic development under his leadership that contained six pillars: the development of small business and entrepreneurship, the exploitation of the potential for research and development, the greater involvement of educational institutions in economic growth, the modernization of traditional industries, the diversification of the provincial economy through service industries and tourism, and selective infrastructure development. These initiatives were consistent with the characteristics of the new regionalism discussed in chapter 3.

Thus, the enduring policy legacy of provincial activism dating to Premier McKenna created an institutional path that coincided with ideas emerging in the mid-1990s about how to engage and facilitate the modern economy (Canadian Institute for Research on Regional Development 2002). By the mid-1990s, the centrepiece of the New Brunswick government's economic development strategy became promoting innovation through knowledge production, technology promotion, and skills development.[5] As discussed in chapter 3, innovation policy leading to economic growth and development is considered to thrive in systems where high levels of interaction and collaboration exist among economic and community stakeholders. At the centre of this policy environment are social clusters of knowledge production, dissemination, and utilization facilitated by interaction through knowledge networks and relationships at the local level. Thus the shift in emphasis towards innovation in New Brunswick resulted in more decentralized governance frameworks as mechanisms conducive to economic success. These policy shifts are analyzed below, with a focus on their implications for ACOA's governing mandate and strategies in New Brunswick.

By the turn of the millennium, the New Brunswick government was defining the provincial policy vision in bolder terms with longer-range planning. In 2002, Premier Bernard Lord unveiled New Brunswick's Prosperity Plan. The plan was a ten-year strategy (2002–12) that focused on the economic fundamentals of innovation, productivity, and export orientation – perceived determinants of success in a knowledge-driven economy (Government of New Brunswick 2002). By making the plan longer-term, the provincial government hoped to strengthen its control of the direction and pace of economic development. The plan was formed on four main building blocks: investing in people, creating a competitive fiscal and business environment, embracing innovation, and building strategic infrastructure. Three main implementation strategies are integrated across the four building blocks: economic diversification and clustering; community economic development; and strategic partnerships with government, business, universities and community colleges, workers, and communities. In general, the Prosperity Plan was seen by the New

Brunswick government as essential to the economic transformation of the province into a leading regional, national, and international economy.

Another dimension of the policy shift towards innovation in New Brunswick was the identification of key cities, such as Moncton, Saint John, and Fredericton, as critical loci of market governance and cities of strategic importance to the new focus on a knowledge-driven economy (Atlantic Provinces Economic Council 2001). The unique geographic importance of Moncton as a hub of complex networks of road and air transportation in the Atlantic region, as well as between the region and the eastern seaboard in the United States, adds to the strategic significance in the new policy environment of the municipal level itself. The notion of innovation clusters emphasizes local aspects of social capital and knowledge networks. Fostering these networks requires equipping cities with a certain coordinating authority and granting them the legitimacy to provide more active and strategic leadership. Moreover, the coordination of knowledge clusters is considered best handled at the local level, and cities in New Brunswick are eager to capitalize on these ideational shifts.

For instance, the Economic Development Office of the City of Moncton has been mandated with the planning, organization, coordination, and execution of initiatives to identify economic development opportunities for the municipality and to create an environment that is attractive to new businesses (City of Moncton 2009). The department has developed its own strategic plan for economic development – the Economic Development Strategy (published in 2005),[6] which is separate from the provincial government's plan. Moncton's Economic Development Strategy was developed with the stated purpose of enabling the "city to take more direct control of its economic development."[7] In the strategy, the city identifies its five key challenges: changing demographics (aging population and workforce and weak immigration), limited post-secondary education opportunities for anglophones, lack of challenging employment opportunities in knowledge-based industries and the creative economy, weak attractiveness factors crucial to making a city more appealing to the younger generation, and weak national and international visibility. The Strategic Plan also works to attract new investment to Greater Moncton, recruit skilled workers to the region, foster new industrial growth, create diversity in the local economy, strengthen existing business partnerships, and seek out new growth opportunities. Part of this plan includes fostering public and private associations with other public agencies and non-governmental entities pursuing economic development initiatives.[8] In particular, the department has targeted facilitating knowledge or innovation networks consisting of participants drawn from the local, provincial, and national levels to coordinate and maximize efforts around economic development for Moncton. For instance, one of the main priorities targeted in the document is for the city to provide leadership in supporting and enhancing the cooperation between the major players involved in economic development such as Enterprise Greater Moncton, the Greater Moncton Chamber of Commerce, Downtown Moncton Centre-ville Inc (DMCI), and the Moncton Industrial Development (MID).

A key part of the city's economic development governance framework, therefore, is to maximize public and private relationships with other individuals and groups pursuing economic development initiatives, as well as to manage relationships with all stakeholders at the local, provincial, and national levels to coordinate and maximize efforts around economic development for Moncton. From the perspective of the multi-actor framework, the city of Moncton is seeking to engage in strategic leadership that mirrors the federal (or ACOA's) and provincial governments' efforts through its Economic Development Office. It is worth recalling in this context the discussion in chapter 3 concerning how the increasingly assertive role of municipalities, legitimized by the concept of innovation-driven economies, calls for policy alignment across levels of government through the development of frameworks of policy governance that gives a central importance to "local spaces" not only as geographical but also institutional constructs.

A specific example of the intergovernmental and inter-sectoral partnership located within the institutional framework of the city can be found in the Southeast New Brunswick Education and Industry Council. The purpose of this council is to formalize the collaboration needed to ensure a strong education (including post-secondary education) presence in the region that is aligned with and responsive to labour force needs in the business community. The council was formed as a result of two Education and Industry Forums held in 2007 that opened the way to the sustained dialogue and concerted effort involving the education sector, industry, and government in seeking to meet the current and future needs of industry in south-east New Brunswick while supporting the growth potential of this region. In addition, in December 2006 the Moncton Technology Planning Group (MTPG), commissioned by the city's Economic Development Office, released an economic development action plan aimed at accelerating a knowledge-based economy in the Moncton area (City of Moncton Deptartment of Economic Development 2007). The central emphasis in the strategy is the growth of Moncton's existing information and communications technologies (ICT) sector strengths and the existing and emergent research capacity in area institutions. A significant characteristic of innovation systems or clusters is that they tend to be geographically concentrated and locally driven ecosystems or networks that support and sustain the creation and dissemination of new ideas and ventures. This trend has reinforced the growing importance of the Greater Moncton region as a distinct jurisdiction in its own right, with governance systems involving networks of government, business, community, and civic actors (Bourjeois and Trepanier 2010).

A further example can be seen in the New Brunswick city of Saint John. The city's Economic Development Service helps to create an environment for prosperity in local communities.[9] The main agency responsible for carrying out the economic development mandate is Enterprise Saint John, a not-for-profit agency funded by the City of Saint John, and the municipalities of Grand Bay-Westfield, Quispamsis, Rothesay, and St Martins. Enterprise Saint John focuses on issues such as workforce expansion, supporting and growing businesses, assisting the start-up of new businesses, and attracting new companies and investments. Through Enterprise Saint John, the city serves as a geographical node for a complex multi-actor intergovernmental and public-private partnership. Government partners include the Town of Quispamsis; the Town of Rothesay; the Town of Grand Bay-Westfield; the Village of St Martins; the Province of New Brunswick Population Growth Secretariat; the Province of New Brunswick Department of Post-Secondary Education, Training, and Labour; the Province of New Brunswick Department of Business New Brunswick; Service Canada; the Atlantic Canada Opportunities Agency (ACOA); and Industry Canada. In this regard, the city provides strategic policy leadership in which ACOA is only one of its partners.

Enterprise Saint John's wide range of private sector partners includes the following: the Atlantic Centre for Energy (which identifies, supports, and promotes opportunities in Saint John's energy sector); PropelICT (a private sector, non-profit organization dedicated to the growth of entrepreneurship, innovation, and the expansion of the Information and Communication Technology sector); the Saint John Board of Trade (dedicated to fostering an economic climate that encourages growth, prosperity, and an improved quality of life in the community); the Saint John Waterfront Development Partnership; the Business Community Anti-Poverty Initiative; and the Eastern Marine Development Corporation (helping businesses expand and develop new markets). Through these partnerships, Enterprise Saint John provides an arena for intergovernmental coordination by serving as an operational conduit for the Province of New Brunswick and the Atlantic Canada Opportunities Agency (Enterprise Saint John 2010). It provides a mechanism of horizontal collaborative governance between the public, private, and community sectors whereby enterprises in the private sector in a particular region can be seen less as objects of economic development and more as agents of adaptation to global and local changes.

Because of space constraints, the present discussion cannot provide a detailed examination of economic development initiatives in other regions of New Brunswick. It is worth noting, nevertheless, that the city of Fredericton (one of the province's three large cities) has undertaken economic development initiatives similar to those in Greater Moncton and Saint John. Like their provincial and federal counterparts, these cities' economic development plans and strategies emphasize the role of municipalities in fostering collaboration and cooperation among business, non-profit, and government sectors. Each city envisages a primary role for municipal leadership in governing the innovation clusters, in particular, and the new economy, in general, by seeing itself as a fulcrum for the coordination of initiatives aimed at economic development.

As the multi-actor implementation framework indicates, understanding economic development policy implementation in the major cities of New Brunswick requires a greater appreciation for the complexity of the operating environment consisting of multiple powers, authorities, and organizations. The gravitational pull of policy governance within the emergent context of New Brunswick is towards greater decentralization, the devolution of responsibilities, and the restructuring of accountability relationships towards municipalities and beyond the once sacrosanct boundaries of the public sector.

Also, economic policy governance mechanisms emphasize building coalitions of strategic alliances in successfully managing the many dependencies that are a natural and necessary component of implementing policies in environments characterized by a multiplicity of actors. The New Brunswick government seems increasingly aware of these developments and their implications, as reflected in the strategic significance attributed to cities in its 2002 economic development plan (Government of New Brunswick 2002). Although municipalities are still creatures of the provinces in Canada, the New Brunswick government's Prosperity Plan figures them not merely as residual institutions for performing rudimentary tasks like road maintenance and garbage collection, as was the case in previous decades, but rather as indispensable partners in the search for local innovation and adaptation.

Local government actors in the province are now considered essential participants in the governance arrangements of a knowledge economy that prioritizes nurturing innovation clusters in every sector in the province. In particular, the provincial government seeks to engage municipalities in a comprehensive framework to invest in institutional infrastructure that will more closely integrate rural, northern, and urban regions in the province's pursuit of economic development (Canadian Institute for Research on Regional Development 2000). This partnership, as will be shown later in the provincial government's International Trade Strategy, is also considered germane to the successful pursuit of New Brunswick's ambition to become Atlantic Canada's energy hub, a leader in energy efficiency, and a world-class producer of goods and services for the global energy sector (Government of New Brunswick International Trade Strategy 2009).

A related development in New Brunswick during the latter part of the 1990s was the expression of discontent in rural and northern regions about the constraints of community or grassroots participation in the market governance processes in the province (Canadian Rural Development Institute 2004; Blake 2003). Local communities became more articulate about their desire to take responsibility for their own economic development, which was fuelled in part by the emergent focus on nurturing "innovative communities" in nonmetropolitan areas (Goldenberg 2008; New Brunswick Regional Development Corporation 2010). A particularly interesting irony that was accentuated by this development is the absence of local governance for most of the province's rural regions. As Pierre-Marcel Desjardins (2002) observes, well before 1987 the Robichaud government of New Brunswick (1966–87) adopted an initiative that became known as the Programme of Equal Opportunity, whereby it was assumed that all residents should have access to basic standards of services regardless of the fiscal capacity of the locality. The purpose of the program was to centralize a number of key government functions to reduce regional disparities. This led to the elimination of the county councils and the creation of a new level of local administration by cities, towns, villages, and local service districts. Ironically, while the government was trying to establish greater equity among the regions, a large portion of New Brunswick's population and land mass ended up in unincorporated areas with no local government (Desjardin 2002).[10] In those areas, services were then authorized and coordinated by the provincial government. This state of affairs often becomes an obstacle to development, since affected local communities find it difficult to take responsibility (Canadian Institute for Research on Regional Development 2000, 2002), with the result that development decisions (on issues of land use for farming or residential or commercial development, for instance) tend not to be determined by local residents. About 40 percent of the province's population lives in unincorporated areas. The result is a lack of county-like jurisdictions that could serve as intermediaries between the cities/towns and the provincial government. This example of governance constraint is rendering the community economic development (CED) model extremely difficult (OECD 2007).

Against this backdrop, one can appreciate the growing expression of discontent in the rural and northern regions of New Brunswick. Viewed through the lens of governance literature, such developments in rural and northern New Brunswick pose some opportunities and challenges for economic development policy in particular and policy delivery in general. Trends in modern governance include shifts in political culture (including the assertive politics of identity), with a consequent emphasis on issues of diversity and local control as a central feature of public policy (Pal 2006; Pierre and Peters 2005). The most significant implication of these shifts is a re-visitation of visions of the role of government at the local level, the feasible tools at its disposal for dealing with grassroots problems, and how best to organize the administrative machinery of government to achieve those ends.

The provincial government has initiated a process of local governance reform in New Brunswick to correct the historic oversight that rendered rural municipalities and regions incapable of effective self-governance (Government of New Brunswick 2010; Atlantic Provinces Economic Council 2006). Part of the provincial government's response was to create community economic development agencies (CEDAs), which replaced regional economic development commissions. This initiative, supported by ACOA and some municipalities in the province, was designed to stimulate greater local, especially rural, participation in economic development. Each CEDA has an advisory board, providing a permanent forum for local stakeholders to take part in decision making. Local communities are also taking matters into their own hands. For instance, the Acadian Peninsula region adopted a joint-action approach earlier this decade bringing together various stakeholders with the aim of achieving more effective strategic planning and local participation in fostering local community innovation and economic development (Canadian Institute for Research on Regional Development 2000).

In addition to these developments in rural and northern New Brunswick, the provincial government released a policy document in 2010 dedicated to the development of its northern regions – the Action Plan for Self-Sufficiency in Northern New Brunswick 2010–2013 (Government of New Brunswick 2010). The new three-year plan is a response to assertive communities in the northern and rural region, and also a recognition of the existing vulnerabilities of resource-based regions that have been severe victims of seismic shifts in global resource markets. In particular, the plan envisages new global opportunities for northern New Brunswick in three targeted areas: modular fabrication and component construction industries, industrial development, and resource-based industries. The implementation of the plan is being coordinated by the Regional Development Corporation (RDC) in partnership with Business New Brunswick, a provincial department.

The plan follows the introduction by the New Brunswick government in 2009 of the $50 million Northern Economic Development Fund (NEDF) and the $100 million Northern New Brunswick Infrastructure Initiative (to help develop, diversify, and expand the economy and communities of the region) (Government of New Brunswick 2010). The NEDF provides incremental assistance of $50 million over a three-year period from (2009 to 2012), investing in projects that support the economic development and community building capacity in Northern New Brunswick. The NEDF is designed to help build vibrant communities that attract people and businesses and encourage investment in new activities and employment. It provides assistance to community-driven initiatives in support of the following areas of investment: first, economic development and diversification through initiatives such as small and medium-sized businesses, entrepreneurship, skills and training, and innovation; and, second, community capacity building through investments in physical infrastructure and other related projects.

Also at this time in New Brunswick, the private sector developed an increased desire to be part of a more inclusive and strategic governance framework that focused on longer-term planning (McNiven and Plumstead 1998). The initial shift in mindsets within the private sector is clear in the Fredericton Chambers of Commerce's (FCC) 1994 brief, which expresses the belief that citizen participation, combined with a dedicated innovative approach by a government willing and able to make brave decisions, could distinguish New Brunswick (FCC 1994). The FCC actively promoted the City of Fredericton's Economic Development Commission as the institution to spearhead efforts to nurture knowledge-based industries as an area of expansion. For example, the Economic Development Office was created as a product and a function of the partnership with the City of Fredericton, the FCC, Downtown Development Fredericton Inc., and the Capital Region Development Commission. Innovation policy as the thrust of regional development therefore began to shift the private sector's focus away from subsidies for individual firms and towards the longer-term, cross-sectoral accumulation of strategic resources for R&D and expertise (skills training). Drawing insights from the multi-actor implementation framework, in light of the imperatives of forging cross-sectoral clusters for managing knowledge-driven economies, the private sector's identification with their immediate communities can be leveraged by the public sector for formal mechanisms of engagement and collaborative forms of economic development governance. Inasmuch as the present context of economic development policy implementation requires institutionalized policy subsystems centred on a number of organizations with diverse sources, the dialectics of horizontal engagement between public agencies and non-state organizations must be considered.

By the turn of the millennium, the New Brunswick private sector had consolidated its appreciation for and advocacy towards moving beyond individual-firm grants or subsidies. Their priority became entering into joint governance arrangements with the provincial and federal governments for a longer-term economic diversification strategy based on nurturing knowledge-based industries (Conford 2005). The Chamber of Commerce in New Brunswick has been pursuing a strategy of nurturing a sustained governance network involving both the public and private sectors to address the lack of critical mass in those industries.[11] This is consistent with what Kooiman (2003) refers to as societal steering through processes of coordination within networks. The New Brunswick Chamber of Commerce has initiated several meetings with ACOA and relevant departments in the government of New Brunswick since 2004 to discuss the framework of joint action in the province.[12] Another important recurring theme has been attitude change as a push towards self-sufficiency and self-reliance, with the aim of reversing the negative stereotypes of seeing the province as dependent on federal largesse.

The New Brunswick government's recognition of the strategic significance of the private sector in a governance framework is shown in its call in the late 1990s to the business community to take a leading role in the development of innovative means of accessing capital.[13] This mood was reflected not only in the 2002 Prosperity Plan but also in a major development the following year. In 2003, the government of New Brunswick launched the New Brunswick Innovation Foundation (NBIF) (Government of New Brunswick 2009). Although launched two years later than a similar program by ACOA (discussed in the next section), the NBIF has become a key instrument for stimulating the province's knowledge community and private sector, as well as fostering a self-conscious knowledge network across these sectors. For instance, the NBIF supports innovation and entrepreneurship by making venture capital investments in start-up companies, as well as funding applied research in the development of new intellectual property. Established as an independent corporation, the foundation manages about $45 million and has been able to leverage more than $177 million more from other sources (including ACOA) (Government of New Brunswick 2009). The NBIF focuses on what it considers "strategic industries" in the knowledge sector, industries dealing with information and communication technologies; geomatics and computer engineering; life sciences (in areas such as biotechnology, marine science, and wood science); and advanced manufacturing (such as plastics and rubbers, metalworking, and electronics). The foundation also supports activities in value-added natural resources in agriculture, forestry, minerals, and aquaculture and fisheries and has been capitalizing on making investments in energy and environmental technologies geared towards energy generation from alternative sources such as wind power, solar power, hydro/marine power, bio-fuels, and geothermal power, as well as investments in energy storage; energy infrastructure; and water and waste water management.

One of the most significant implications of the new developments in New Brunswick is that the emergent phenomena suggested a transition towards a more complex multi-actor policy environment that will require concerted action across institutional boundaries, given the multiplicity of actors, loci, and levels. The subsystem of economic development policy in New Brunswick now consists of constellations of ideas and interests within and outside the government (ACOA's Policy Outreach Activities 2004). A key question, then, for policy implementation in the multi-actor governance framework is not what specific formal areas of control the state has retained. Rather, it has become, what types of adaptive instruments and capabilities does the state possess? While coordination and coherence are central to the discourse of the multi-actor governance framework, policy implementation still depends on the capacity and legitimacy of the state to enforce decisions in some ways – something that implies the power of the public sector and its use of legitimate authority to provide policy leadership and direction. The governance approaches suggest a conceptual or theoretical representation of cooperation, coordination, and collaboration as central features of policy implementation. But they do not necessarily imply the demise of the state in that process.

By the first decade of the twenty-first century, the momentum towards provincial leadership in regional economic development was becoming consolidated. In 2006, a new development plan for New Brunswick titled Achieving Self-Sufficiency was unveiled under a new government (Government of New Brunswick 2006). The substance of this plan is similar in many respects to the 2002 plan, except that the 2006 plan has a longer time frame and pays more attention to the inclusion of local and rural regions in the institutional infrastructure of innovation governance. The thrust of the document is concerned with transforming the economy (with a focus on fostering innovation), building the workforce for a knowledge-based economy (mostly through education and training), and reforming the institutions of government (for greater efficiency and effectiveness in service delivery and the adoption of single-window delivery models). Compared to the 2002 Prosperity Plan, the Self-Sufficiency Plan of 2006 has a longer time horizon and seems more exhortative (but the Prosperity Plan remains more concrete in implementation details than the Self-Sufficiency Plan). More importantly, the 2006 plan emphasizes the priority of the provincial government working more closely with critical partners. In particular, it targets the nurturing of relationships with various strategic partners in the private and non-profit sectors and within the public sector in closer partnership with the federal and municipal governments. The emphasis on partnership is consistent with the plan's focus on targeting a number of technology clusters and priority core technologies for support through the development of strategic alliances in the education, training, and recruitment of highly qualified personnel and the attraction of investment by outside sources.

The government's recognition of the strategic significance of collaborative intergovernmental relations is expressed in comments regarding fostering partnership between Business New Brunswick (a highly influential provincial department), the Atlantic Canada Opportunities Agency and the province's Community Business Development Corporations. The stated aim of this collaboration is to provide streamlined access to business support programs at all levels. The provincial government maintains that, together, these agencies will develop standards and implement provincial planning policies to provide planning certainty for developers and put in place innovative incentives to encourage sustainable management of economic development resources.

The institutional framework of governing the new environment as expressed in the plan refers to "transforming government," "renewing the public service," and "improving public service delivery," and all these goals are geared towards making the governance context more proactive, participatory, responsive, and adaptable to the imperatives of governing a complex set of economic goals. Thus the plan recognizes that the institutional framework and implementation processes of government need to reflect the networked cross-sectoral nature of longer-term innovation strategies.

The new emphasis, therefore, is on partnerships across levels of government and between the public and private sector to create networked systems conducive to providing better institutional support for knowledge-driven processes of economic development; the plan emphasizes adaptability and accessibility to the needs of economic actors (Beaudin 2005; Atlantic Provinces Economic Council 2006).

Another example of a greater emphasis on more coordinated and proactive governance can be found in the province's International Strategy Report of 2009 (Government of New Brunswick International Trade Strategy 2009), which "sends a clear signal to all policy actors in [the province] that for New Brunswick to prosper in the new global economy, it will require a focused and coordinated approach – a departure from the scattershot and top-down approach of previous years."[14] A key objective of the international strategy is ensuring consistency between the province's international activities (to increase trade and the number of exporting firms, diversify the market base and sector product lines, increase investment levels, and increase innovation capacity and productivity). The report also envisages – in what it refers to as the "integrated trade strategy" – the promotion of New Brunswick through a close partnership among the provincial and federal governments and with the private sector, the academic community, and local communities.

What does this development mean for ACOA's policy engagement in economic development in New Brunswick? The multi-actor framework draws our attention to emergent changes in the nature of the state when processes of public policy intervention shift from traditional technocratic state control towards more collaborative mechanisms of policy implementation. The new governance literature, for instance, stresses networks, bargaining, and interaction, rather than hierarchies, as the best way to govern and understand governance. As we will see in the next section, this vision of the future direction of governance has analytical and practical implications for ACOA's involvement in economic development in New Brunswick. One of the most significant challenges posed to traditional patterns of governance is the potential to deinstitutionalize governance and "replace" the state with alternative mechanisms of policy formulation and implementation. Therefore, giving consideration to the society-centred arrangements of policy formulation and implementation would require some radical institutional adaptation.

Appreciating the full implications of major socioeconomic changes in New Brunswick over the past decade requires a restatement of the proposition put forward earlier in the book. To recapitulate, the effectiveness of regional development policy governance in environments characterized by policy and political complexity requires that managers establish links across organizations representing different levels of government and outside government, and that they share ideas, resources, and even power with state and non-state actors. Managing regional economic development policy involves operating within and across layers of government, as well as between the public and non-governmental sectors. Moreover, given the dynamic nature of the policy environment, the process is often characterized by the constant evolution of strategies over time. The next section thus analyzes the implications that the emergent environmental context of economic development policy governance in New Brunswick holds for the federal government's economic development agency in the region – the Atlantic Canada Opportunities Agency (ACOA).

NAVIGATING THE NEW INSTITUTIONAL BOUNDARIES

We should recall our discussion in previous chapters in which innovation policy as a framework of economic development policy intervention requires, first, governing institutions and institutional infrastructures that lend themselves to closer intergovernmental coordination and, second, a greater capacity to facilitate joint action that involves local and non-state actors (OECD 2009; Holbrook and Wolfe 2002). Such transitions as observed in New Brunswick since the late 1990s have administrative implications for ACOA's regional economic development intervention in the province. Again, while this chapter focuses on New Brunswick, the events analyzed above are microcosmic reflections of wider phenomena in Atlantic Canada.

For ACOA, the successful implementation of the agency's policy is no longer a merely technical task of program design and delivery; it is also a matter of political negotiation and partnership formation, since it must coordinate its activities with those of emerging actors and with ideas coming to the fore beyond its own confines.[15] Successful policy implementation in New Brunswick thus came to be about how ACOA could make its policy interventions consistent with and supportive of local joint action under provincial leadership (ACOA Research Study: Atlantic Gateway Business 2009). As a senior manager in the agency put it, "ACOA is now striving to facilitate full participation in the New Brunswick economy by shifting towards making investments that build and capitalize on local capacity, foster economic diversification, and help communities transition beyond traditional economic activities."[16] ACOA was beginning to attune its program and service delivery model to the changing imperatives of regional development and the transitions of local phenomena in New Brunswick. For instance, the agency's targeted Special Growth Sectors in the early 2000s were developed only after close consultations with counterparts in the provincial government and the private sector. The resulting document closely reflected the provincial government's strategic focus on the energy and petroleum sectors (ACOA's Five Year Report to Parliament 2003–2008). The agency's articulation of its delivery model shifted towards encouraging disadvantaged regions to maximize their ownership of economic diversification.[17]

ACOA also became focused on intergovernmental initiatives such as fostering greater productivity and public-private collaboration with a range of actors in the region for investing in skills development for a knowledge-driven economy. From the standpoint of the multi-actor implementation framework, ACOA had to focus on a multi-level governance arrangement that could maximize local assets, foster the interaction of local stakeholders, and nurture synergies across various economic sectors. By the turn of the millennium, in the face of the aforementioned developments in New Brunswick the attention of ACOA turned toward overcoming administrative boundaries and facilitating better networks with the provincial and municipal governments, as well as with non-state actors such as the private sector and community actors.[18] Since the early part of the new millennium, ACOA has been placing a key emphasis on strengthening partnerships and mobilizing stakeholders to work on its economic development priorities (ACOA Five-Year Report to Parliament 2003–2008; Treasury Board Secretariat 2009). And this focus on collaborative policy implementation continues to characterize the agency's strategy of policy penetration in the region. For instance, the agency's 2011–12 projection "Plans and Priorities" indicates a commitment to work with provincial governments, businesses, and academia to increase the volume of research and development conducted in New Brunswick and the rest of Atlantic Canada, as well as to implement initiatives to help commercialize technology developed in the region (ACOA's Report on Plans and Priorities 2011–2012).

In a preamble to its 2009 program document, ACOA makes a commitment to coordinating its policy activities with partners drawn from other federal agencies administering a comprehensive array of programs and services that support business and economic development in the region (ACOA's Fact Sheets and Brochures 2009). These agencies include Foreign Affairs and International Trade Canada, the National Research Council, Transport Canada, and Industry Canada. ACOA also identifies its public sector provincial partners in New Brunswick as consisting of two key agencies responsible for economic development in New Brunswick: Business New Brunswick (BNB) and the Regional Development Corporation. As indicated above, ACOA is building close working relationships with non-governmental regional stakeholders from academic institutions (like the University of New Brunswick and the University of Moncton) and research centres, community groups (mostly the CEDA discussed earlier), and local economic development organizations (such as the various Enterprise Networks and Economic Development Corporations) within the municipalities (ACOA's Report on Plans and Priorities 2011–12). A specific example of the agency's focus on collaborative models of policy intervention is its work with Springboard Atlantic Inc. (ACOA's Departmental Performance Report 2009–2010). Established in 2004 by the Association of Atlantic Universities, Springboard Atlantic encourages commercialization of university research. ACOA has closely partnered with this organization, which has resulted in tripling the number of technology transfer professionals, industry liaison officers, and others engaged in activities to support this effort; doubling the number of disclosures, patents, and commercialization agreements, and doubling revenues; and increasing the research budgets of Springboard members from a total of $225 million to $280 million (ACOA Five-Year Report to Parliament 2003–2008). Moreover, in line with what is referred to as the Global Commerce Strategy, ACOA has committed to working with its provincial partners in promoting Atlantic Canada as a competitive business partner and valuable link in the global supply chain (Policy Research Initiative Roundtable Synthesis Report 2006). Similarly, through the Atlantic Energy Gateway initiative, ACOA seeks to facilitate the development of Atlantic Canada's clean and renewable energy sector through inter-jurisdictional and inter-organizational alliances. The agency sees multi-actor alliances as critical instruments in the pursuit of new technology-based growth sectors and the competitiveness of resource industries (ACOA's Policy Outreach Activities 2005).

By the middle of this decade, ACOA and the New Brunswick government were adjusting their parallel delivery models to the exigencies of the new economy. In the words of an ACOA senior official, the agency "is shifting focus from delivering individual business subsidies to stimulating growth in productivity and competitiveness in the region by fostering research and development, technology adoption, business skills development, and trade and investment."[19] A sectoral focus for firm subsidies or loans was seen as outdated and ill-suited to a knowledge economy. Public agencies across levels of government were required to work more closely to provide the institutional framework for nurturing network clusters, fostering backward and forward linkages among firms, and exploiting knowledge spill-over from one sector to another. Between 2003 and 2008, ACOA funded over 230 R&D projects involving more than $70 million (ACOA Five-Year Report to Parliament 2003–2008; Treasury Board Secretariat 2009). It has supported more than 85 technology-adoption projects involving more than $21 million in assistance. From 2003 to 2007, as part of its work in promoting and developing export capacity, the agency led seven Team Canada Atlantic trade and investment missions, engaging more than 230 small and medium-sized enterprises (SMEs) throughout the region and generating in excess of $10 million in immediate-export sales. See appendix 1 for more details on ACOA's current program architecture and resource allocation.

Another significant structural element of ACOA's new framework of policy intervention appears in relation to community groups in the region through the Regional Economic Development Organizations (REDOs). The REDOs, which are created by ACOA, play a leadership role by bringing communities together to plan, develop, and implement economic development efforts. The REDO in New Brunswick is the Enterprise Network. In all, ACOA works with and provides funding to fifty-two Regional Economic Development Organizations (REDOs) located throughout Atlantic Canada, including fifteen Community Economic Development Agencies in New Brunswick, twenty Regional Economic Development Boards in Newfoundland and Labrador, eleven Regional Development Authorities in mainland Nova Scotia, two Regional Development Authorities in Cape

Breton, and four Community Economic Development Corporations in Prince Edward Island. The role of these organizations is to foster and drive economic development at the local level in partnership with other federal, provincial, and municipal governments; economic development organizations; and other stakeholders. Along with the provincial and municipal governments in New Brunswick, ACOA not only supports the Enterprise Network mechanism but jointly provides the framework, policy direction, and funding for each of the Enterprise agencies across the province. An important example is that Enterprise Greater Moncton is jointly sponsored by ACOA and the provincial and local governments. This arrangement also allows for an institutionalized engagement of intergovernmental coordination at the city or local level with input from non-state actors in the private sector and the community. ACOA's approach to community development is based on the principle that the problems facing communities, such as unemployment and economic instability, can best be addressed through a holistic and participatory process. ACOA has invested over $316 million in more than nine hundred community-based projects through the Innovative Communities Fund and its predecessor, the Strategic Community Investment Fund. These investments have leveraged an additional $359 million from other partners (ACOA Five-Year Report to Parliament 2003–2008).

As these examples indicate, building synergies among a constellation of public agencies and private organizations has become the order of governance in New Brunswick (Government of New Brunswick 2002). Managing the province's economic development policy ambitions in a complex environment requires a process of policy delivery involving multiple agencies analysing and learning from each other across levels of government, the private sector, and local stakeholders. ACOA has positioned itself, in this regard, as a strategic partner with provinces and, even, municipalities.[20]

A significant characteristic of ACOA's strategy in pursuing collaborative policy intervention is to provide a rather supportive role behind provincial leadership in economic development. The Atlantic Innovation Fund (AIF) initiative is an example. In recognition of the prevalence of innovation policy within New Brunswick and the rest of Atlantic Canada, in 2001, ACOA launched the AIF, which is designed to work jointly with the provincial and municipal governments as well as with the private sector in New Brunswick (and other provinces in Atlantic Canada) to compete in a global knowledge-based economy through the development of new ideas, technologies, products, and markets (ACOA's Departmental Performance Report 2001–2002). The AIF aims to support research and development leading to the launch of new products, processes, and services. It also seeks to improve the province's capacity to commercialize R&D. Through the AIF, ACOA has made strategic investments aimed at deepening partnership with the government and non-state actors in New Brunswick, particularly the chambers of commerce and universities, to increase the innovation capacity of the province.

ACOA continues to foster R&D through the AIF, which was renewed in 2005 with an additional $300 million in funding (ACOA Five-Year Report to Parliament 2003–2008; Treasury Board Secretariat 2009). The government of New Brunswick's launch of the NBIF two years after the AIF can be seen as testament to the success of ACOA's pursuit of collaborative governance. The AIF and the NBIF complement each other not only in the substance of their policies but also as intergovernmental funding mechanisms. ACOA also plays an essential role in the co-ordination and development of the Atlantic Gateway, and it leads trade development initiatives that increase the exposure of Atlantic Canadian firms in foreign markets, thereby generating new economic opportunities.

A further instance of organizational adaptation on the part of ACOA is the agency's delivery of the national Economic Action Plan (introduced after the major 2007–2009 global recession), which is consistent with its emphasis on strategic collaboration with a range of partners drawn from the public sector and non-state actors in the community, the private sector, and the universities. ACOA essentially now manages many such programs, but *not alone*. An example is the Community Adjustment Fund (CAF), which provides funding for projects that will create jobs and employment opportunities in communities that are hard hit by the economic downturn. Activities supported by the fund include science and technology initiatives, community transition plans that foster economic development, and other measures to promote economic diversification in affected communities. Another such project is Recreational Infrastructure Canada (RInC), which provides funding for projects to rehabilitate recreational facilities across Canada, including upgrades and repairs of existing assets and new construction that adds to or replaces existing recreational infrastructure. Other examples include the Innovative Communities Fund (ICF), which invests in projects that lead to long-term employment and economic development of the community. Not-for-profit organizations, municipalities, cooperatives, educational institutions, economic development organizations and business, technology, and industry associations are all critical co-producers of the ICF. Moreover, the Building Canada Fund provides funding for municipal infrastructure projects, particularly in smaller communities. It focuses on improving infrastructure in areas such as water, wastewater, culture, and recreation. The fund is also cost-shared; the Government of Canada contributes, on average, one-third of the total eligible cost of each project, while the provincial government and the municipality contribute the balance.

ACOA also has a program for Official Languages Minority Communities (OLMCs) through which the agency collaboratively strengthens the vitality and economic development of francophone minority communities throughout Atlantic Canada. As part of this mandate, ACOA is responsible for implementing the Economic Development Initiative (EDI) in the Atlantic region. The EDI falls under the Government of Canada's Roadmap for Canada's Linguistic Duality, which is supposed to demonstrate the government's commitment to promoting linguistic duality and enhancing the vitality of official-language minority groups. In addition, through intergovernmental initiatives such as the Aboriginal Business Services Network (ABSN) and Aboriginal Business Canada (ABC) in New Brunswick, tangible illustrations of joint policy action all point to evidence of an emerging framework of economic development policy governance that is a fundamental departure from top-down models to collaborative networks models. Another dimension of ACOA's adaptation to local phenomena in New Brunswick was its re-visitation of its organizational mandate. By the early part of 2000, the agency had revamped its hitherto latent mandate on policy analysis, advocacy, and coordination.[21] Even the goals and performance indicators of ACOA reflect the agency's adaptation to the new discourse of regional development. For instance, in its recent report on program activities the agency placed greater emphasis on growth in new industries in aerospace and information technology (ACOA Performance Report, Treasury Board Secretariat 2010–2011). Even the agency's growing investment in value-added products in traditional industries (wood, food, paper) had the funding criteria of innovation.[22]

In order to carry out its revived mandate more effectively, ACOA metamorphosed into a larger organization (far beyond the intent of its designers in 1987) with greater institutional clout and human resource capacity (ACOA Performance Report, Treasury Board Secretariat 2009–2010). With its larger size and greater capacity for intelligence gathering, ACOA plays an even larger role in innovation policy. Although the agency continued with elements of the former paradigm of economic development in its direct business incentive programs, ACOA's program became focused on longer-term partnerships with provincial departments, research and academic institutions, and trans-sectoral associations of private sector interests. Even the agency's Enterprise Development and Community Development programs began to reflect the logics of innovation, productivity, and skills development, rather than grants, loans, and subsidies. It is not that these firm subsidies no longer exist; what is new is the emphasis on cross-sectoral and longer-term investment strategies.

ACOA also sought to position itself as a credible conduit through which the opportunities and challenges of the Atlantic economy could be channelled onto the federal policy stage (Strategic Outcomes for ACOA 2009). The agency became more assertive about its advocacy role to ensure that New Brunswick's (and Atlantic Canada's) interests are recognized in the development of other federal departments' policies and programs. In contrast to the situation just over a decade ago, when various federal departments were operating their distinct programs in New Brunswick, ACOA has gradually become a credible lynchpin around which the economic development-related activities of other federal departments in the region could be coordinated and aligned with the interests of the provincial government, the private sector, and other local actors. A key element in the successful adaptation of ACOA since the 1990s, therefore, has been the agency's ability to recognize changing policy trends, identify the shifting bases of power, and proactively exploit opportunities for more collaborative partnerships with the provincial government and local actors. The agency has placed priority on forming sustained alliances with the local business community, other community economic development organizations, and public policy organizations (including academic research institutions). The main challenge for ACOA will be to constantly maintain its identity and survive as a relevant federal agency operating within provincial jurisdictions in the face of dramatic political and economic changes in its operating environment.

SUMMING UP

Drawing insights from the multi-actor implementation framework, the discussion in this chapter has analyzed how the effectiveness of regional development policy implementation is more than ever intertwined with the ability of ACOA, as a federal public agency, to nurture and maintain policy partnerships with other levels of government, as well as with non-state actors and community groups. Underlying the agency's activities over the past decade have been the challenges of program coordination and the navigation of complex institutional boundaries. The effectiveness of policy delivery by a federal agency like ACOA operating in a provincial jurisdiction largely rests on its capacity and legitimacy for inter-jurisdictional and inter-organizational alliances in joint policy engagement.

The present context of ACOA's economic development policy intervention in New Brunswick can be rightly referred to as collaborative governance of innovation policy involving various levels of jurisdiction and the multiple ideas and resources of non-governmental stakeholders. The process is also highly dynamic in the sense that within the two decades since the creation of ACOA, various stages of institutional evolution have marked the transition from a bureaucratic delivery of firm subsidies to collaborative and decentralized networks of economic development policy governance in New Brunswick. The present and future challenge for ACOA in such a complex and dynamic policy context is protecting its mandate and organizational identity as a federal agency, while also navigating the murky waters of diverse organizational cultures and interests across several levels of government, as well as sharing ideas, resources, and power with non-state actors. These trends, as will be seen in later chapters, are not unique to ACOA but are shared by similar federal agencies.

Several lessons about regional development policy in multi-level systems can be drawn from the experience of ACOA. First, current efforts aimed at promoting economic development should be framed as consistent with the imperatives of globally integrated knowledge-driven economies where cluster growth strategies and knowledge production, dissemination, and commercialization determine the success of a region. Rather than merely relying on individual firm subsidies or grants, the dictates of the new economy require that resources be directed toward the creation or support of knowledge clusters and industrial network activities. Second, ACOA's adaptation over the past decade indicates that economic development policy intervention seems most conducive at the local level, since knowledge or industrial cluster activities tend to be geographically concentrated. This means that sub-national jurisdictions in New Brunswick and elsewhere are gaining greater salience and leadership in economic development policy intervention. And sub-national jurisdictions are becoming increasingly willing and eager to actively decide the course of their economies.

Third, organizational restructuring – such as that introduced in 1987 – is not sufficient on its own to create institutional infrastructures that lend themselves to more effective policy intervention in complex systems. ACOA's experience illustrates that the organizations must use certain strategic adaptations geared towards closer intergovernmental and inter-jurisdictional coordination that facilitate joint action. In theory, one of the key advantages of a decentralized policy implementation process is greater coordination of programs among public agencies of different jurisdictional levels, but the initial relationship between ACOA and the New Brunswick government (immediately following the 1987 restructuring) did not strongly evidence such coordination. The culture and strategies of public agencies must adapt over time to the demands of inter-jurisdictional and inter-organizational coordination. Fourth, optimizing program output does not necessarily indicate an effective approach to regional economic development. For instance, ACOA's initial focus on delivering more programs to prove its effectiveness was exploited by the New Brunswick government. The agency's resources were used to fund any conceivable provincial scheme that was ostensibly for development (Savoie 1997). ACOA realized this vulnerability and adapted towards coordinating its programs more closely with the provincial government. The success of regional development policies in complex and multi-level jurisdictions increasingly requires the support of those who can affect the program delivery from other levels of government and from outside the public sector.

Finally, and in a nutshell, the multi-actor implementation framework fits well with the complexity of economic development policy in New Brunswick's emerging knowledge-driven economy. The multi-actor implementation framework views policy implementation as encompassing diverse expressions of inter-jurisdictional and inter-organizational cooperation among public agencies, on the one hand, and between state agencies and organized interests within the market and society on the other. These efforts aimed at joint policy action are strategic networks of complex and evolving relationships among agencies with similar mandates from different levels of government, and state-society partnerships incorporating community development organizations and business groups.

6

Canada-Manitoba Cooperation on Regional Economic Development

INTRODUCTION

This chapter continues the effort of previous chapters to analyze how the increasing complexity of policy implementation processes is shifting attention towards fostering inter-jurisdictional and inter-organizational partnerships involving mechanisms of joint policy action across institutional boundaries. Policy implementation is increasingly seen as a problem not simply of bureaucracy per se but also, frequently, of governance. This chapter examines the manifestation of these emergent governance frameworks within the context of economic development in the province of Manitoba, because it shares many of the broader features of policy assertiveness at the sub-national level that were observed in New Brunswick in the preceding analysis. But a distinct characteristic of the Manitoba case is the exclusive use of contractual mechanisms for managing intergovernmental cooperation in regional economic development. While the discussion focuses on the contractual arrangements between a federal economic agency and the Manitoba government, the analytical emphasis concerns how the contractual instruments have adapted to facilitate policy delivery in an increasingly complex economic and political system within the province over the past two decades. The contractual mechanisms of inter-organizational cooperation across different levels of government have experienced dramatic transitions over the years, reflecting the exigencies of the emergent policy environment in Manitoba. The implications of these changes are also analyzed.

The population of Manitoba consists of just more than one million people living in an area of approximately 650,000 square kilometres.

Table 6.1
Demographic and Economic Characteristics of Manitoba

Capital	Winnipeg
Largest city	Winnipeg
Largest metropolitan area	Winnipeg
Total area	649,950 km² (250,950 sq mi)
Population (2010)	1,232,654
Total GDP (2009)	C$50.973 billion
GDP per capita	C$38,001

Source: Courtesy of Statistics Canada.

Winnipeg serves as the province's administrative and commercial capital (Government of Manitoba 2011a). Table 6.1 summarizes the province's key characteristics; figure 6.1 provides a map of the province. In addition to having a diverse economy, relative to the rest of the other western provinces, Manitoba enjoys a strategic geographic advantage in being located in the centre of North America. This position provides the province with significant competitive natural conditions that can be (and are) leveraged through a number of policy instruments of economic development.

The 1987 restructuring that gave birth to the Atlantic Canada Opportunities Agency (ACOA) in New Brunswick also resulted in the creation of the Western Economic Diversification Agency (WD). Like ACOA, the WD is a department of the government of Canada, but it is established under a distinct provision – the Western Economic Diversification Act of 1987 (Government of Canada 1987b). The WD is headed by a federal minister with the title Minister of State for Western Economic Diversification. Its head office is in Edmonton, Alberta, while regional offices are located in each of the other western provinces – Winnipeg, Saskatoon, and Vancouver – along with a liaison office in Ottawa.

The Western Economic Diversification Act empowers the WD to promote the development and diversification of the economy of Western Canada by pursing policies and programs related to industrial development and diversification. The agency's mandate under its founding legislation is therefore quite broad. As we will see, this feature of the WD's founding document proved critical to the eventual strategic adaptation of the agency in the face of assertive provincialism over the past two decades. Like its sister agency, ACOA, the in-built flexibility created by the WD's founding mandate reflects

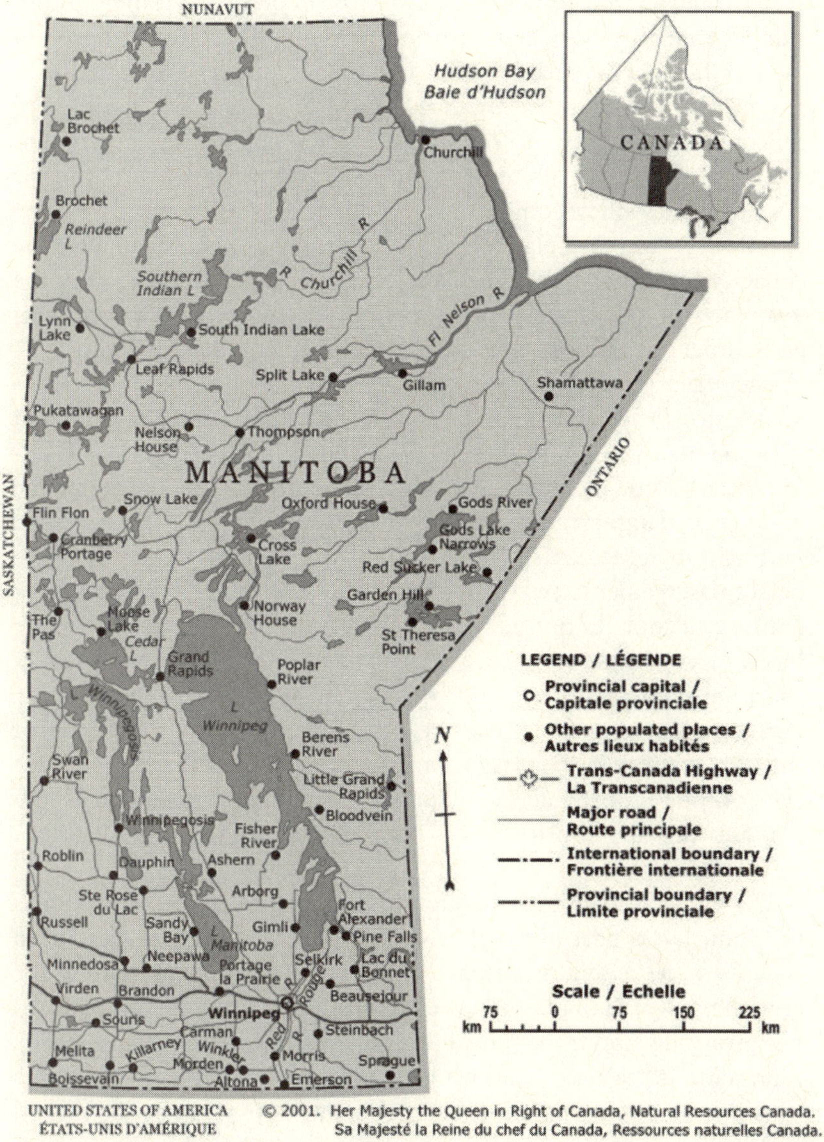

Figure 6.1 Map of Manitoba. Courtesy of Natural Resources Canada

the fact that the agency was considered partly a response to the administrative and political discontent expressed by the provinces with respect to the perceived centralized administration of regional development (Webster 2002).

As noted in the previous chapter, the federal government considered that the 1987 restructuring of regional economic development policy governance provided certain advantages associated with decentralized administration in that programs are easily modified to reflect local circumstances (McGee 1995). The rationale was that assigning the responsibility for the federal government's economic development policy commitment to agencies whose mandates pertain directly to particular regions (and provinces) could enhance the capacity for closer federal-provincial cooperation. In the case of the WD, each of the western provinces could engage with the federal government in tailored contractual arrangements for joint action.

The WD adopted what before 1987 were called General Development Agreements (GDAS) and Economic and Regional Development Agreements (ERDAS) (as discussed in chapter 4). The agency's funding mechanisms include partnership agreements, direct agreements, and national agreements (WD's Western Canadian Fact Sheets 2011). Partnership agreements – referred to as the Western Economic Partnership Agreements (WEPAS) – constitute the majority of the WD's grants and contributions and are delivered in partnership with other levels of government. These partnerships allow the agency to cost-share initiatives that respond to regional needs and opportunities. For instance, current WEPAS are cost-shared equally with each of the four western provinces; a total of $200 million ($25 million for each of the four provinces) is allocated to initiatives identified as federal and provincial priorities (WD's Reports on Plans and Priorities 2011–2012).

The Canada-Manitoba Economic Partnership Agreement (MEPA) in Manitoba is part of the WEPAS. The past three MEPAS have been signed by the federal minister of the environment (representing the government of Canada) and the Manitoba minister of competitiveness, training, and trade (now entrepreneurship, training, and trade), representing the provincial government. A management committee (made up of two members or co-chairs, one appointed by the federal and the other by the provincial minister) is responsible for the general administration and management of the agreement.

Using contractual documents to articulate expectations for and commitment to intergovernmental collaboration provided a convenient instrument for managing a policy field involving two levels of jurisdictions. The MEPA contracts provide a unified, co-financed, and multi-year funding mechanism for collective intervention and shared responsibility (Government of Canada 2003). A single fund helps clarify spending and financial incentives. Multi-year budgeting tends to reduce uncertainty in the planning process and to ensure continuity. In this regard, compared to ACOA's initial experience in New Brunswick, the WD seems to have enjoyed greater inter-governmental joint policy action since its inception and into the early 2000s. This relatively simple world of intergovernmental coordination did remain the same, as we shall see later in the chapter, but the nature of the contracts provided a mechanism for strategic adaptation over time.

The WD's contractual model provided a mechanism for forging a more collaborative working relationship with the government of Manitoba. The contracts identify in advance the mandates and resources of the WD and its relationship with its wider institutional and political environment. The MEPAS provided terms of commitment with some measure of flexibility that allowed for a coordination of policy delivery in ways that are not only technical but also political.[1] In particular, the contractual arrangements between the WD and the Manitoba government acknowledged the complexity of interdependency between national and sub-national jurisdictions in as highly contingent and nebulous a policy area as economic development (WD Departmental Performance Reports 2004–2005). Therefore, the notion of a contract in this context can be viewed loosely as a governance mechanism for managing what the multi-actor framework refers to as interdependencies across institutional boundaries in multi-level governance systems. A contract allows for customized arrangements that reflect regional and temporal contingencies.

SHIFTS TOWARDS THE "NEW ECONOMY" IN MANITOBA

By the latter part of the 1990s, however, developments very similar to those discussed in Atlantic Canada were taking place that would add further complexity to the federal government's joint economic development initiatives with Manitoba. This section sketches the range of key actors and their specific demands and highlights the implications of these trends for economic development policy intervention in the province. These trends in Manitoba were microcosmic reflections of broader trends in Western Canada (Canada West Foundation 2008), but for analytical depth and clarity, the discussion focuses on Manitoba. The following discussion analyzes the

WD's adaptations to these developments over the past decade, which required certain organizational changes for the WD to maintain its capacity and legitimacy for effective policy penetration in the province (and by extension, the region of Western Canada).

In particular, shifts in thinking about economic development were changing policy perspectives on regional development within the province of Manitoba and the rest of Canada. A major paradigm shift during this time was the emergence of a new discourse about knowledge-driven economies (Conference Board of Canada 2009). As discussed in chapter 3, the rationale of economic development policy intervention became geared towards building systems capacities for the development, dissemination, and application of knowledge rather than delivering direct subsidies to individual firms. Policy interventions aimed at specific businesses, for instance, are considered distortional, whereas cross-sectoral assistance to knowledge production in whole industries with the aim of promoting innovations in products, process, services, and markets is viewed positively (Industry Canada 2009). Policy instruments (such as innovation systems management) aimed at the successful development and application of knowledge, that is, instruments that lead to the development, adaptation, or improvement of products, process, services, markets, governments, institutions, and ideas are viewed as consistent with the imperatives of a globally integrated economy such as Canada's (Canada West Foundation 2007).

By the late 1990s, regional development instruments packaged as "innovation policy" began to emerge more prominently in Manitoba in the provincial government's increasing initiatives to direct the course of its own economy (Government of Manitoba 2003). The promotion of innovation thus became a central pillar of Manitoba's economic development. The government of Manitoba incorporated this message into its annual budget speeches, thus repeating and stressing the importance of innovation as critical to creating an environment that sustains economic growth and job creation. But Manitoba differed from New Brunswick in one major respect – although still classified by the federal government as a socio-economically disadvantaged region, by the turn of the millennium, Manitoba had become one of the most diversified economies in Western Canada (WD's Research and Market Studies 2008, 2009a). The province also boasted certain structural advantages, such as low energy costs, a relatively low cost of living (compared to Canada's two central provinces and two far west provinces), a skilled labour force, and competitive business taxes (Government of Manitoba 2011a; 2011b. Manitoba's labour productivity growth is among the strongest in Canada and the Conference Board of Canada (2009) projected that Manitoba's economic growth of 3.7 percent would lead all other provinces well into the next few years. Manitoba is also home to growing innovative industry sectors such as alternative energy, digital media, information and communications technologies, and life sciences. These areas represent opportunities for tremendous growth based on innovative local companies, world-class research, and skilled workforces (Government of Manitoba 2011c).

The Manitoba government has, therefore, been in a relatively stronger position to exploit the shift in the instruments of economic development policy intervention in knowledge-driven economies. The government began defining the province's policy vision in more ambitious terms with longer-range planning. For example, around the turn of the millennium, the government of Manitoba took stock of the state of the economy in the province, with a particular focus on its innovation assets, and it reviewed challenges and opportunities accordingly (Government of Manitoba Budget 2008). The result of this effort was the Manitoba Innovation Framework, which identified key actions to enhance the innovative capacity of the economy and foster an environment to support sustainable economic growth and job creation.

Another critical element of the Manitoba Innovation Framework was its basis in information gathered in consultation with business and community leaders, including the Premier's Economic Advisory Council; Century Summit (2000), involving Manitoba leaders from business, the community, and academia; Biotechnology Tours to California (2001) and Germany (2002); and Smart Tours to leading innovative countries, including Singapore (2000) and Ireland (2001) (Government of Manitoba Budget 2008). This process indicates that rather than delivering and directing, the legitimate role of government in the emerging complexity of a province's economy is facilitation and empowerment. Target groups once considered merely beneficiaries or recipients of government programs are viewed as policy actors in their own right. Policy intervention in this regard is neither primarily about public agencies undertaking policy governance themselves nor about shifting such responsibilities completely to non-state actors. Through the lens of the multi-actor framework, the process that led to the Manitoba Innovation Framework is consistent with building synergies for joint action with partners drawn from the private and other non-governmental sectors. Within such a context, governments act as partners and facilitators, providing support and frameworks that empower other actors.

The 2003 Manitoba Innovation Framework focuses on identifying the key drivers of the emerging sectors of its economy. And in 2003, the Manitoba government released the province's "Action Strategy for Economic Growth" (closely related to the Manitoba Innovation Framework), which became the official document setting out the province's vision for economic development (Government of Manitoba 2003). The Action Strategy contains a "Six-Point Action Plan" consisting of

1 Developing a skilled workforce that meets the needs of an ever-changing economy,
2 Investing in research that builds on Manitoba's economic strengths,
3 Investing in technology commercialization activities that develop and attract opportunities,
4 Connecting communities to ensure that all Manitobans have the opportunity to participate in innovation activities,
5 Strengthening the environment for business innovation opportunities, and
6 Fostering a service philosophy and spirit in government that is citizen-driven, innovative, and results-oriented.

As the Manitoba government was busy articulating its innovation strategy, the province was confronted with the rather "dark" realities of Manitoba's economy – existing structural constraints on the full participation of northern and rural residents in the province's economy (Silver and Loxley 2007). The challenges of the rural and northern regions are physical as well as institutional. Some of the challenges of rural communities in the province (and much of the country) include the following: geographic isolation, poor transportation, a dispersed population, the out-migration of the young, limited communication, weaker institutions of governance, constrained access to basic essential services, depressing employment opportunities, poor infrastructure, disturbing social conditions, and lower access to education (Canadian Rural Development Institute 2004).

These challenges tend to be interrelated and to reinforce one another. For instance, some distant rural and northern communities in Manitoba still rely on winter ice roads and air transportation for shipping. As a result, the costs for food, clothing, lumber, and fuel are much higher in these regions. Access to health, education, and other social services often require costly travel. Many young people must leave home for educational opportunities, and most never return.

Charting a future course for the province's economy, therefore, means responding to the demands of northern and rural residents to eliminate or reduce their socio-economic disenfranchisement. This imperative became even more pressing in light of the government's stated commitment in the Action Strategy of 2003 to connect communities to ensure all Manitobans have the opportunity to participate in innovation activities (Government of Manitoba 2003).[2] Moreover, Manitoba's heavy reliance on agriculture, tourism, energy, oil, mining, and forestry makes the rural sector a critical component of public policy governance in the province, which means that integrating residents of these regions more closely into emerging policy discussions about charting the course of a new economy in the province is absolutely necessary. The abundant natural resources of Manitoba provide considerable opportunities for economic diversification and development, which could sustain successful adaptation of the province's rural regions to the forces of global economic change. Eco-tourism, fishing, hydroelectric development, and value-added forestry are key examples of major sectors and potential drivers of service-oriented and knowledge-driven economic diversification in rural and northern Manitoba (Government of Manitoba 2009).

Given the provincial government's new narrative of a comprehensive innovation policy for all sectors and regions of the provincial economy, the participation of local government and non-state actors is essential to the province's economic development policy governance arrangements.[3] As noted in chapter 2, critical trends in modern governance include shifts in political culture (including the assertive politics of identity) with a consequent greater emphasis on issues of diversity and local control as a central feature of public policy. Indeed, by the turn of the millennium, as the discourse of rural development became infused with the paradigms of locally driven processes in a knowledge-based economy, the Manitoba government began to see its rural regions and their governance structures differently. This development is closely reminiscent of a similar phenomenon in New Brunswick. Rural municipalities and other jurisdictions are gradually considered less as residual institutions for performing rudimentary tasks and more as indispensable partners in the search for local innovation and adaptation (Government of Manitoba 2003).[4]

For example, the 2003 Action Strategy for Economic Growth also includes leveraging the increased strategic importance of rural regions in a knowledge-driven global economy. In particular, the document identifies the need to equip non-metropolitan regions and municipalities with a certain coordinative authority and the legitimacy to provide active and strategic leadership. Even more important, the strategy indicates an appreciation for the fact that the coordination of knowledge clusters is best handled at the local level. A more concrete example of the effort by the provincial government to respond to the demands for new governance arrangements was the Aboriginal Summit in 2000, which highlighted the many ways in which Manitoba's growing Aboriginal population represents an important resource for the province's growing economy. The Aboriginal Summit of 2000 led to an integrated strategy for Aboriginal economic development based on institutionalized partnerships between the provincial government, Aboriginal communities, and businesses (Government of Manitoba 2009; 2011d).[5] The process grew out of recommendations drawn from wide consultations under the leadership of the Premier's Economic Advisory Council (PEAC). The PEAC consists of a broad cross-section of community and private-sector leaders from across Manitoba. Some other key initiatives that have emerged from this partnership include the Manitoba International Gateway Council Initiative, which seeks to pursue opportunities to use Manitoba's unique northern rail route and the deep sea port of Churchill to develop trade links with northern Europe and Asia.

Since the present book conceptualizes policy implementation as involving institutionalized policy subsystems centred around a number of organizations with diverse sources, an important analytical element is to consider the governance literature's concern with the dialectics of horizontal engagement between public agencies and non-state organizations. The central concern shared by policy implementation research, organization theory, and the governance literature is to understand how government organizations interact with their external environment in the delivery of policies. Over the past decade the Manitoba government has appeared to be keen to work in partnership with rural communities to add value to the natural, cultural, and physical resources of the province, as well as to provide infrastructure to help rural communities grow and develop. Another significant development indicative of this new approach is the province's adoption of a strategic plan titled "Creating Opportunities Action Plan," released in 2006.[6] This plan identifies rural economic development initiatives in six areas: alternative energy, tourism, agriculture, natural resources, industry services and manufacturing, and Aboriginal and northern initiatives.

Manitoba's Ministry of Agriculture, Food and Rural Initiatives (MAFRI) is one of the most significant agencies in the province's effort to respond to the demands of rural regions in enhancing the economic capacities of rural communities (Government of Manitoba 2011b).[7] For example, their programs include assistance for farm and rural families with the goal of enhancing their knowledge and skills in leadership and management, marketing, sustainable production, adding value, diversification, and economic development options within the agricultural sector. The Rural Economic Development Initiatives (REDI) are another significant initiative of the agency; they promote economic development for diversification and long-term sustainability.[8] REDI programs and funds enhance business and co-operative development, create opportunities for youth, support industry, and help rural communities and organizations to address priorities and needs. REDI programming includes the Community Works Loan Program, Rural Entrepreneur Assistance Program (REAP), the CED Tax Credit Program, and the Community Adjustment Assistance programs, among others.

The Rural Entrepreneur Assistance Program provides an interesting illustration of the emergent context of policy engagement in the province. While the bulk of REAP is directed at providing loan guarantees (over $20 million), the focus of the government's delivery strategy is on third-sector engagement in co-production (Government of Manitoba 2011b). The model of policy implementation within this framework further reinforces the government's awareness of the transition from simply delivering and directing to facilitation, coordination, and empowerment. Under REAP, the provincial government has identified the strategic imperative of partnering closely with rural development corporations to promote business development and support regional initiatives. Moreover, there has been an increase in collaborative market-scanning activities involving the government and local business and community groups to identify trade issues and to simplify and strengthen the interprovincial as well as international trade process for Manitoba's agrifood companies.[9]

There has also been a noticeable increasing emphasis on nurturing productive innovation clusters in the rural economy of Manitoba. For example, the Economy and Rural Development Branch of MAFRI fosters the development of co-operative enterprises among rural, northern, and urban Manitobans. This approach is considered by the branch to be critical to the social capital and network linkages of adaptable rural regions in the knowledge-driven economy. In pursuit of the concept of innovation clusters and social capital within rural economies, MAFRI has been organizing annual conferences – the most recent one was titled "Capturing Opportunities 2011."[10] The conferences are designed to create knowledge exchange among entrepreneurs and researchers about new ideas and resources within the bio-based economy. The 2011 conference, for instance, focused on four key areas within the bio-economy where Manitoba is a leader: food and health, bio-products, energy, and agriculture.

As shown in chapter 3, one of the significant characteristics of the modern economy is that innovation systems or clusters tend towards geographically concentrated and locally driven ecosystems or networks that support and sustain the creation and dissemination of new ideas and ventures. These systems need not be restricted to metropolitan areas or technology-intensive sectors and economies but also relate to innovation processes in the rejuvenation and growth of traditional economic activities in sectors such as resource-based products (Holbrook and Wolfe 2002). In Manitoba's relatively peripheral rural and northern regions, opportunities are being identified in the emerging bio-economy such as, forest-based biomass, bio-plastics, agri-fuels and biopharmaceuticals.[11] Moreover, these regions' natural assets could generate opportunities in renewable energy, water technologies, and other environmental technologies. Furthermore, the digital economy creates new opportunities for regions once isolated and cut off from the global value chains because of distance. Now, once geographically peripheral regions of Manitoba are expanding their access to economic diversification opportunities.

Another particularly significant initiative reflecting the new paradigm of rural economic development in a knowledge-based economy is the development of an assistance program for Brandon University's Rural Development Institute to support rural research and development projects.[12] Furthermore, through the Northern Development Strategy of the Manitoba Ministry of Aboriginal and Northern Affairs, the province has committed about $45 million in capital funding for the University College of the North to support service expansion at the two main campuses in The Pas and Thompson, as well as offering a northern community economic development diploma through Red River College, in partnership with the University College of the North. Also, the provinces Broadband Communications North program has been increasing the potential for economic development, health, and education services. Of sixty-seven northern communities, fifty-two are now connected to a broadband network.

Another policy initiative of crucial importance to northern and rural economic development in Manitoba is the Northern Development Strategy (NDS) (Government of Manitoba 2009).[13] The NDS is a long-term plan that identifies opportunities to develop the human and natural resources in the North through five key priorities: education and training, economic development and partnerships, transportation, health services, and partnerships to improve housing. The NDS was initiated by the northern MLEs in April 2000 in response to pressure from their constituencies for a more proactive and collaborative approach to rural and northern economic development. It is also based on previous consultations, including the Northern Mayors and Chiefs Conference and the Report of the Northern Manitoba Economic Development Commission. The economic development initiatives for northern Manitoba contained in the Northern Development Strategy have been identified in six areas: alternative energy, tourism, agriculture, natural resources, industry services and manufacturing, and Aboriginal and northern initiatives.

One of the most critical tests of the new paradigm of rural and northern economic development policy governance in Manitoba, however, will be the extent to which policy initiatives like the Action Strategy for Economic Growth, The Rural Economic Development Initiative (including REAP), and the Northern Development Strategy provide real and sustained opportunities for collaborative and bottom-up processes of program delivery. One encouraging sign is that each of these documents envisages the pursuit of economic development through collaborative mechanisms involving partnerships drawn from the affected communities. In this regard, if implemented according to stated priorities and instruments, these new policy initiatives may serve to correct the historic tendency of provincial governments to pursue uncoordinated initiatives in rural and northern regions.[14]

Another development in Manitoba since the turn of the millennium, which mirrors events in New Brunswick, is the growth of the private sector's desire to be part of a more inclusive and strategic governance framework that focuses on longer-term planning for a knowledge economy. The successful performance of the province's economy over a period of two decades has strengthened the confidence of the private sector.[15] The manufacturing sector is the largest in the province's very diversified economy, claiming over 12 percent of Manitoba's total GDP (WD's Research and Market Study 2009a). The province also hosts many major service sector operations. In particular, the province's multi-faceted economy consists of strong sectors not only in agriculture and food processing but also in aerospace, mining and hydroelectric generation, transportation equipment, pharmaceuticals, film and sound, commercial printing, transportation and distribution, and information and communication technologies.

Within the emergent context of the province's economy over the past two decades especially, the Manitoba private sector has sought to be part of a joint governance arrangement for longer-term economic development strategy based on nurturing knowledge-based industries.[16] For instance, industry and business groups under the umbrella of the Manitoba Chamber of Commerce have recommended that the province place greater emphasis on collaboration and innovation-focusing energies in technology commercialization and high-tech business development.[17] Specific advice from the Business Council of Manitoba urges the government to establish an Innovation Council to collaborate with education and research institutions and the private sector in developing an innovation strategy that strengthens the link between research and its commercialization (Business Council of Manitoba 2003). The Manitoba government seems eager to reciprocate the private sector's desire for closer participation in market governance.[18] For instance, the government acted on the advice of the private sector and appointed a Manitoba Innovation Council whose task is to guide the development of an integrated approach to innovation and technology commercialization in the province.[19] The rationale is that this approach will strengthen collaboration between industry, entrepreneurs, and researchers to create a stronger culture of innovation in the province (Government of Manitoba 2011c).

Another dimension of Manitoba's emergent context of economic development policy engagement is the increasing strategic importance of Winnipeg as the critical locus of industrial and trade policy coordination in the province (Economic Development Winnipeg Inc. 2011). As is the case elsewhere in Canada, although municipalities are "creatures" of the provinces, they have been assuming greater policy responsibility and attendant policy autonomy and discretion, especially in the governance of local economic development. Unlike New Brunswick, which struggles to create a demographic centre consisting of a critical population mass to support innovation clusters, Manitoba already enjoys a comparative advantage in Winnipeg. With a population of just over 700,000, Winnipeg claims about 60 percent of the province's residents. The unique demographic concentration of Manitoba's population within three hours' drive of the city adds to the strategic significance of the municipal-level jurisdiction in the new governance environment (WD's Research and Market Study 2009b).

Over the past decade, Winnipeg's knowledge-based industries have matured into significant forces in the provincial economy (Economic Development Winnipeg Inc. 2011). For example, the city is home to forty life sciences companies and thirty research and development groups with expertise in areas such as health, environmental, and agricultural biotechnology. The sector generates more than $500 million in annual revenue and employs in excess of four thousand people (Government of Manitoba 2011c). Winnipeg's notable biotech and research organizations include Innovative Magnetic Resonance Imaging Systems (IMRIS), Monteris, Manitoba Institute of Cell Biology, Medicure, the International Centre for Infectious Diseases, the Canadian Science Centre for Human and Animal Health, and the National Microbiology Laboratory. Evidence of the increasing strategic significance of the municipal-level jurisdiction in Manitoba as a characteristic of the new governance environment is best illustrated by a brief elaboration of the activities of the city's municipally mandated economic development corporation – Economic Development Winnipeg Inc. (EDW). The EDW is a not-for-profit organization led by a private sector board of directors.[20] The primary aim of the agency, which consists of two divisions – Economic Development and Tourism Winnipeg – is to lead, facilitate, and promote Winnipeg's economic development efforts. Strategically focused on stimulating economic growth and development for the city, EDW is a policy leader in its own right but "embraces a collaborative approach in its day-to-day activities, aimed at minimizing fragmentation and garnering the collective wisdom in stakeholder synergies to produce positive results."[21] An official succinctly describes the agency's ultimate goal as geared towards "diligently serving as systems integrators and enablers of collaboration."

In addition to its three-year rolling business plan, titled "A Foundation for Success" (which provides a concise overview of the organization's priorities, sectors, strategies, and structure), EDW is currently developing a targeted strategy for attracting foreign investment. In attaining consensus and alignment among stakeholders, the agency projects that the initiative will result in a five-year growth strategy for key industry sectors, complete with an action plan specifying tools and processes for 2011 and 2012. Moreover, EDW has developed a pilot program for the provision of direct service benefits to selected firms to help develop and advance their business enterprise through expert financial coaching services. This program will also demonstrate the value of financial-literacy education and enterprise-training services and explore the best delivery mechanism for providing such services on a long-term sustainable basis to the Winnipeg business community.

In April 2011, Economic Development Winnipeg Inc. hosted its annual general meeting, where it laid a new groundwork for future growth and development (EDW 2011). The centrepiece of the framework is providing locally grounded institutional mechanisms for stimulating economic growth in the city. Part of this novel thrust is a restructuring of the new Economic Development Winnipeg and Tourism Winnipeg brands, as well as a clearer and more concise organizational framework through which to move forward. The new strategic framework also emphasizes collaboration as the new competitive advantage. An interesting piece of the emphasis on collaboration is that in its effort to attract new foreign investment and trade, Winnipeg is joining Canada's eleven largest cities in launching newly unified brand and bilingual websites (ConsiderCanada.com and CanadaEnTete.com) that provide comprehensive information for global companies considering expansion into North America.[22] Moreover, consistent with Richard Florida's (1995) notion of attractive cities for international knowledge workers, the city of Winnipeg is engaged in a range of activities such as downtown revitalization through upgrading its Millennium Library, the MTS Centre, and Red River College's Princess Street Campus.

As a corollary to these trends in Winnipeg, the city of Brandon, though much smaller in size and significance, is also positioning itself as a region of agri-based innovation excellence in Manitoba and Canada.[23] The city of Brandon is the second largest city and service centre in Manitoba and serves as a major hub for the surrounding agricultural area. Although it has a metropolitan population of only about 50,000, its commercial area and influence spread over an area of between 100,000 and 150,000 residents. The city's economic industry is largely a reflection of its agricultural history: most major industries are related to agriculture, agri-foods, and agri-businesses (including fertilizer and animal husbandry). In addition, because it serves as a major hub for the surrounding Westman region of southwest Manitoba, Brandon boasts a large number of retail and government services well out of proportion to its actual size. It even hosts Brandon University and Assiniboine Community College – two critical institutions that anchor the city's research facilities and knowledge-generating services for related economic activities. Through its Department of Economic Development, the city of Brandon has been exhibiting ambitions and a policy assertiveness that are similar to those of Winnipeg.[24] This clearly indicates the keen competitive pressures with which cities of various shapes and sizes are confronted (WD's Research and Market Study 2009b).

The imperatives of knowledge-driven economies, as noted in earlier chapters, emphasize local aspects of social capital and knowledge networks (Holbrooke and Wolfe 2002). Fostering networks of geographically concentrated innovation clusters, for instance, requires equipping cities with a certain coordinating authority and the legitimacy to provide more active and strategic leadership. In this regard, the systems capacity of knowledge-driven economies is considered best handled at the local level (Roy 2007). Innovation thrives in systems where high levels of interaction and collaboration take place among economic and community stakeholders. Therefore, what is observed in Manitoba is a reflection of broader systemic transformations in which cities act like "city-states," complete with institutional capacities for effective policy engagement in economic development (WD's Research and Market Studies 2009b, 2010). An interesting dimension of these developments in Manitoba is that the provincial government seems to reinforce the institutional implications of these trends in Winnipeg and other smaller cities in the province (Western Centre for Economic Research 2004). In 2005, for example, the provincial government established the Building Manitoba Fund, which expanded the personal income and corporation income tax revenue-sharing arrangements with municipalities and provided municipalities with additional sources of growth revenue. These socio-economic changes in the economy were, therefore, creating new bases of power in the province.

Overall, these developments have significant implications for the WD's contractual arrangement under the MEPAS between the agency and the Manitoba government. The emergent knowledge-driven economy in both urban and non-metropolitan regions of the province has resulted in a complex set of locally grounded policy processes involving reviewing and setting new goals and challenges for the future. However, the more complex the policy instruments and the task environment, the more dynamic are the political processes involved in managing the implementation process. The more sources of uncertainty or contingencies for multi-actor policy contexts there are, the more power bases exist in a given policy subsystem.

What used to be managed through basic inter-governmental contracts must now be solved through shared adjustments involving horizontal collaborative processes. Market governance in the province is becoming more diverse and complex as northern and rural interests, Aboriginal organizations, private sector associations, and municipalities adopt the economic development policy vision and the need for networked forms of governance to nurture clusters of creativity and competitiveness. In this emerging context of market governance in the province, the capacity and legitimacy of contractual mechanisms of intergovernmental collaboration are confronted with new local realities. Although the federal government's constitutional responsibility under section 36 of the Constitution Act, 1982 (Government of Canada 1982) and its financial resources accord it a central place in the governance of economic development and innovation policy in Manitoba, since 2000 ownership and control over the process seem to have been shifting towards the provincial government and other bases of power outside the public sector. These transitions are further legitimized by the fact that the Canadian constitution grants primary responsibility for economic development to the provinces. The implications of these transitions for the WD's engagement in the province are analyzed in the next section. A useful lens through which to appreciate the full nuances of the federal government's economic development policy engagement in the province is the multi-actor implementation framework. Since this framework, as discussed in previous chapters, looks at a multiplicity of actors, loci, and levels of policy action, it connects the politics of public policy and the procedural preoccupation of public administration, demonstrating a greater appreciation for the complexity of the operating environment consisting of multiple actors and perspectives.

ADAPTING THE MEPA CONTRACTS TO A COMPLEX POLICY ENVIRONMENT

It is important to reiterate at this point that while events in Manitoba have been the focus of analysis in this chapter, they are a microcosmic reflection of broader forces of change in the country. In fact, although the aforementioned events are woven through the tapestry of the actors' preferences and subsequent policy responses in the province, the broader contours of the events in terms of the emergence of a range of actors are very similar to what we observed in New Brunswick in the preceding chapter. The next chapter on Northern Ontario will further confirm the systemic nature of the emerging characteristics of environmental complexity and dynamism for public policy delivery in the country (Industry Canada 2008). In the context of Manitoba after 2000, the key imperative for the WD's adaptation was the evident assertive leadership of the provincial government in defining the policy vision and governance framework of economic development.

The environment of the WD's economic development policy intervention in Manitoba is also characterized by an emergent constellation of actors (from the public and non-governmental sectors), each with its own conception of, and specific interest in, economic development. In economic development policy governance in the province over the past decade, therefore, the WD is increasingly engaged in the search for effective program interventions according to criteria of contractual rationality, yet surrounded by complex interdependencies of actors within the province posing profound uncertainties that threaten the logic of contracts. A federal public agency like the WD must deal with the complexity that inevitably accompanies realizing the goals of multiple organizations as disparate members of the task environment increasingly demand participation in the selection of instruments and the delivery of policy goals. A consequence of such challenges to contractual instruments of coordination is the clash of organizational cultures in the navigation of institutional boundaries. As the federal government's main conduit of economic development intervention in the province, the WD's relevance and survival increasingly thus rests on its ability to adapt to the exigencies of the above-mentioned socio-economic changes in the province of Manitoba. The effectiveness of the WD's policy intervention in such settings requires that its managers are able to make connections across organizations, bridge diverse cultures across levels of government and outside government, and share ideas, resources, and power with state and non-state actors.

An important element of inter-organizational networks is that they are often managed by an "inner circle" within an apparently complex policy subsystem (OECD 2007). The inner circle revolves around one or two public agencies with the capacity (resources, knowledge, etc.) and legitimacy (mandates and authority) to set the terms of implementation and provide leadership as governance processes evolve. What this suggests is that although the federal government's role in regional economic development is changing (away from the Weberian archetype of top-down policy implementation that dates back to the 1960s), the federal government still possesses certain resources that other sub-national actors seek to share or appropriate for their own preferences and interests. This reality tends to serve as a check on the excessive enthusiasm of sub-national policy assertiveness. Collective actions for solving economic policy problems in Manitoba are increasingly taking place within networks based on inter-jurisdictional and inter-organizational forms of management but still characterized by a considerable degree of federal influence as represented by the WD.

It should be noted that even since 2000, the WD and the Manitoba Ministry of Entrepreneurship and Trade have continued to be primary players in the MEPA and have managed to form the inner circle within an increasingly complex subsystem of economic development policy in the province (WD's Departmental Performance Reports, 2001–2002, 2004–2005, 2007–2008). But their leadership is becoming ever more symbolic. Other key ministries whose activities coalesce around the provincial government's growing economic policy assertiveness and rather aggressive pursuit of emerging economic priorities are the Ministry of Innovation, Energy and Mines; the Ministry of Agriculture, Food and Rural Initiatives; and the Ministry of Aboriginal and Northern Affairs (Government of Manitoba 2011). Inasmuch as effective multi-actor policy implementation often requires agreed common goals, joint decision making over more than the short term, cross-sectoral work, and shared responsibility and accountability structures, the more manageable bilateral contracts of federal-provincial economic partnerships before 2000 have taken on a more complicated texture involving multiple actors. For the WD, policy delivery has become fraught with costly coordination in terms of program ownership and control as multiple and sometimes conflicting local interests in diverse sectors of the urban and rural economy project their own narratives and visions of economic development in the province. The WD now works with a wide range of organizations in the public, non-profit, and private sectors, including academic and financial institutions, research centres, not-for-profit organizations, and other levels of government.

In particular, over the past decade, the WD's policy intervention now contains a mixed range of contractual policy instruments principally consisting of what the agency refers to as "partnership agreements," "direct agreements," and "national agreements" (WD's Departmental Strategy 2009; see appendix 2 for more details of the WD's current strategic outcomes and program activities architecture.) The majority of the WD's grants and contributions are still delivered through the economic partnership agreements (MEPAs in Manitoba). But these agreements, such as the Urban Development Agreements (UDAs), now consist of a multi-lateral partnership involving the federal, provincial, and municipal governments working in collaboration on broad issues such as inner city revitalization, strengthened innovation, or sustainable economic development.

Under its direct agreements, the WD allows itself a measure of flexibility and policy manoeuvring in responding to a wide range of disparate demands without being bound to the terms of the MEPAs. Through the direct agreements, for instance, the agency enters into various forms of partnership with other organizations such as universities and other research institutes, industry associations, and other not-for-profit organizations. An example of direct agreements is a suite of contracts aimed at strategic longer-term investments in innovation, business development, and entrepreneurship and community economic development (WD's Reports on Plans and Priorities 2011–2012). While the direct agreements do provide the WD with some measure of flexibility in a highly crowded and complex policy space, the main demerit of such a strategy of policy delivery is that it is prone to the danger of being subject to an incoherent set of programs that are at best opportunistic responses to the exigencies of politics rather than the result of sound policy rationales. For example, the WD's community economic development model of policy intervention has been criticized as fragmented and lacking policy coherence.[25] It is viewed as a tool of political visibility to deflect the criticisms of grassroots communities. But a good example of contractual arrangement is the WD's Direct Agreements scheme is the Western Canada Business Service Network (WCBSN). The WCBSN in Manitoba (and across Western Canada) is a group of several independent organizations that receive funding from the WD to provide a range of services to help create and build small businesses in the province (WD's Departmental Performance Report 2009–2010).[26]

In addition to the partnership agreements and the direct agreements, as noted earlier, the WD now also has "national agreements" consisting of a number of national programs that the agency delivers in the Western provinces. The most popular among these are the set of programs developed under Canada's recent Economic Action Plan (EAP) (WD's Report on Plans and Priorities 2010 –2011). They include the Community Adjustment Fund (CAF), the Municipal Rural Infrastructure Fund, the Recreational Infrastructure Canada (RInC), and the Community Economic Diversification Initiative. The implications of some of these programs and how they fit into the new framework of WD's policy engagement in Manitoba will be further analyzed later in this section.

The important point is that through its range of "agreements," the WD now collaborates not only bilaterally with the provincial government but also with industry, municipal, and community partners in investments that support a range of activities, including support for knowledge clusters in the province (WD Departmental Performance Report, Treasury Board of Canada 2009–2010). The WD's emergent focus on multi-dimensional and multi-lateral partnerships, therefore, now constitutes a fundamental characteristic of the agency's delivery strategy not only in Manitoba but across Western Canada. The contracts thus tend to incorporate multiple stakeholders in the provinces. The WD actively reaches out to multiple partners all at once, thereby blurring the once sacrosanct boundaries of the public sector in what constituted inter-governmental agreements (WD Departmental Performance Report, Treasury Board of Canada 2009–2010). This adaptation is consistent with the open-systems perspectives in organization theory, which emphasize the permeable boundaries of most public organizations, recognizing that public agencies are not as concrete and fixed as the mechanistic model of policy intervention had supposed. The open-systems perspectives draw our attention to public management as an exercise of collective action within cooperative social systems. This approach in organization theory broke fundamentally from the machine models (closed-systems) view of policy implementation, focusing instead on the imperatives of the broader political context within which public agencies such as the WD operate.

Another significant adaptation of the WD to the trends in Manitoba is the agency's emphasis on "fostering learning networks among multiple policy stakeholders."[27] Since 2000, for example, the MEPAs have become highly flexible and "relational" contracts. Relational contracts can be best understood when juxtaposed with technical or legal contracts, in the sense that the latter are enforceable in a court of law, whereas the former are viewed rather loosely as a sort of memorandum of understanding among the "contracting" parties. In particular, in the 2003 MEPA the contractual document emphasizes mutual learning through joint monitoring and evaluation mechanisms (Government of Canada 2003). The WD's agreements also began to emphasize the need to create "room for improvement," and to view both successful and unsuccessful experiences as triggering "motivation for further improvement." Viewing the federal-provincial partnership agreements as instruments for governing learning networks reflects the increased complexity of this new environment (WD's Departmental Performance Reports 2004–2005). This should necessarily be necessarily viewed as a sign of weakness in the agency model of policy delivery. Classical contracts have proved ill-equipped to deal with the issues of uncertainty, information asymmetry, and interdependency in the modern context of policy delivery (Atwood and Trebilcock 1996).

Moreover, as the multi-actor framework indicates, in a policy environment such as the one in Manitoba in recent years, the rationalistic underpinnings of public management as a process of planned change are bound to be confronted with unanticipated contingencies, some of which, ironically, are created by the ambitions of those seeking to control organizational activities in a deliberate fashion. The new governance literature, for instance, stresses networks, bargaining, and interaction, rather than hierarchies, as the best way to govern and the best way to understand policy intervention in complex multi-level systems. Kooiman (2003), as noted in chapter 2, refers to governance as societal steering through processes of coordination within networks. The most significant implication of the governance discourse for our understanding of the WD's economic development policy implementation in Manitoba is a re-visitation of visions of the role of government and the feasible tools at its disposal for dealing with public problems. Effective policy intervention in such a complex multi-actor setting as that of post-2000 Manitoba requires considerable investment of time and resources in reaching agreed common goals and in monitoring joint decisions that are implemented over more than the short term, and it would involve considerable cross-sectoral work, as well as shared responsibility and accountability structures. Relational contracts are thus becoming essential instruments of joint action by multiple organizations. Unlike classical contracts, they enable partners to plan a course of joint action that allows for constant adaptation of management systems to dynamic changes in the environment. It should be stressed that the general objectives of the WD's contractual agreements still remain to further strengthen and diversify the economies of the provinces and to build on their existing economic strengths. But the emphasis now is on "promoting regional development in accordance with the key strategic areas periodically identified by all parties."[28]

A further characteristic of the WD's adaptation to the complexity of its operating environment is that the agency began to interpret its contractual relationship with Manitoba as "supportive of local joint action under provincial leadership."[29] As the theoretical framework in chapter 2 suggests, part of public agencies' adaptive behaviour in complex multi-level systems is to enter "marriages of convenience" in order to reduce the potential for contestation that comes with operating in turbulent and assertive provincial and local jurisdictions. The WD increasingly sees itself as a strategic partner (in rather supportive roles) with the provincial government and, even, the municipalities in the province (WD's Departmental Strategy 2009). Inter-organizational collaboration in Manitoba had to make more room for local actors in joint action with the various levels of government. As one of the WD's senior management officials put it, "the emphasis of the earlier framework of the agency's policy delivery was to provide a mechanism for achieving equal federal-provincial cooperation in realizing the economic and regional development potential of the province of Manitoba, whereas now we see value in demonstrating our support for the province's policy priorities … they seem eager to get somewhere, and we're going with them … the important thing for us is that we're all in the same boat."[30]

In particular, the WD's agreements since 2000 increasingly reflect a policy thrust consistent with elements identified in the provincial government's innovation strategy. The 2003 MEPA Agreement, for instance, focuses on five strategic areas of regional economic development closely reflective of the provincial government's Action Strategy of 2003, namely, support for knowledge-based research and development, an increase in value-added production, support for trade and investment promotion, enhancement of productivity and competitiveness, and promotion of economic development through tourism opportunities. Similarly, the 2009 MEPA Agreement strongly resonated with Manitoba's Action Strategy for the province's economy in its emphasis on nurturing critical masses of knowledge networks that could serve as dynamic engines of innovation (Government of Canada 2009a). In this sense, they provide a legal framework for intergovernmental coordination consistent with a framework of regional development governance in which the provincial government takes on more active leadership.

The Action Strategy thus provides a de facto framework for guiding the contract between the province and the federal government. Even a range of policy initiatives delivered in Manitoba under the framework of "national agreements" are indicative of this shift: some of the main national agreements, as indicated earlier, include Recreational Infrastructure Canada and the Community Adjustment Fund. What these programs have in common is delivery framework designed by WD to maintain some level of flexibility in their implementation in order to allow for a rather strong provincial and municipal input (WD's Corporate Business Plan 2010). While the federal government remains keen on maintaining some level of visibility, the flexibility of its delivery rule is supportive of provincial policy leadership in order to allow for critical spaces of adaptation for manoeuvring around inter-jurisdictional complexity.

Moreover, the policy time frames of the WD's agreements since 2000 have tended to reflect medium- to longer-term goals rather than short-term subsidies to businesses.[31] There seems to be a more strategic focus on softer goals, such as support for institutional capacity building (like research capacity) geared towards long-term economic productivity and competitiveness. Although the WD is technically empowered by its founding mandate to engage in direct assistance programs, the agency's operational emphasis is less on proposal-based programs whereby the public can apply and access funds for business projects. For example, in the agency's 2010–2011 Report on Plans and Priorities, the WD identifies what it refers to as "operational priorities," which include "technology commercialization," "trade and investment," and business productivity and competitiveness, all aimed at softer goals such as private capacity building over the long term (WD Report on Plans and Priorities, Treasury Board of Canada 2011–2012).

For example, through the WD's "trade and investment" operational priority, the agency has entered a long-term partnership with the provincial government and Economic Development Winnipeg (EDW, a semi-autonomous economic development corporation of the city) in a project called Yes Winnipeg.[32] The goal of the partnership is to work together over the long term (no horizon specified) to foster the attraction and retention of foreign investment capital in Manitoba. A similar partnership undertaken by the EDW under its business competitiveness and trade "operational priority" involves an agreement with the Canadian Manufacturers and Exporters (CME) association in Manitoba.[33] The WD (along with a number of provincial ministries) works with the CME over an undefined time frame on issues like training small and medium-size business managers about global market systems and processes.

These examples demonstrate how the general focus of the WD is now more on programs involving joint longer-term strategic investment decisions alongside the private sector, the non-profit sector, and public sector organizations (WD's Research and Market Study 2010). The WD is thus focusing less on providing funding directly to businesses and instead supports a network of policy actors within the market economy. The agency's pursuit of its new operational priorities is consistent with the open-systems perspectives of organization theory, since the WD's attention seems focused on forging a cooperative social system through longer-term projects that enhance collective action. This emphasis breaks fundamentally with the machine models of earlier years in which contractual agreements were often given shorter maturity and termination terms. The WD is now more willing to make open-ended commitments without specific time frames for conclusion. This is a considerable compromise of its policy ownership but a reasonable expenditure to adapt to the imperatives of a highly dynamic economic development policy environment in the province.

An even more poignant indication of this new strategic thrust is the agency's pursuit of its "policy advocacy and coordination mandate" (WD's Departmental Strategy 2009). The WD has seen itself more and more as a "convening power" bringing a number of federal players in the province together to work around a number of strategic issues.[34] For instance, in 2010 the WD spearheaded a tri-level committee consisting of six federal departments, four provincial ministries, and the city of Winnipeg to work on the CentrePort Canada project, which is aimed at building an in-land port around the Winnipeg Airport (Economic Development Winnipeg Inc. 2011). The federal departments involved were Transport Canada, Industry Canada, Foreign Affairs and International Trade (DFAIT), Export Development Canada (EDC), the Canada Revenue Agency (CRA), and the Canada Border Services Agency (CBSA). The provincial departments were Entrepreneurship, Training and Trade; Finance, Infrastructure and Transport; and Local Government. The city was represented by the Department of Development and Planning. In addition, the WD also serves as "chair" (coordinator and lynchpin) of the Federal Council in Manitoba,[35] which consists of approximately forty senior-level public servants from all the federal departments in the province. These examples indicate attempts by the WD to exercise its perception of its authority to pursue a more concerted policy action by serving as the "golden thread" that weaves together the federal government's economic development policy engagement in the province.

Sometimes, however, in pursuing its policy advocacy and coordination mandate, the WD is faced with the stark realities of federal politics. It does serve as a sort of lynchpin for coordinating federal agencies in the region, leveraging a reservoir of expertise, perspectives, and resources from the federal departments for the province. But the province does not always appreciate this "outside" expertise and these perspectives, especially when they sit uneasily with the preferred line of action of the provincial government. For example, the 2012 decision of the Conservative government of Stephen Harper to terminate the monopoly of the Canadian Wheat Board on marketing wheat and barley has raised considerable objections within the province of Manitoba. The province's main concern is that the federal government has not developed any plan to address the devastating blow this decision will deal to the economy of Churchill, which relies almost exclusively on the transportation and storage of grain in its port under the current Wheat Board's system. The WD is caught between the competing policy visions of the federal and the provincial government and often has to perform political gymnastics to maintain its credibility as a policy conduit.

But despite such occasional difficulties, the WD has been able to maintain considerable legitimacy in representing the interests of the province in Ottawa while serving as the economic development window of the federal government in Manitoba. As a senior policy official at the agency puts it: "No one is able to do anything alone successfully anymore – things have become too complex and multifaceted, and so they must be done in partnership."[36] Moreover, the WD's challenges are made easier by the fact that, macro-economically, Manitoba (like most of the provinces) is in such a fiscal squeeze that any "outside" resources tend to be given the "red carpet."[37] The province seems reluctantly aware of this reality and succumbs to the expediency of a complex mesh of expertise and perspectives that inherently bring with them some resources and useful insights.

In spite of the rather impressive demonstration of strategic adaptation to the turbulence of a highly dynamic and complex operating environment, another major limitation in the WD's current operations in the province is a lack of policy coordination with other agencies involved in rural and northern development (WD's Corporate Business Plan 2010). As noted earlier, the WD's current operational priorities for Manitoba (and the rest of Western Canada) include the commercialization of technology, trade and investment, and business productivity and competitiveness (WD's Report on Plans and Priorities 2011–2012). The WD's fourth priority, rural economic diversification, has been removed from the agency's strategic plan over the past two years. However, the WD is still involved in rural and northern development through its sixteen Community Futures Development Corporations (CFDCs) and seventeen CDEMs (or Conseil de développement économique des municipalités bilingues du

Manitoba). The CFDCs and CDEMs work with local community development corporations (although CDEMs focus solely on bilingual municipalities) with the goal of promoting economic development and successful businesses in disadvantaged rural and northern communities.

There is still considerable fragmentation and duplication of economic development programs in northern and rural Manitoba. For example, Agriculture and Agri-Food Canada (Agric-Canada) and Indian and Northern Affairs (INAC) (the WD's sister federal agencies in the province) have very similar programs that fall within the WD's mandate.[38] Although Agric-Canada does not necessarily have a rural development mandate, its agricultural mandate in the province is intrinsically connected to rural development. The department has a five-year partnership framework with the provincial government called Growing Forward, under which initiatives for the rural economy are cost-shared. The initiatives include business risk management programs, innovation and science programs, business development programs, and environmental development programs. Under the Growing Forward partnership framework, the province has developed a suite of programs, including the Advancing Agric-Innovation Program, the Agric-Extension Innovation Program, Business Development Management, the Agri-Food Research and Development Initiative (ARDI), the Farm Innovation and Diversification Centres Program, and the Northern Agriculture Program.

Other provincial program initiatives for rural and northern regions delivered by the Ministry of Agriculture, Food and Rural Initiatives (MAFRI) include the creation of Regional Development Corporations, the Rural Economic Development Initiative (REDI), Rural Entrepreneur Assistance Guarantees (REA), and the Skill Development for Young Entrepreneurs Program. The seven RDCs, for instance, serve to encourage regional development initiatives in rural and northern Manitoba (Government of Manitoba 2011b). Moreover, the provincial Ministry of Aboriginal and Northern Affairs (ANA) manages a number of Northern initiatives such as the Community Economic Development Fund, the First Peoples Economic Growth Fund, and the newly created Métis Economic Development Fund (Government of Manitoba 2011d). The federal government's Indian and Northern Affairs Canada (INAC) also has its own community economic development programs. Under the Gathering Strength initiative, for instance, INAC manages a suite of programs for remote communities and Indian reserves, including the commercial development of lands, human resource development, economic development, infrastructure, and business ventures.

In short, each of the departments has developed a rather impressive suite of programs for the rural and northern regions of the province. The problem is that the institutional context of the WD's rural economic diversification policies and programs is fragmented because each of the departments mentioned above, including the WD's own federal counterparts, maintain their operational silos, or "stovepipes." This creates program duplication and potential resource waste – a problem acknowledged by some of Manitoba's MAFRI officials and the province's Rural Development Institute in Brandon.[39] The WD's CFDC activities, for instance, duplicate the province's RDCs with geographical and functional overlaps in their operations. There is even a tendency towards rivalry and jurisdictional turfs among the front-line delivery agencies. The RDCs are viewed as the poorer cousins of the well-funded CFDCs, and the RDCs often seek to demonstrate their relevance by undertaking programs for which they lack the resources. The WD has seemingly left the CFDCs to fend for themselves in a rather crowded and fragmented policy space. The irony is that this fragmentation and duplication at the front line persist despite the presence of the Rural Secretariat located in Agriculture and Agri-Food Canada, which should, in principle, serve as a focal point for pursuing partnership and coordination among agencies and target populations. Compared to the other examples of the WD's attempt to synchronize its program activities with a range of partners in emerging priority sectors, there is no evidence of an effort by the WDs to partner with the province in pursuing greater institutional coordination at the front lines of rural and northern economic development policy delivery.[40]

The unfortunate result is that the most disadvantaged regions of the province, those with the highest need for concerted policy action, are not given the same level of attention as is given to innovation and technology commercialization in emerging sectors of the urban economy. The implication is a potentially incoherent framework of rural economic development leading to less effective policy intervention, as sectoral policy interventions tend to be logically inconsistent with the complex and interrelated nature of regionally defined problems in rural and northern Manitoba. Against this backdrop, in 2009 the agency decided to remove rural economic diversification from its operational priorities, claiming they had been fused into the other priorities – namely, technology commercialization, trade and investment, and business productivity.

The evidence of the WD's successful strategic efforts to make necessary adaptations to synchronize its program activities with other partners in the province in the areas of technology commercialization, trade and investment, and business productivity indicates that these stated priorities are being given due attention. Programs for rural and northern Manitoba that are not expressly included in the agency's priorities have fallen through the institutional cracks. This strategic choice largely reflects structural trends in the modern economy, where focus shifts considerably towards building systems capacity for high-performing knowledge clusters. In this regard, the limitation of the WD's rural and northern program activities, ironically, can be seen as a legitimate function of a small and resource-limited agency's strategic choice to prioritize its activities based on the current emerging sectors in the province's economy.

Notwithstanding the limitations in its execution of a rural and northern development mandate, the WD has made considerable strategic adjustments over the years to adapt to the changing imperatives of its operating environment. Given the federal government's historic power struggle with the provinces for visibility and credit for its regional development programs, preserving federal agencies' organizational integrity and policy mandates is an intrinsic aspect of federal politics in Canada. The direction taken by the WD since 2000, however, seems to have dissipated its agency identity and policy control. The WD appears to be conducting collaborative management with the province of Manitoba from a position of relative weakness compared to just over a decade ago. Indeed, the ideational and structural shifts over the past decade have given the Manitoba government a certain advantage over the WD with respect to Manitoba's greater knowledge of local economic and political realities and its greater legitimacy (by virtue of proximity) for coordinating the multiple emergent bases of power within a complex knowledge economy. Moreover, the apparent dissipation of the WD's policy identity and program mandate may indicate the general tendency of decentralized agencies. The decentralized structures created in the 1987 reorganization of regional development agencies may finally be taking effect, even if this means a loss of policy control on the part of the federal government.

Flexibility is thus both the WD's blessing and its curse. The agency's strategic adaptation to the exigencies of dynamic changes in its operating environment means that it must try to be everything to all stakeholders. Policy and operational coherence become the casualty in such contexts. Like all federal departments, the agency is required to state its operational priorities in its annual "Reports on Plans and Priorities" to the Treasury Board Secretariat. But in reality, these plans and priorities are like "today's special" in a restaurant menu. The full range of items on the menu are being served to stakeholders – the imperatives of strategic adaptation to a highly politicized policy subsystem means that the menu may continue to grow larger (with potential fragmentation and duplication) while the operational "specials" remain relatively small.

On the other hand, even though the mechanisms of multi-actor policy delivery in Manitoba since 2000 may appear to dissipate some of the WD's control over its perceived constitutional mandate and legislated policy domain, the legitimacy of the agency's policy intervention in Manitoba is enhanced through a willingness to invest in building trust with local partners. Also, because the WD serves as the federal government's main conduit of economic intervention in the province, it remains a significant player whose program preferences are given serious consideration by local partners, including the provincial government. And because it carries the institutional authority of a federal agency, the WD continues to draw on symbolic or "soft" power to influence the direction of program development and implementation in the province. In this regard, the WD remains part of the inner circle within a complex policy subsystem. Finally, the current complexity of horizontal collaborative market governance consisting of multiple partners in Manitoba serves the WD's organizational interest insofar as, in addition to it drawing from the strengths of many perspectives, there are many heads to share the blame when policy expectations exceed outcomes, as they sometimes do.

The central thread that weaves through this analysis of the WD's adaptation is a concern shared by policy implementation research, organization theory, and the governance literature – to understand how public agencies interact with their external environment in the delivery of policies. Emerging from this shared concern is the need to re-conceptualize power and authority among public and non-state organizations in the policy environment. Regional economic development policy implementation in Manitoba over the past decade has been a complex mix of hierarchy and collaboration. Rather than delivering and directing, the role of the WD has become to act as a facilitator and an empowering agency. Target groups once considered beneficiaries or clients of government programs are now viewed as policy actors in their own right. Policy implementation in this regard is neither primarily about public agencies undertaking policy implementation by themselves nor about shifting such responsibilities completely to non-state actors. The focus becomes building synergies for joint action with partners drawn from the private and not-for-profit sectors. Within such a context, governments act as partners and facilitators by providing support and frameworks that empower policy actors to solve problems and manage change.

CONCLUSION

This discussion has analyzed changes in the framework of economic development policy intervention from the "administration" of bilateral contracts to the "governance" of complex policy networks involving a constellation of actors drawn from several jurisdictions (including municipalities), the private sector, community groups, and research institutions. This chapter highlights the forces behind these transitions in regional economic development policy implementation in the province of Manitoba, tracing the ideational changes among policy actors as the emphasis of regional economic development shifts towards knowledge or innovation capacities as the foundation of productivity, competitiveness, and growth. Through the lens of the multi-actor framework, the present context of economic development policy intervention in Manitoba is based in the collaborative governance of innovation policy involving various levels of jurisdiction, with multiple lenses of interpretation (including those of non-governmental stakeholders).

Using the multi-actor framework as an analytical lens has allowed us to track and understand the capacity and legitimacy of the WD in light of the broader imperatives of its operating environment. Organization theory, for instance, directs our attention to the willingness or ability of the WD to reorganize its culture and operations in ways that involve sharing authority and power, as well developing a learning culture. How the WD as a federal agency operating in a provincial jurisdiction seeks to adjust its mission to reflect the changing values and interests of the local environment thus becomes an important consideration in our understanding of regional economic development policy governance in the province.

The governance literature calls our attention to the emergent phenomenon of non-state actors' engagement in co-production. The institutional and ideational forces underlying the shift in the province of Manitoba is best understood as an emergent transition away from simply delivering and directing to one of facilitation, coordination, and empowerment. The expectations and demands of organized actors in the province outside the public sector imply that the external environment is not simply a set of variables to be manipulated by the WD. Building legitimacy for effective policy intervention requires the WD to identify the main actors within the province and their specific demands and then to re-think its use of contracts to coordinate the various bases of power. The structure of support and established feedback loops that the agency maintains with local organized actors are crucial factors for success. The effectiveness of economic development policy implementation requires the WD to make connections across organizations – within and across layers of government, as well as between the public and non-governmental sectors – as they constantly evolve over time.

This discussion has thus analyzed the WD's demonstrated dexterity and flexibility in pursuing its organizational mandate and goals under conditions of extreme uncertainty and complexity. The relevance and integrity of the WD's contractual agreements under the current governance arrangements in Manitoba over the past decade rest on the adaptive capacities of the agency in the face of complexity and change. Since changes in thinking about economic diversification and development in modern markets are still emerging, it is fair to project that the WD's continued capacity and legitimacy to influence the direction of economic development policy implementation in Manitoba rests increasingly on the agency's ability to navigate the murky waters of inter-jurisdictional and inter-organizational arrangements for joint policy action. This requires greater willingness on its part to adjust its policy goals and contractual instruments to the changing ideas and power relations within its operating environment.

At a broader level, the Manitoba case also illustrates the use of contracts as instruments for managing joint policy action across institutional boundaries in dynamic multi-level systems. As the case indicates, intergovernmental contracts in multi-level systems are best seen as relatively flexible "relational" instruments to facilitate joint action in solving complex problems. Such intergovernmental agreements should not be confused with classical contracts. Classical contracts tend to be rigid, with a very strict interpretation, and the signatories are inclined to resort to the courts if a perceived infringement of the terms of the contract occurs. Classical contracts are thus ill-equipped to deal with the issues of uncertainty and interdependency in the public context of policy governance. Unlike classical contracts, relational contracts (such as the one increasingly used by the WD) enable partners to plan a course of joint action that allows for the constant adaptation of management systems to dynamic changes in the environment.

Finally, the experience of the WD provides useful lessons on intergovernmental coordinating processes in policy delivery, because the transitions observed in Manitoba reflect broader economic, social, and institutional changes in Canada and the world. The environment of public agencies is increasingly characterized by a complex network of organizations (public and non-governmental), each with its own goals, instruments, resources, and accountability structures. An additional challenge to the coordination of most multi-actor policy networks is the dynamic nature of the environment within which public agencies must operate.

The practical implication of this analysis is that the effectiveness of public policy implementation now, more than ever, requires that public managers and other policy stakeholders are able make connections across organizations, bridge diverse cultures across levels of government and outside government, and share ideas, resources, and power with non-state actors. Policy intervention aimed at successfully solving complex problems in most domains involves collaborative governance arrangements that transcend layers of government, as well as bridge the once sacrosanct boundaries between the public and non-governmental sectors.

7

The Federal Economic Development Initiative for Northern Ontario

INTRODUCTION

The effectiveness of the multi-actor implementation framework discussed earlier chapters is illustrated here by analyzing the Canadian government's pursuit of economic development in Northern Ontario over the past two decades. As in the preceding two chapters, the discussion focuses on how the federal government's main economic development agency engages with its provincial and local counterparts, as well as with organized community and private sector groups within the region.

Since this chapter focuses on a region within a province rather than on the province as a whole, the reason for including it as a distinct case needs further elaboration. Northern Ontario is a region with a vast land mass and a small population. Table 7.1 provides a summary of key characteristics of the province of Ontario as a whole. Figure 7.1 provides a map of the province as a whole, whereas figure 7.2 highlights the main regions of Northern Ontario. Although it covers approximately 800,000 square kilometres, representing almost 90 percent of the Ontario land mass, the region has a total population of only about 786,500 – only 6 percent of the population of the province (Government of Ontario 2009). This rugged and varied land includes towns, cities, farmland, forests, muskeg, and rock (McGillivray 2007). The region's socio-economic development (or underdevelopment) has been shaped over the past hundred and fifty years by its staples economy (Nelles 2005). Forestry, mining, and to a minor extent agriculture have been the essential features of the region's economy, in contrast to the advanced industrial activities of its southern counterpart.

Table 7.1
Demographic and Economic Characteristics of Ontario

Capital	Toronto
Largest city	Toronto
Largest metropolitan area	Greater Toronto Area
Total area	1,076,395 km^2 (415,598 sq miles)
Population (2010)	13,210,667
Total GDP (2009)	c$578.2 billion
GDP per capita	c$43,847

Source: Courtesy of Statistics Canada.

The administrative divisions of Southern and Northern Ontario illustrate one of the historic disadvantages of the latter: while Southern Ontario's municipal units are situated within larger municipal structures called counties or regional municipalities, Northern Ontario's settled areas are mostly incorporated into municipal structures called districts, which have relatively weaker jurisdiction for undertaking local development activities (Southcott 2006). Northern Ontario now consists of the Regional Municipality of Greater Sudbury (the only one of its kind in the region) and the following districts: Kenora, Rainy River, Thunder Bay, Algoma, Cochrane, Manitoulin, Sudbury, Timiskaming, Nipissing, and Parry Sound.

The region as a whole (as indicated in table 7.2) consists of 144 municipalities, 106 First Nations, and more than 150 unincorporated communities. These communities are diverse, ranging from remote settlements of a few hundred people to large cities, and they can be divided into three distinct types of communities: small and medium-sized cities; resource-dependent communities; and Aboriginal communities (Government of Ontario 2011a; Southcott 2006). Table 7.3 provides a comparison of the rural and urban demographic distributions for Northern and Southern Ontario. The Northern region's economy is dominated by its five large population centres: Sudbury, Thunder Bay, Sault Ste Marie, North Bay, and Timmins.

Since the formal inception in the early 1970s of economic development policy mechanisms for Northern Ontario, the region has been considered a "slow growth" or "lagging" region in the province (Government of Ontario 1973). Some of Northern Ontario's main economic challenges include declining employment opportunities in primary industries, lower population and labour force increases owing to higher rates of out-migration, labour participation rates

Figure 7.1 Map of Ontario, Courtesy of Natural Resources Canada

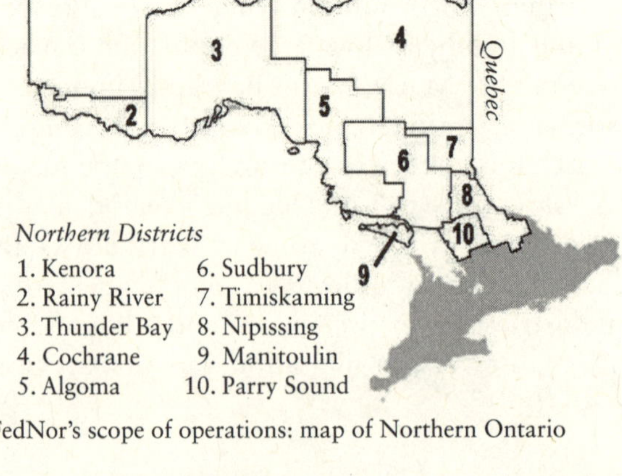

Figure 7.2 FedNor's scope of operations: map of Northern Ontario

Table 7.2
Key Facts about the Administrative Divisions of Northern Ontario

- 10 territorial districts
- 144 municipalities
- 106 First Nations
- Over 150 unincorporated communities, including 44 Local Services Boards
- Population of 807,509
- Land area of 802,396.06 km^2
- Francophone population of 139,010
- Aboriginal population of 97,930

Source: Courtesy of the Ontario Ministry of Northern Development, Mines and Forestry.

Table 7.3
Comparison of Southern and Northern Ontario: Rural/Urban Population Distribution (percentages)

	Rural	*Urban*
Southern Ontario	11	89
Northern Ontario	34	66

Source: Statistics Canada, 2009 *Annual Population Estimates.*

that are lower than those in the rest of Ontario, high levels of unemployment, the relative absence of significant manufacturing activities, and lower average incomes than the provincial average.

Northern Ontario is currently in the midst of economic change, crisis, and transition (Government of Ontario 2011a). The issues affecting its performance include the presence of a declining sector linked to older industry, aging populations, out-migration of the younger population, and the absence of coherent strategies to drive economic growth (Di Matteo 2006). The history and structure of industry in the region confirm a trend of persistent decline in the mainstays of the economy, mostly primary resource industries, with a gradual shift towards service industries. There has been a general decline in industrial activity and a traditional weakness in secondary manufacturing and service industries (the presence of pulp and paper mills notwithstanding) (Bollman, Beshiri, and Mitura 2006). The share of employment in primary and manufacturing industries declined from 28 percent in 1981 to 16 percent in 2001 (Southcott 2006). The picture of industrial stagnation and decline is reflected in socio-economic indicators such as a high unemployment rate, a low average income, and net outmigration relative to the rest of the province.[1]

For example, from 1996 to 2006 the population of the region decreased by 4.8 percent, while the rest of the province of Ontario's population grew by 6.1 percent and Canada's by 4 percent. Between 1996 and 2006, the number of people employed in Northern Ontario decreased by 0.4 percent, but Ontario's number increased by 12.5 percent. In general, the average income per capita of the region is three percentage points below the provincial average, and unemployment is four percentage points above the provincial average. Also, the industrial structure gives us a clearer indication or explanation for the difference between Northern Ontario and the rest of the province. While the manufacturing sector represented 16.4 percent of all industry jobs in Ontario in 2001, this sector represented only 10.7 percent of jobs in Northern Ontario, despite the presence of a large number of sawmill and pulp and paper industries in the North.

Before 1987, the federal government's economic development initiatives for Northern Ontario were indirect; funds for rural and northern development in the region were channelled through the provincial government (Government of Ontario 1973). The Canada-Ontario General Development Agreements of the 1970s, which were administered by the then Department of Regional Economic Expansion (DREE), provide a particular instance of this framework (see chapter 4 for more details). With the major 1987 restructuring of regional economic development in Canada, a special federal agency was created for Northern Ontario – the Federal Economic Development Initiative for Northern Ontario (FedNor). The creation of FedNor was a clear indication that the federal government had decided to deliver its own economic development programs directly (Industry Canada 1987).

FEDNOR IN NORTHERN ONTARIO

FedNor's mandate, broadly speaking, is to promote economic growth, diversification, and job creation in Northern Ontario (Government of Canada 1987). The agency's creation in 1987 exacerbated an existing political disequilibrium and complexity already emerging in Northern Ontario. In principle, FedNor was given a mandate to deliver its own programs as both a facilitator and a catalyst of economic development in the region. In fact, however, the federal government was reacting to the perceived tendency of the provinces across Canada to use the federal government's financial resources for regional development while taking credit themselves (Savoie 1997).

Although FedNor was created under principles of administrative restructuring guided by the stated value propositions of institutional decentralization, the agency (as an offspring of intergovernmental politics) was eager to proceed with the implementation of its own program and ensure political visibility (FedNor 2003).[2] FedNor's policy intervention during the early years of its operation was by all accounts inconsistent with the principles of concerted action across institutional boundaries suggested by the multi-actor implementation framework discussed in earlier chapters. While the agency's engagement in the region affected two levels of policy jurisdictions (provincial and municipal), as well as a large numbers of actors, FedNor's early activities were characterized by somewhat "top-down" processes that reflected a mechanistic orientation towards program delivery.[3]

FedNor boasted two main programs, the Northern Ontario Development Program (NODP) and the Community Futures Program (CFP) (Industry Canada, Reports on Plans and Priorities, 1998–1999). Appendix 3 provides further details of FedNor's full range of programs. The NODP seeks to promote economic development and diversification by providing repayable and non-repayable contributions to not-for-profit organizations and small and medium-sized enterprises (SMEs). As an all-embracing program, it covers almost every economic sector. The other component of FedNor's programs is the Community Futures Program. This program supports twenty-four Community Futures Development Corporations (CFDCs) in Northern Ontario, which are part of a larger national program supporting community economic development and small business growth in disadvantaged regions. Both the NODP and the CFP have been designed to address some of the structural, sectoral, and community economic development challenges facing the region by improving small business access to capital and supporting community economic development endeavours, as well as providing business information and market intelligence for the private sector.

One of the distinct features of FedNor that initially shaped the agency's model of economic development policy implementation is that whereas other regional development agencies like ACOA and the WD enjoyed considerable departmental autonomy, FedNor has largely been subsumed under the purview of Industry Canada

(Government of Canada 1995). (See figure 7.3 for an organogram depicting FedNor as a delivery unit within Industry Canada.) This structural characteristic of FedNor means that although the agency is, in principle, mandated to work with the private sector, community partners, and other organizations, it lacks policy discretion to sustain credible partnerships at the front lines (Industry Canada Performance Report 1998–1999).[4] FedNor's model of policy delivery was, however, consistent with the normative preferences of the "top-down" approach to policy implementation in the prevalent scholarly literature of first-generation research described in chapter 2. Since FedNor's programs were based on policies developed within Industry Canada, the agency's ability to adapt was constrained by the imperatives of its external environment. This constraint did not mean, however, that FedNor officials were opposed to working with local partners. In fact, in the early to mid-1990s, FedNor officials made efforts to work with community groups in program delivery (Government of Canada 1995), but the agency's model of governance was perceived as too hierarchical (or "top-down" in the terminology of first-generation implementation research).[5]

FedNor's efforts to create an environment of consultation and partnership involving communities, businesses, and other levels of government were hindered by the fact that the agency was principally a program delivery organization and lacked the authority to develop its own policies or deviate from those set within the framework of Industry Canada, its parent department (Industry Canada Performance Report 1997). Thus, although a principal feature of the new policy and organizational configuration of 1987 was the decentralization of administrative and policy functions away from Ottawa and towards the regions, this was not strictly the case for FedNor in Northern Ontario. If the new approach after 1987 allowed for more direct interaction between local federal agencies and the community in the design and implementation of programs, FedNor was given no practical authority to engage in it.

The operational framework of FedNor's mandate is what the first-generation critiques of top-down models of policy implementation describe as excessively mechanistic and unable to do justice to the realities of policy delivery in democratic societies or complex multi-level jurisdictions. Also, within organization theory, open-systems analysts would refer to FedNor's mandate as fundamentally a machine model or closed-systems view of policy implementation

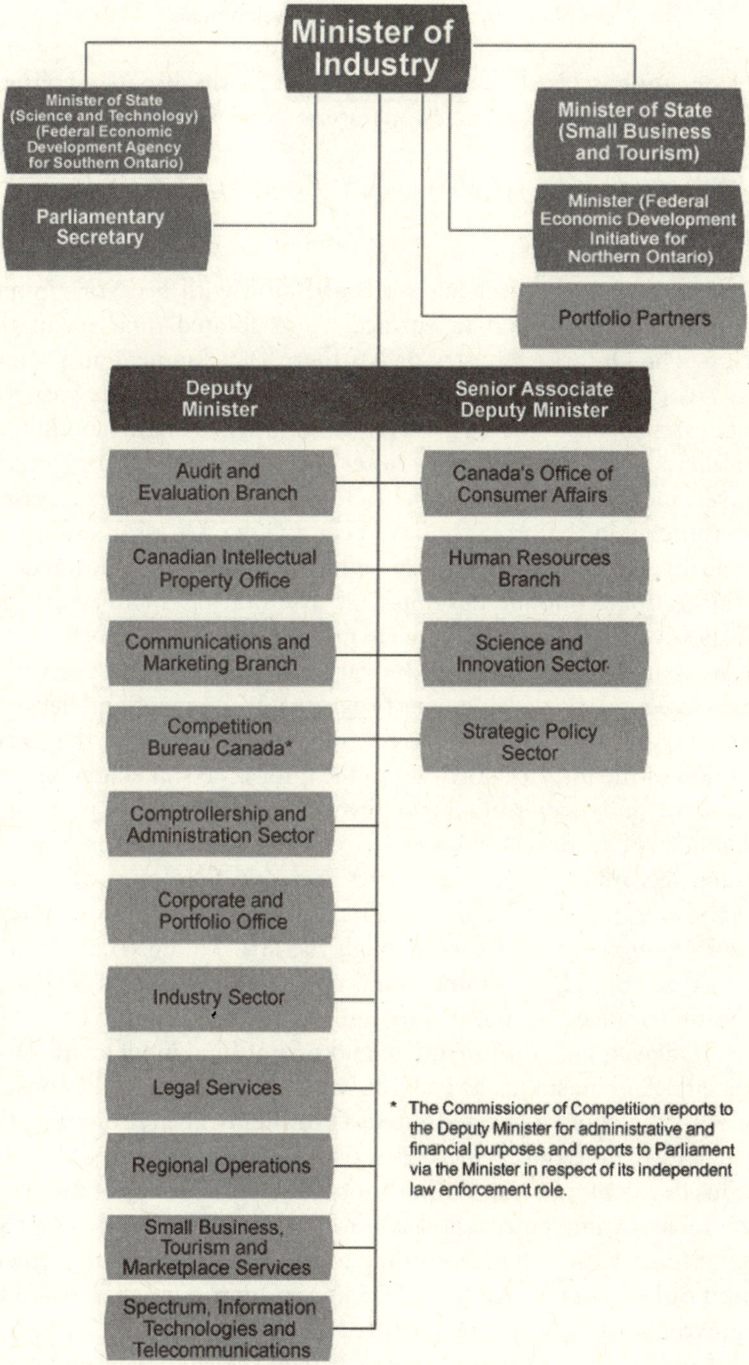

Figure 7.3 FedNor's structural link with Industry Canada

that de-emphasizes the complex relations in the broader political context within which agencies operate.

THE EMERGENCE OF POLITICAL AND IDEATIONAL PERTURBATIONS

In the early 1990s sentiments of disaffection with FedNor's implementation model began to surface from isolated quarters in the region. The Ontario Ministry of Northern Development and Mines (MNDM) (whose name has changed several times over the past five decades) has been the provincial government's main conduit of economic development policy intervention in Northern Ontario (Government of Ontario 2011b). Since the late 1960s successive governments in the province have been involved in promoting economic diversification in northern Ontario. Before 1987, most federal resources for economic development in Ontario's socio-economically disadvantaged regions were channelled through the MNDM. This meant that the MNDM enjoyed a rather hegemonic and unrivalled status in economic development program development and delivery.

In fact, the MNDM (now referred to as the MNDMF, after the recent addition of the forestry portfolio to the ministry)[6] still enjoys hegemonic status in Northern Ontario. Over the past decade in particular, the ministry has developed a range of programs in the forestry and mining sectors of the region. In the 2009–10 fiscal year, the provincial government invested over $1.2 billion in Northern Ontario's mineral and forestry sectors through the MNDMF (MNDMF Annual Report 2010). This amount alone considerably dwarfs FedNor's operating budget of about $40 million for the region. Thus, the MNDM viewed FedNor's mandate and operational model with some curiosity. And inasmuch as FedNor wanted its mission to be consistent with the core values and interests of the local environment, the agency took note of the MNDM's jurisdictional sensitivities.[7]

This development can be understood through the lens of the emergent focus of implementation research on concerted action across institutional boundaries. According to this approach, the implementation of FedNor's programs in Northern Ontario would have to be contextualized within Canada's federal system, with different levels of policy action for the federal, provincial, and even municipal jurisdictions. A significant manifestation of the challenges of intergovernmental coordination is apparent in FedNor's relationship with the Northern Ontario Heritage Fund Corporation (NOHFC).[8] The NOHFC is the program delivery agency of the Ontario Ministry of Northern Development and Mines (MNDM) (Government of Ontario 2009). With an annual budget of about $100 million (more than twice that of FedNor's), the NOHFC performs functions similar to those of FedNor, such as providing financial assistance and advisory services to business, primarily through industrial and regional development programs designed to fill gaps in capital markets. The NOHFC also supports industries in manufacturing and related activities, tourism operations, and exporters.

The NOHFC continues to be an important instrument of the MNDMF in Northern Ontario, and since October 2003 the agency has committed more than $506 million to the region (MNDMF Annual Report 2010). About $193 million was invested in local community infrastructure development and enhancement projects through the NOHFC's Infrastructure and Community Development Program; $30 million was invested through the Youth Internship and Co-Op Program, which created over fifteen hundred internships and co-op placements that span the entire North, including remote Far North communities; over $84 million was invested through the Enterprises North Job Creation Program aimed at creating jobs and positioning small and medium-sized businesses in the North for success; and about $90 million was invested through the Emerging Technology Program.

Thus, FedNor had to work around structural constraints to incorporate more intergovernmental coordination with the MNDM. For the MNDM, however, intergovernmental coordination meant that FedNor had to incorporate considerable elements of the former's policy vision into the latter's development programs.[9] This meant that policy direction for FedNor could not simply come from outside the region. A better way to understand this apparent complexity is provided by open-systems analysts within organization theory. Their focus is on the relationship between a particular public agency and its strategic (or external) environment. In their rejection of the machine models (closed-systems) view of policy implementation, open systems analysts emphasize the complex relations between public agencies and the broader political context within which they operate. The assumptions of order and control that may preoccupy Industry Canada's relationship with FedNor, for instance, are viewed as simplistic and set up for FedNor's potential failure. A way out of this impasse is for FedNor to assume the authority to re-examine its policy intervention in the region of Northern Ontario as a highly complex process in which the agency must engage other organizations such as the MNDM and its affiliate agency (the NOHFC).

By the turn of the millennium, other provincial ministries (in addition to the MNDM) began making assertive penetration into Northern Ontario. For instance, the Ontario Ministry of Natural Resources (MNR) and the Ontario Ministry of Transportation (OTR) began to assume greater responsibility for economic development in the region.[10] These ministries were empowered by the ideas surrounding the new regionalism that emphasized a role for every sector of a region's economy within an integrated governance framework. As discussed earlier, the strategy of the old paradigm of economic development policy intervention tended to focus on sectoral or, even, individual firm approaches, whereas the new paradigm is integrated and cross-sectoral, seeking to position regions as niches within the global economy. For example, rather than focusing on the pulp and paper industry in isolation, the new paradigm builds a complex and intricate fabric of regional clusters of inter-sectoral innovation, production, and exchange systems. These cross-sectoral systems of cooperation extend beyond industries within the private sector. This system of co-production among a network of actors constitutes a key element of the new paradigm of regional development.

The MNR thus started building its policy capacity for greater development intervention in the forestry sector in Northern Ontario. Innovative ideas and programs like ecotourism and multi-use forestry were adopted by the MNR, providing justification for greater intervention in the region.[11] Other provincial ministries, such as Energy and Transportation, increased their engagement in the region as the concept of alternative and renewable energy systems became increasingly predominant in the region over the past decade. Since the new framework of regional development policy intervention calls for more integrated and cross-sectoral approaches, these ministries felt justified in increasing their activities in a region once considered the exclusive domain of the MNDM.

In its 2008 "Mid-Term Evaluation of the Northern Ontario Development Program (NODP) Final Report," Industry Canada's (2008c) Audit and Evaluation Branch noted a somewhat lengthy list of economic development programs for Northern Ontario, which included the NODP; the Northern Ontario Heritage Fund;

the Ontario Trillium Foundation; the Rural Economic Development Program of the Ontario Ministry of Agriculture, Food and Rural Affairs; the Ontario Job Creation Partnerships; Human Resources and Social Development Canada; the National Research Council; Indian and Northern Affairs Canada; and programs for municipalities (Industry Canada 2008). Clearly, within this context the adaptive abilities of FedNor became extremely important to the agency's success at navigating intergovernmental tensions. The challenge for FedNor is balancing the imperatives of its relationship with Industry Canada while also addressing jurisdictional sensitivities at the front lines of its operations. What makes the challenges of intergovernmental coordination even more significant for policy intervention from FedNor's standpoint is that Canadian federalism makes the provinces the primary players in regional economic development (Simeon 2006). Major areas where the provinces have flexibility in developing policy include determining which resources will be developed, how, to what extent, and by whom, and determining the extent of local public input into policies and plans and of participation in implementation. A long history of province-building in Canada has led to the development of strong, wilful provinces bent on pursuing provincially defined economic strategies that sometimes seek to compete with or displace the federal government wherever and whenever possible (Simeon 2006).

These and other challenges similar to those experienced by ACOA in New Brunswick and the WD in Manitoba confronted FedNor's model of program delivery. As was evident in Manitoba and New Brunswick and across much of Canada, one of the principal challenges for FedNor emerged from municipalities in Northern Ontario. Around the late 1990s, ideational shifts in the conceptualization of economic development made community economic development the prominent paradigm (Goldenberg 2008). Paradoxically, local regions seemed more eager to manage their own economic destinies in the face of globalization (Roy 2007). In Northern Ontario, major municipalities such as Sudbury, Thunder Bay, Sault Ste Marie, and Timmins began to take more assertive stances in demanding that the provincial government rethink its engagement with local entities (Conteh 2011).

Since 1973, upper tiers of government, especially the government of Ontario, have provided special support grants for Northern Ontario municipalities, which were viewed as creatures of the provinces, and their status in Northern Ontario, as noted earlier in this chapter, was even weaker not only because of their high dependence on provincial grants but also because of their weaker policy jurisdictions as districts. Paradoxically, this unique weakness of the municipalities eventually turned into an asset. In the absence of any statutory organization such as the county system in southern Ontario, the municipalities of Northern Ontario have maintained inter-municipal relationships, mostly through District Associations, as a way of presenting a united voice to the provincial capital in Queen's Park. Also, in 1974 Municipal Advisory Committees (MACs) were established, one for the Northwest and one for the Northeast, to provide the provincial government with comments and advise on regional development strategies.

Three municipal associations in Northern Ontario have played considerable roles in forging a regional identity over the years – the Northwestern Municipal Association (NOMA), formed in 1947, consisting of representatives from the Districts of Kenora, Rainy River, and Thunder Bay; the Federation of Northern Ontario Municipalities (FONOM), formed in 1960; and the Association of District Municipalities (ADM), formed in 1976, which acts as a liaison between NOMA and FONOM. Their united fronts were designed to make up for their individual weaknesses. The continuous existence of these associations over time has institutionalized a culture of collective action among municipalities that enabled them to exploit the emergent concepts of city-regions as institutional and geographic nodes of economic development in the knowledge-driven economy. Each of these municipalities seeks to find its own role and place in the emerging Northern Ontario economy by viewing itself as the economic and service hub of various sub-regions (Northern Ontario Growth Plan 2011; Conteh 2011). Some of these communities are keen on positioning themselves as points of convergence for major infrastructure, including transportation, energy, information, and communications technology, and community infrastructure.

By the turn of the millennium, this trend was reinforced as municipalities in Northern Ontario (as in other regions of the country and around the world) no longer wished to be treated simply as "clients" of economic development programs. They saw that they were better equipped in terms of institutional and organizational capacities to serve as conduits of economic development in the region (Northwestern Ontario Municipal Association 2000). Municipalities were closest to the problems of local economic development and, therefore, believed that they should be viable partners with germane insights in policy development, program design, and project delivery. Consequently, municipalities increasingly expect to be part of any policy and governance structure aimed at addressing the ills of their regional economy.[12]

In essence, FedNor was confronted with another wave of demands for the agency to work more closely with other levels of government. The complexity created by the inclusion of municipalities, as well as the province, in FedNor's policy space is the ideal image of what implementation research calls the challenges of concerted action across institutional boundaries. The three orders of government, each with its competent jurisdiction, constitute the multiplicity of actors, loci, and levels that Hill and Hupe (2003) described in chapter 2. Although municipalities in Canada are technically creatures of the provinces, FedNor's concern about political legitimacy in the region meant that the risks of failing to respond to the municipalities' demands for closer partnership could not be ignored. FedNor was faced with the challenge of reconciling Industry Canada's national frame of reference in policy development with the particular nature of the municipalities' approach to local economic development. An example is provided by FedNor's close engagement with the City of Greater Sudbury in a project to assess under-serviced industrial land related to future development (Government of Canada 2009b). In the past, part of FedNor's approach was to consult with Industry Canada officials to prevent local projects from conflicting with departmental policies. Rather than setting preconditions or dictating the terms of the project, the framework of implementation was designed to enable municipal authorities to make projections and plans about the industrial future of their city. It was not a completely "bottom-up" framework either, because as a partner, FedNor could influence the direction of industrial assessment and planning in the city.

Furthermore, other developments were emerging outside the institutional boundaries of the public sector. In particular, Aboriginal communities, represented through their treaty organizations within Northern Ontario, were increasingly demanding a role in the region's economic development planning framework as distinct jurisdictional entities (Nishnawbe Aski Nation 2009). Significant numbers of Aboriginal people are relocating to the urban centres of

Sudbury, Thunder Bay, Sault Ste Marie, Timmins, Kenora, and Sioux Lookout as they seek further education and employment opportunities. Their participation is deemed crucial to any forward-thinking approach to the economy of the region (Abele 2006). A recent report (Rosehart Report 2007) sponsored by the Ontario government concludes there is a strong recognition within the region that all future development initiatives by higher levels of government, municipalities, businesses, industries, and other stakeholders must be carried out in concert with the First Nations. The expectations and demands of Aboriginal groups are too deeply rooted in the fabric of Canadian politics for FedNor to see them as just another set of variables to manipulate. Building legitimacy for effective policy intervention in a region with First Nations communities requires careful identification of their existing community governing structures, and then coordination with the various bases of power they potentially command. But Aboriginal communities are not the only mobilized community groups. Other grassroots interests now include the Thunder Bay Economic Justice Committee and the Food Action Network, among others.

As was the case in New Brunswick and Manitoba, the private sector also added to the complexity of FedNor's policy environment by maintaining that businesses have increasingly been thinking in terms of the "market of regions" in their investment calculations (Northwestern Ontario Associated Chambers of Commerce (NOACC) 2009). Like municipalities, the private sector, through its umbrella chambers of commerce (Northern Ontario Chambers of Commerce (NOCC) and NOACC), viewed participation in the governance infrastructure of the region as crucial to prosperity. For instance, the NOACC maintain that domestic and international market pressures require a framework of regional development that goes beyond disparate project funding. Establishing more permanent feedback loops between public agencies and the private sector, the argument goes, would be more conducive to inter-sectoral and longer-term economic planning for the region.

An insightful way to understand the implications of the emergence of non-state actors in FedNor's engagement with Northern Ontario is drawn from the governance literature discussed earlier. According to this research, FedNor's activities are best contextualized within an intricate web of state-society relations, with the latter consisting of groups within society mobilized by a desire for self-governance.

FedNor faces an institutionalized policy subsystems environment characterized by a number of organizations within and outside the public sector. The dialectics of horizontal engagement suggests that policy implementation must take into consideration the perspectives and actions of organized target groups and other societal interests in less hierarchical policy settings. Some governance scholars will view FedNor's policy intervention in northern Ontario as an instance of a dominant public agency being constrained by a constellation of organized societal actors within a relatively complicated policy subsystem. Others will view the whole region as a highly complex system in which the adaptive ability of FedNor is crucial to successful interaction with the emerging organized interests in the region.

FEDNOR'S FUTURE – SINK OR SWIM

In the wake of the above-mentioned changes to its policy landscape, FedNor recognized the need to revisit its regional development policy framework. Clearly, the bases of power within the region were changing quickly, becoming not only more diverse but also multi-layered and complex. One advantage FedNor enjoyed over the provincial government was its nimbleness as a small agency compared to the much larger departmental structure of the MNDMF and other provincial agencies in the regions (FedNor 2006). When FedNor realized regional penetration down to the community level was in its interests in implementing its programs, it immediately did so.[13]

Part of the agency adaptation was a de facto restructuring of its intra-organizational processes that allowed for greater autonomy from Industry Canada in the early part of this decade (FedNor 2003). FedNor's increased operational autonomy by the turn of the millennium granted authority to formulate or adapt policies. This significant development allowed for a more credible pursuit of community partnership and close consultation with other agencies (Industry Canada Performance Report 2009). FedNor's adaptation to the exigencies of the local environment cannot, however, be seen as a complete break from the policy influence and control of Industry Canada. Rather, the agency's recent emphasis on multi-actor negotiations and inter-organizational implementation models is a complex mix of hierarchy and collaboration.

The combined perspectives of policy implementation research, organization theory, and the governance literature reinforce our understanding of policy implementation in modern political systems as based in cooperation and conflict as public agencies navigate various levels of constitutional and policy jurisdictions. While doing so, these agencies strive to gain legitimacy and positive feedback from non-state policy stakeholders. Within the context of a structured hierarchy, FedNor was confronted with the need to adjust its processes to environmental imperatives of horizontal management to maintain system stability, manage change, and deepen the impact of their policy intervention. In this light, the multi-actor implementation framework views FedNor's latest strategy of policy implementation as consisting of inter-organizational cooperation between FedNor and other public agencies, on the one hand, and between the agency and organized societal interests on the other.

In 2009, for example, the government of Canada committed $9.5 million through FedNor's Northern Ontario Development and Community Futures Programs to support economic development throughout Northern Ontario (Government of Canada 2009b). Although the money was accompanied by broad policy directions for use in economic development, the rather vague terms of the directives allowed for considerable local flexibility. FedNor's framework of implementation included a distinct emphasis on working with Aboriginal and other community groups, as well as with the private sector, to "develop a responsive, business-ready infrastructure" for the region.[14] Given the complex, inter-sectoral, and highly local nature of regional economic development, FedNor had to adjust its limited policy discretion to achieve wider environmental imperatives while remaining conscious of existing accountability structures within Industry Canada. These ongoing tensions meant that FedNor's culture became that of a learning organization.[15] As a learning organization, FedNor could hope to exploit emerging feedback loops with the local constellation of organized actors in the region, thereby deepening its policy intervention (FedNor Business Plan 2010–2011).

The gains from operational flexibility and adaptation have been more than symbolic for FedNor. For instance, the agency is better positioned to deal with yet another major development that started in the middle of this decade. In 2005 the Ontario government adopted a broader and more ambitious vision of regional economic diversification for Northern Ontario. Under the MNDMF's leadership, the Growth Plan (finally published in 2011) for Northern Ontario was set in motion by the provincial Places to Grow Act (2005). The Growth Plan, with $3.5-billion earmarked for its implementation, offers a set of policies, programs, and actions structured around six theme areas: the economy, people, communities, infrastructure, the environment, and Aboriginal peoples. It calls for comprehensive planning across all the sectors in the region, with a long-term projection of twenty-five years. An administrative framework supporting the Growth Plan has also been established, consisting of an interministerial forum known as the G-North Ministers Table (Government of Ontario 2009). This special committee of sixteen provincial Cabinet ministers, with mandates related directly to issues of economic development in Northern Ontario, coordinates the Ontario government's approach to policy, planning, and direction-setting in the region.

A significant element of the Growth Plan is that it calls on the federal government (primarily FedNor) and municipal governments to partner with the provincial government in realizing the "shared visions" of the plan, including maximizing the economic benefit of increased mineral exploration and strengthening the mineral industry cluster by bolstering partnerships among colleges, universities, and industry to support research; educating and training residents of the regions for careers in emerging fields such as advanced manufacturing, the digital economy, renewable energy, and water technologies and services; building a new relationship with Aboriginal people to increase participation in the future economic growth of Northern Ontario and achieve better health status for aboriginal communities; developing complete networks to support stronger communities, such as an inter-regional transportation network, enhanced broadband service, and a broader transmission network to increase capacity for renewable energy development; and creating regional economic zones to help communities plan collaboratively for their economic, labour market, infrastructure, land-use, cultural, and population needs (Growth Plan for Northern Ontario 2011). The Growth Plan is the culmination of the policy assertiveness of the Ontario government in the region, which has been unfolding rapidly, gaining great momentum and much publicity over the past decade. In 2004, the minister for northern development and mines introduced the Northern Prosperity Plan. In the same year, the Panel on the Role of Government in Ontario issued its report "Investing in People: Creating a Human Capital Society for Ontario" (Segsworth

2009). The panel argued that the provincial government, local governments, and regional authorities should recognize the realities of decline in small and remote communities and develop strategies to accordingly.

One of the concerns about the 2004 Prosperity Plan was that it displayed a hierarchical approach by the government of Ontario. Earlier, in 2005, the Northwestern Ontario Municipal Association (NOMA), and the Federation of Northern Ontario Municipalities (FONOM) had called for a review of the approach to regional economic development in the north involving extensive consultation. "Creating Our Future: A New Vision for Northern Ontario"[16] argued that "the current approach to regional economic development in Northern Ontario is not producing the desired results." The document also called for a more collaborative approach involving all orders of government to pursue a new vision for Northern Ontario through coordinated strategies and actions. At the end of the consultation process, a Northern Ontario Summit was proposed.

By 2007 the government of Ontario had responded to these concerns and challenges by establishing a process under the 2005 Places to Grow Act to produce a new plan for northern Ontario development. Over the course of three years, the government received input from "more than 2,500 northerners ... in over 80 events across the north including 13 regional forums, 13 technical tables, a Think North Summit, 20 meetings with Aboriginal communities and organizations and workshops engaging more than 200 youth" (Segsworth 2009). The "Proposed Growth Plan for Northern Ontario" was published and announced as open for comment in the fall of 2009, with a view to revision, and the final plan was released in March of 2011.

The Growth Plan for Northern Ontario was an attempt to respond to the perceived need for better coordination in the development of policy. Two lead ministries, the MNDMF and Energy and Infrastructure, worked with fifteen other provincial ministries on the development of the plan. However, the policy development did not appear to provide any concrete measures regarding how to include all three levels of government as partners; consequently, concerns about duplication, overlap, and lack of coordination and responsiveness to local development planning remain valid concerns (Segsworth 2009). Moreover, judging by the cacophony of voices at the 2009 and 2011 summits, which led to the publication of the Growth Plan, it is clear that the provincial government still has challenges ahead.[17]

The province is still bent on establishing its presence as the main policy conduit in the region. The ministry has also created a Northern Advisory Committee (NAC) consisting of two pilot groups from Northwestern and Northeastern Ontario. Each of the pilot groups is made up of individuals with different backgrounds and expertise to oversee the development of five-year action plans for implementing the twenty-five year vision of the Growth Plan. As one critique puts it, it will take at least five years to implement a plan that took more than three years of planning to complete.[18] Moreover, the Northern Ontario Heritage Fund Corporation (NOHFC) has provided $5 million for the creation of a Northern Policy Institute, which is supposed to serve as a think tank and coordinating centre for various policy ideas and initiatives within the framework of the Growth Plan for the region. As a creation of the province, however, some feared that the allegiance of the institute would be too closely tied to the MNDMF's public relations interests and would not act as an objective conduit for an evidence-based policy critique in the region – but it is still too early to confirm such fears.

In addition to the Growth Plan, the MNDMF has been placing increased priority over the past several years on improving relationships and engagement processes with Aboriginal peoples through "enhanced information sharing and communication projects."[19] For example, since 2003, the government has invested over $34 million in Aboriginal communities through NOHFC programs, including Telehealth Services expansion, waterfront development, and cultural attractions (MNDMF Annual Report 2010). An interesting element of this development is that FedNor views its engagement with Aboriginal and single-industry communities as one of its critical policy niches in the region.

In general, whether FedNor views these developments in the province as threats is unclear. But what is clear is that FedNor officials have participated in all the consultation and planning conferences leading to the Growth Plan and have openly expressed support for the new provincial initiatives.[20] This public show of support for the MNDM's leadership may seem at odds with a public agency's jurisdictional impulse and ambitions, but it is a strategic investment in building legitimacy within its external environment by forming a united front with other public agencies. Moreover, the province, in turn, has openly committed to "collaborate with the federal government," even if the exact terms remain unclear, as well as with "business and industry, municipalities, Aboriginal communities and organizations, the education and research sectors, and community organizations on economic development strategies for existing and emerging priority economic sectors" (Growth Plan for Northern Ontario 2011). FedNor, therefore, cannot be seen as opposed to these developments. Moreover, although it is a much smaller agency than the MNDMF, FedNor's participation in the new governance framework increases its chances of carving a policy space within the rapidly changing bases of power in the region.[21] FedNor can maintain some institutional capital to influence the terms of regional development policy and program coordination in the new environment.

The new framework also seems consistent with FedNor's program interest. It allows public agencies across the levels of government to overcome program fragmentation and duplication resulting from intergovernmental rivalry. In the past, criticisms about duplication, fragmentation, and waste have often hurt the image of all public agencies (Report of the Auditor General 1995). FedNor continues to pursue regional economic development through the delivery of its two core programs: the Northern Ontario Development Program and the Community Futures Program (FedNor Business Plan 2009–2010). Since 2006, FedNor has approved more than $156 million in support of nearly nine hundred projects through the NODP alone. But the agency now promotes its NODP and Community Futures programs as part of a broader strategic investment in the region, complementing efforts of the Growth Plan and other initiatives by municipalities and the private sector to help communities make the transition to a diversified economy (FedNor Business Plan 2009–2010; 2010–2011). Even in implementing a range of new programs under the federal government's Economic Action Plan (EAP), such as the Community Adjustment Fund and the Economic Development Initiative (a program aimed at strengthening the vitality of Official Language Minority Communities), FedNor is emphatic about synchronizing its delivery operations with the multiplicity of actors both within and outside the public sector (FedNor Business Plan. 2009–2010; Industry Canada 2007, 2009). The political context of economic development in Northern Ontario has obviously changed considerably over the past two decades.

The one major limitation of the agency is its small size relative to the larger players surrounding it. Although, ironically, that characteristic proved to enhance its nimbleness and adaptability in the past, in fact, organizational size and resource clout may be important characteristics in an increasingly complex and crowded policy subsystem. Moreover, in addition to its size, FedNor's inability (like that of the NOHFC) to "roll over money from previous budgets" into subsequent fiscal operating years raises questions about the agency's ability to make credible long-term commitments with its range of partners.[22] As the framework of policy engagement with the policy stakeholder increasingly moves away from disbursing funds to supporting longer-term and more strategic investment in building knowledge clusters and regional growth hubs, FedNor's rigid budget structure may prove to be a constraint (FedNor 2008). The legitimacy of collaborative ventures is enhanced when partners can commit financial and other resources over the long-term.

In spite of its size and resource constraints, nevertheless, FedNor's recent approach to policy implementation validates the proposition that the political legitimacy and coordinating capacity of public agencies are indispensable elements of policy implementation. The open-systems perspective within organizational theory suggests that the success of policy implementation is a function not merely of public agencies' intra-organizational integrity, expertise, and coherence, but also of their adaptation to the imperatives of the operating environment. The governance literature draws our attention to the phenomenon of increasing societal mobilization and engagement in policy formulation and implementation. These two perspectives thus enrich discussions about implementation research in seeking to explain the institutional and ideational forces underlying the emergent shift in policy implementation. The integrated insights of these analytical traditions affirm the observed transition of policy implementation processes as shifts from delivering and directing to facilitation, coordination, and empowerment. In cultivating legitimacy for successful policy intervention, public agencies such as FedNor must identify the main actors within their field of operation and seek ways to coordinate the bases of power within that policy subsystem.

FedNor has come a long way in its attempts to adapt its model of policy implementation to changes in its external environment. It now emphasizes economic development through partnerships among levels of government and, with First Nations, other non-governmental organizations and the private sector (FedNor 2004, 2011). The ongoing effort under the Northern Ontario Growth Plan to move towards a more collaborative governance framework can be seen as the culmination of a long under-current of change in the region, and these changes are still unfolding. FedNor's willingness and ability to adapt to these emergent contexts will continue to be tested, and if past trends are any indication, FedNor may have reasons to believe it can survive the complexities of change and remain an effective player in the economic future of Northern Ontario. In the end, it seems, a small federal agency like FedNor operating in a complex and dynamic provincial jurisdiction may have to exercise considerable restraint in the politics of visibility and credit-taking in order to engage in effective policy penetration through collaborative mechanisms.

CONCLUSION

The case study in this chapter has assessed the changing dynamics of intergovernmental and state-society relations in the implementation of economic development policy in Northern Ontario. Using the multi-actor implementation framework, consisting of insights drawn from implementation theory, organization theory, and the governance literature, the discussion examines various dimensions of FedNor's relationship with its provincial and local counterparts, as well as with organized community and private sector groups in the region. Regional economic development policy in Northern Ontario is propelled by the imperatives of political legitimacy and administrative coordination in policy planning and delivery systems. Policy implementation is a function not merely of public agencies' intra-organizational integrity or expertise but also of their engagement with, and adaptation to, the external environment. The foregoing discussion illustrates how regional development policy implementation processes in Northern Ontario have been moving towards diverse expressions of intergovernmental relations and state-society co-production.

To recapitulate the theoretical discussion in chapter 2, as implementation research continues to undergo a conceptual transformation in favour of concerted action across institutional boundaries, integrated analytical frameworks drawing from the strength of other research traditions could enrich our understanding and explanation of implementation phenomena in complex and dynamic systems. By analyzing the changing process of policy implementation through the multi-actor implementation framework, the present chapter has reinforced the contribution of the preceding chapters by identifying and establishing the missing link between politics and administration.

Finally, a general extrapolation from FedNor's experience in Northern Ontario over the past two decades exists in that inter-organizational and inter-jurisdictional collaboration are dynamic forms of partnerships designed to enhance the governance of economic, social, and political transactions. Such collaborations involve some measure of surrender of jurisdictional authority by partners. Moreover, they are democratizing arrangements whose technologies of decision making may conflict with the pyramidal structure of most public agencies. This means surrendering governance over opportunism and opportunistic behaviour, which may compromise the interests of potential partners or maximize credit and visibility. Inter-jurisdictional and inter-organizational collaborative ventures bring out the tensions between the ambitions of centralized, hierarchical, and multi-layered authority (such as exist in federal systems) and the imperatives of coherent and meaningful policy engagement in complex systems. Front-line public servants who operate at the strategic interface of organizational boundaries, therefore, need to be assured by senior-levels within their organizations that some level of surrender to joint policy action does not mean an absolute loss of autonomy, interference, weakness, or even failure for an organization.

Moreover, these collaborative joint policy actions are best viewed as dynamic, transitory, and evolving rather than as static and permanent. As FedNor's shifting strategies indicate, policy intervention across organizational boundaries consists of economic, social and political relations that are as living and dynamic as the actors who make up the policy subsystem. Efforts to make the inter-jurisdictional linkages permanently tied to one particular form risks disabling leadership and reducing flexibility and effective adaptation and response to challenges and opportunities.

8

The Federal Economic Development Agency for Southern Ontario: Prospects and Challenges

INTRODUCTION

In chapter 4 we saw that from its humble beginnings in the creation of a plethora of uncoordinated boards and agencies in the 1960s, regional development has remained a persistent feature of public policy governance in Canada over the past five decades (Savoie 1981, 1997; Careless 1977). The preceding three chapters illustrate the resilience and adaptability of this policy domain in Canada through analysis of three respective federal regional development agencies' changing strategies of policy intervention in the face of increasing complexity and turbulence in their respective operating environments.

The most recent federal agency to join Canada's regional economic development policy domain is the Federal Economic Development Agency for Southern Ontario (FedDev). The question that naturally comes to mind, one that has been raised at a number of conferences in the province is, Why would such a relatively wealthy and diversified region like southern Ontario (the industrial and financial capital of the country) need a federal regional development agency?[1] The most immediate impetus for the creation of FedDev in October 2009 was the response by the federal government to Southern Ontario's economic challenges during the major global recession that began in 2007 (Industry Canada Report on Plans and Priorities 2010–2011). FedDev is part of the federal government's Economic Action Plan, which seeks to encourage the nation's economic recovery from the recession by providing some short-term stimulus to the hardest-hit communities and some long-term funding to promote economic growth, job creation, and innovation.

Moreover, as discussed in chapter 2, the modern rationale and justification for the continuation of regional economic development policy intervention is that it provides institutional support for the competitiveness and productivity of knowledge-driven economies at a time of seismic global economic restructuring (Council for Canadian Academies 2009). Among the key challenges confronting all major industrialized economies are the following: first, the intensification of global competition, especially with the rapid rise of what is referred to as the BRIC countries (Brazil, Russia, India, and China); second, the demographic time-bomb of Canada's and other OECD countries' aging populations, which threatens productivity growth as the proportion of the working age population plateaus and begins to decline; and third, but not least, unfolding and outstanding developments in the transformative technologies of information and communications, life sciences, and advanced materials, which are providing new and immeasurable opportunities and an arena of intense international competition. In short, most industrialized nations (including the emerging economies of China and India) are engaged in the aggressive cultivation of innovation capacities to gain a productivity edge over their competitors. The world is in the midst of a major post-industrial revolution, and any nation that adopts a laissez faire attitude towards the restructuring of its economy risks falling behind its competitors (Broome 2007; OECD 2009).

Therefore, as discussions predating and surrounding the creation of FedDev in 2009 clearly attest, although regional economic development policy has seen its share of controversy in Canada, it has also proven quite resilient. Regional economic development has come full circle since the emergence of the growth-pole concept in the 1960s. However, the current focus is on intangible assets – knowledge creation, dissemination, application, and commercialization (Holbrook and Wolfe 2002; Bradford and Wolfe 2010). Thus, a relatively wealthy Canadian region like southern Ontario can now boast its own federal economic development agency, because knowledge-driven economies require governmental institutional support systems for the creation of globally competitive inter-sectoral innovation clusters (Florida 1995).

The rest of this discussion analyzes FedDev through the analytical lens of the multi-actor implementation framework. Given that FedDev is a relatively new agency with no sufficiently accumulated experience of policy implementation, the best that can be done at the moment is to analyze the prospects and challenges confronting the agency by situating its existence, mandate, and instruments within the emergent ideational and institutional context of regional economic development – or the new regionalism. In this way, comparative lessons can be drawn from the experience of the other federal agencies discussed in previous chapters to make tentative projections about FedDev's challenges and opportunities.

FEDDEV IN SOUTHERN ONTARIO

Southern Ontario consists of about 92 per cent (or 12.1 million) of the total population of the province (13.1 million), compared with the less than 1 million residents in Northern Ontario (Government of Ontario 2011a). Chapter 7 contains more comparative figures and tables about the two regions of the province. In sharp contrast to Northern Ontario, the population of Southern Ontario consists of about 12 million people living in an area of about 140,000 square kilometres. Several factors account for this highly skewed population distribution between the two regions, including the South's gentler climate; highly developed and well-networked land, air, and water transportation infrastructure, larger area of arable land, and relative proximity to large metropolitan areas in the Northeastern and Midwestern United States. Southern Ontario's boundaries with the North are demarcated by the French River and Algonquin Park. (See figure 7.1 for a map of Ontario.) Though the idea is sometimes contested, it also includes the popular tourist belts of Parry Sound and the Muskoka districts. In general, the line between the counties and regions of the South and the districts of the North forms the boundary between Southern and Northern Ontario.

Southern Ontario consists of four major sub-regions, namely, the Golden Horseshoe (which includes the Greater Toronto Area – Canada's industrial capital and largest urban concentration), Eastern Ontario (which contains the national capital, Ottawa), Southwestern Ontario, and Central Ontario (FedDev Ontario 2009). Administratively, Southern Ontario is divided into forty census divisions made up of twenty-two counties, eight regional municipalities, nine single-tier municipalities, and one district. Major cities in southern Ontario (counting by census metropolitan areas, or CMAs) include Toronto (with a population over 5 million), Ottawa (about 1 million), Hamilton (almost 700,000), the London-Windsor corridor (500,000),

Cambridge-Kitchener-Waterloo (500,000), and St Catharines–Niagara (about 400,000). Other large city-regions include Oshawa, Windsor, Barrie, Kingston, Guelph, Brantford, and Peterborough.

With an allocation of more than $1 billion over five years, FedDev was mandated to "support economic and community development, innovation, and economic diversification, with contributions to communities, businesses and non-profit organizations" aimed at positioning them to take advantage of opportunities as economic growth recovers in Canada and around the world (FedDev Ontario 2009). The agency's mandate is thus consistent with what the OECD (2009) describes as geographically delineated development activities calculated to spur economic growth and development using instruments to promote the development, application, and commercialization of knowledge, which leads to the adaptation of, or improvements to, products, processes, and services within a given region.

Created as a delivery unit within Industry Canada (see the organogram in figure 7.3 – FedDev and FedNor have the same structural links to Industry Canada), FedDev's programs consist of five broad categories: the Southern Ontario Advantage Programs, the Economic Development Programs, the Stimulus Programs, the Infrastructure Programs, and the Partnerships and Third-Party Delivery program. (See appendix 4 for more details of FedDev's program activities.) The Southern Ontario Advantage Programs (one of the five broad categories), contain activities like the Applied Research and Commercialization Initiative, Investment in Business Innovation, the Graduate Enterprise Internship, Scientists and Engineers in Business, the Technology Development Program, the Prosperity Initiative, and Youth STEM.

Under the Prosperity Initiative, FedDev has allocated $210 million within its first two years of operation to support three different strategic goals: economic diversification, productivity enhancements, and competitive advantage.[2] A range of sectors such as science and technology, energy, health and sciences, food and beverage, and information and communication technologies are targeted for productivity enhancements, the goal of which involves fostering the adoption or adaptation of new processes, skills, or technologies to enhance productivity in businesses in Southern Ontario. As outlined under the Prosperity Initiative, competitive advantage involves the expansion and development of strategic economic groups to increase Southern Ontario competitiveness and build on the strengths of the region to serve the global economy. Part of the goal targets labour productivity through long-term employment and high-value skills training. It also includes activities that increase the capacity of various sectors within the region's economic sector to expand and access new markets through the development of new infrastructure, increased diversification, and improved competitiveness.

FedDev's operations reflect the changing currents of policy ideas concerning the role of the state in the economy. Another dimension of these trends is the creation of certain apparent contradictions or paradoxes whereby a globalized world with integrated markets has witnessed the emergence of policy frameworks supportive of local communities to exercise more control over their socio-economic destinies. Accordingly, FedDev's activities contain elements of this attention to local economic development.[3] For example, one of the five broad categories of FedDev's programs – the Economic Development Program – is essentially the Southern equivalent of some of FedNor's key programs in Northern Ontario – these are the Southern Ontario Development Program, the Eastern Ontario Development Program, the Community Futures Program, and the Economic Development Initiative (FedDev Ontario 2009). They fit within the emergent framework of community-driven local economic development.

The Community Futures program, as noted in preceding chapters, is part of a nation-wide initiative aimed at economic diversification in small communities (Industry Canada Report on Plans and Priorities 2010–2011). Under this program, FedDev provides funding to thirty-seven Community Futures Development Corporations in rural Eastern and Southern Ontario in support of community economic development and small-business growth. The Southern and Eastern Ontario Development Programs as well as the Economic Development Initiative are also aimed at community economic diversification in the region. The Southern and Eastern Ontario Development Programs were established as core programs of FedDev Ontario (as with the Northern Ontario Development Program (NODP) of FedNor). Approximately $100 million was allocated to the Southern Ontario Development Program in 2009–10 to build upon the assets and strengths of communities to create an environment where businesses can thrive and maximize Southern Ontario's potential to succeed in a knowledge-based economy.[4] Funding under this program goes towards projects that can stimulate local economies and enhance the growth and competitiveness of local businesses and communities, including about $20 million through an intake for the food and beverage processing sector; $15.75 million for the Canadian Manufacturers and Exporters' (CME) SMART Program to fund an estimated three hundred projects that will help small- and medium-sized manufacturers increase their productivity and competitiveness in the global economy; and about 1.6 million for the Ontario Chamber of Commerce's Export Market Access Program to help build managerial and marketing capacities in Southern Ontario businesses that will increase international sales.

Another characteristic of the ideational shift in regional economic development policy toward innovation are discussions among scholars and practitioners of public policy about the administrative processes of economic development policy implementation (Hale 2009; Roy 2007). FedDev's mandate reflects the changing physiology of government towards emphasis on co-production network arrangements between the public sector and non-state actors. For example, currently in its second year of operation, FedDev is projecting the next phase of its policy initiatives; its model of operation aims to provide tools that facilitate the building of partnerships with a range of actors for the creation of local conditions for the region's global competitive edge (FedDev's Report on Plans and Priorities 2011–2012). One such partnership is the strategic alliance involving the National Research Council Canada, the Industrial Research Assistance Program, and the Business Development Bank of Canada.[5] Also, the agency has set aside some funding for angel investor networks (i.e., agencies that provide capital for business start-ups) and their associations to attract new investment and support the growth of angel investment funds. The Prosperity Initiative under the Southern Ontario Advantage program also supports market development and expansion efforts to build greater diversification regionally through collaborative strategic alliances or initiatives.

The prevalent paradigm of regional innovation systems management policy has thus directed a growing emphasis to collaborative governance mechanisms of policy delivery, with the understanding that policy implementation tasks in complex policy systems are best viewed as strategic, and not merely operational. These governance mechanisms, as noted in chapter 3, are distinguished from traditional administrative processes in that policy implementation or program delivery primarily involves building partnerships with various agents across different levels of government and with non-state actors in other institutions and in the private sector. Acknowledging the importance of collaborative governance, therefore, entails accepting that the boundaries of the public sector are more porous than ever and also that policy implementation must involve multiple agencies and groups working in concert.

For example, FedDev's Applied Research and Commercialization program aims to address the gap between research and commercialization in Southern Ontario by positioning itself as a lynchpin in new collaborations between small and medium-sized enterprises (SMEs) and post-secondary institutions (FedDev's Report on Plans and Priorities 2010–2011). The agency's Technology Development Program also provides financial support to encourage research and innovation organizations, the private sector, post-secondary institutions, and not-for-profit organizations to work together to accelerate the development of large-scale, advanced technologies that will result in new market opportunities for Southern Ontario businesses. Similarly, the Graduate Enterprise Internship provides financial support to not-for-profit organizations and post-secondary institutions in Southern Ontario for internships with structured mentoring opportunities with SMEs for graduate students and recent graduates of programs in science, technology, engineering, and mathematics.[6]

Another significant characteristic of the "new economy" is the building of a complex and intricate fabric of sub-national institutional and policy support systems to facilitate regional innovation systems (RIS). We saw in the previous chapters how the currents of policy ideas about the role of sub-national jurisdictions were manifested in assertive provincial and municipal governments eager to gain greater control over their socio-economic destinies. But while in the other regions provincial activism in economic development policy was the result of the seismic structural shift towards globalization and the rise of ideas sympathetic to the role of sub-national jurisdictions as the centres of economic policy intervention, this is not the case in Southern Ontario. The province of Ontario has always been one of the strongest and wealthiest provinces of the Canadian federation, and because of its unique strength relative to most other provinces, it has enjoyed greater control than other provinces, with the exception of Quebec, in economic development and other policy issues (Simeon 2006; Bakvis and Skogstad 2002). The question worth considering, then, is, since FedDev is a relatively new organization (only three years old) and still building its organizational capacities, how did its ambitions to serve as a facilitator of productivity in the region fit into the existing institutional infrastructure of economic development policy governance in Ontario? This question is addressed in the next section using the multi-actor implementation framework to provide a lens for explaining complex multi-level governance systems as they rapidly transition towards more dispersed policy authority between orders of government as well as across loci and sectors.

THE SUB-NATIONAL CONTEXT OF ECONOMIC DEVELOPMENT POLICY

As in the case of regional economic development policy in other parts of Canada, although the federal government has been actively involved in economic development policy intervention in the provinces, in reality, the Canadian Constitution grants de jure responsibility for economic development policy to provincial governments. And while provincial assertiveness is being gradually catalyzed by growing institutional capacity and attendant self-confidence in other regions, Southern Ontario has enjoyed decades of dense institutional support for sub-national policy initiatives (Simeon 2006). As the industrial and commercial heartland of the country, Southern Ontario already has both a concentration of provincial agencies and a long history of active engagement on the part of the provincial government. The activities of two ministries in existence during FedDev's creation – the Ministry of Economic Development and Trade (MEDT) and the Ministry of Research and Innovation (MRI) – are highlighted below to illustrate the provincial government's comprehensive range of programs and services aimed at providing support systems for emerging sectors of its knowledge-driven economy. The services of these two ministries (which, as explained later in the chapter, have now been merged into one) almost duplicate the whole range of programs that FedDev is offering.

Ontario's Ministry of Economic Development and Trade (MEDT) is responsible for working with the province's private sector in expanding its exports and fostering innovation and competition, as well as attracting new investment to the province (Government of Ontario 2011c).[7] The ministry provides one-on-one consulting services, market-specific seminars and workshops, assistance with market research and analysis, help with export strategies and marketing plans, organization of trade missions, and participation in international exhibitions. The MEDT funds two key investment strategies: the Advanced Manufacturing Investment Strategy (consisting of repayable loans to help manufacturers invest in new technologies, products, and processes) and the Ontario Automotive Investment Strategy (a $500 million program that invests in skills training and innovation in the auto industry).[8] In addition, the ministry manages a series of programs and partnership opportunities designed to help business, industries, and communities grow an innovative, sustainable, and competitive Ontario economy; these programs also include the Eastern Ontario Development Fund and the Communities in Transition Initiative. Both initiatives target the building of regional and local development capacity and helping address economic challenges facing specific communities and sectors across Ontario. For example, the Eastern Ontario Development Fund is a grant program intended to attract investment and support job creation in Eastern Ontario through support for capital spending, skills development, infrastructure needs, and other economic development initiatives. Also, the Communities in Transition Initiative assists Ontario communities and industry sectors facing economic development challenges including plant closures, significant job losses, and industry-wide restructuring (Government of Ontario 2011c). Other programs include Energy Connections (supporting long-term partnerships for the province's manufacturers and suppliers across the range of Canada's energy supply chains) and the Ontario Emerging Technologies Fund (a co-investment program that partners with qualified venture capital funds and other private investors).

Do not confuse the programs mentioned above with traditional subsidies and grants to business under the old paradigm of economic development. Canada, like most OECD countries, now acknowledges that the traditional tools of regional economic development have not delivered the expected results (Council of Canadian Academies 2009). In particular, the distribution of subsidies across a large number of lagging industries has been too diluted to sustain economic take-off and has often led to a culture of dependency that has stifled entrepreneurship and distorted markets (Mintz and Smart 2003). On the other hand, more selective assistance has also tended to cause rent-seeking behaviour (i.e., seeking access to economic wealth by manipulating the political environment rather than by creating new wealth through market forces) without necessarily yielding predicted returns. However, as discussed in chapter 3, the recent literature on economic development has questioned assumptions about whether the simple concentration of resources in a particular place will translate into dynamic clusters of economic activities. Several prerequisites, such as a pooled labour market, backward and forward linkages among firms, and knowledge spill-over cannot be ignored. Building these prerequisites factor immensely into considerations of the Ontario government's agencies regarding how different stakeholders interact and how synergies are exploited in different types of industries and sectors.[9] In short, the market does not always achieve this result alone.

As a further example, the Ontario Ministry of Research and Innovation (MRI) is a relatively new organization (2005) with a mandate to make innovation a driving force in Ontario's economy and to project this new Ontario onto the national and international stage (Government of Ontario 2011d).[10] The MRI's program activities are directed at facilitating Ontario's transition to an idea- and innovation-based economy especially supportive of new knowledge-intensive industries. One of the ministry's key programs is the Ontario Network of Excellence, which works directly with entrepreneurs, academia, and businesses to build globally focused, investor-ready companies. This involves supporting researchers, entrepreneurs and businesses as innovators in all stages of the pipeline to help bring unique products and services to market. The ministry's partners are drawn from a range of actors that include research hospitals, universities, entrepreneurs, venture capitalists, businesses, and government agencies. Key programs such as the Research Excellence Program, the Ontario Research Fund, and the Innovation Demonstration Fund all target funding and promoting transformative internationally significant research of strategic value to the province. The Innovation Demonstration Fund, for instance, provides financial support of up to 50 percent of eligible costs to help Ontario companies with the commercialization and initial demonstration of their innovative technologies.[11]

The MRI is even promoting a strategic outreach to emerging markets like China by building partnerships that seek to exploit the strengths that China offers as well as to penetrate its huge domestic market. For example, the Ontario-China Research and Innovation

Fund (OCRIF) supports collaborations between researchers and innovative companies in Ontario and China, collaborations aimed at generating positive economic, technological, scientific, and social impacts for both jurisdictions (Government of Ontario 2011d). In this respect, a key rationale of economic development policy intervention is not only to mitigate the threats of global economic integration but also to leverage the opportunities for regions and sectors of a country's economy to successfully adapt to the imperatives of exogenous and endogenous forces of change.[12] Within this context, as the capacity of states to actively intervene and regulate their economy decreases, the state is viewed less as a regulator of markets and more as a facilitator of market processes led by private corporations (Mackenzie, Sheldrick, and Silver 2010). Thus, while the rationale for the state's role in a highly developed and diversified economy like that of Southern Ontario may be less obvious, it is, nevertheless, actively involved in the promotion and development of the new economy (Roy 2007).

Another important characteristic of the MEDT's and the MRI's activities is that they are granted the official mandate and responsibility for public policy domains such as economic development, even though these mandates are increasingly shared with non-governmental organizations, including the private sector and the universities.[13] The example of the Ontario Centres of Excellence program described earlier is a case in point. Jointly funded and administered by the MEDT and the MRI, the program bridges the gap between academia and industry, linking universities, industry (including emerging entrepreneurs), and government to help turn science and technology innovation into successful business endeavours. As mentioned, the MEDT and the MRI were recently merged into one ministry to become the Ontario Ministry of Economic Development and Innovation (MEDI).[14] The MEDI has taken on the combined role of the two ministries, rationalizing its mandate as focused on supporting the growth of a strong and innovative provincial economy in a fast-changing global economy (Government of Ontario 2011e). The ministry's operational strategy emphasizes a facilitative role that involves "bringing together entrepreneurs, academia and investors to help build globally focused, investor-ready companies." Its operations are a continuation of MEDT and MRI functions, which consist of promotional activities ("selling" Ontario to the world as a place to do business and actively luring businesses to invest in the province) and support activities (which focus on strategic sectors that constitute industry-leading clusters in the province).

The ministry's list of programs and funding further illustrates the continuation of the activities of its predecessors (except now under an integrated organizational structure). Some of the main programs and funding include the Ontario Research Fund, the Innovation Demonstration Fund, and the the Research Excellence Program. Newer programs now include the Investment Accelerator Fund (for eligible start-up companies to develop their technology and gain entrepreneurial expertise to bring their product or service to market), the Ontario Innovation Agenda, the Ontario's Life Sciences Commercialization Strategy, and the Green Focus on Innovation and Technology (GreenFIT).[15] The GreenFIT is an interesting addition because it is projected to facilitate critical technological leadership that will serve as part of the engine of Ontario's new green economy. It has the potential to support and encourage the introduction of innovative and sustainable solutions into the local and global marketplace. More broadly, however, the MEDI continues the MEDT's and the MRI's operational emphasis on leveraging the competences of non-governmental organizations, including the private sector and the universities, to carry out its mandate of promoting and supporting economic development and innovation in the province. These kinds of partnership are central to the successful pursuit of strategic economic adaptation and growth, whether through the stimulation of increased productivity and innovation; the active promotion of a given geographical space as a place to invest, innovate and trade; or the support of strategic sectors as drivers of regional growth.

The governance of innovation systems, in particular, requires a governance architecture that transcends and integrates the various levels of government, as well as one that institutionalizes a network governance framework. Some of the major institutional players in this governance infrastructure are local private and public research-intensive firms, research universities, and government labs. This trend has given rise to the growing importance of sophisticated local network governance systems involving government, business, university, community, and civic actors. Innovation governance systems, for instance, presuppose dense geographically concentrated linkages and dynamic interactions among key actors. This co-production of actors constitutes interdependence among the key public private and civic sectors. In this regard, public management is about multi-sector and multi-actor engagement energized by global forces. The tensions and complements in the connection between global phenomena and national governance arrangements can be leveraged by public managers to stimulate creativity, innovation, and adaptation (Roy 2007). Economic development policy intervention increasingly relates less to the issues within particular public sector agencies and more to understanding new models of public service delivery that consist of co-production between the public and private sectors as well as across levels of government.

The implications of pre-existing collaborative policy outreach on the part of public agencies in Southern Ontario are demonstrated by the fact that the region is already a highly crowded policy space with strong institutional and administrative capacity at the sub-national level. Within such a context, therefore, a small federal agency like FedDev's value would be better demonstrated by focusing on partnerships, rather than trying to create its own niche and running the risk of duplication and potential organizational rivalry. FedNor's early experience in Northern Ontario serves as a useful lesson for the agency as it designs future policy engagement in the region. Competition for visibility and the pressures of intergovernmental politics can be potentially costly to the agency's capacity and legitimacy as a relevant player within its operating environment.

The multi-actor implementation framework draws our attention to the rapid transition towards more dispersed policy authority between orders of government, including local governments. Although municipalities and other sub-provincial jurisdictions are creatures of the provinces in Canada, in reality, however, cities, as we observed in other regions, are increasingly becoming critical loci of economic development policy governance. A function of this imperative is the de facto decentralization of authority to cities in order to carry out a number of functions entailing greater responsibility and policy discretion in promoting local economic development. For example, the Niagara region and the London-Windsor corridor are each struggling to revitalize their local economies after massive industrial restructuring (including plant relocation and downsizing) in the automobile and other hard-manufacturing industries (Industry Canada Business Plan 2010–2011). Other more prosperous regions, such as Greater Toronto and Kitchener-Waterloo, are also seeking to build or advance their comparative advantages in the face of intense global competition from emerging markets around the world. Each of these sub-regions is engaged in frantic efforts to build infrastructural and institutional capacities for more effective participation in the global economy. A few examples from some of these sub-regions should provide a clearer context of the multi-level jurisdictional complexity in FedDev's operating environment in southern Ontario.

The Waterloo region is a globally recognized advanced technology cluster that also boasts of the highest concentration of manufacturing activity among Canada's metropolitan areas.[16] The business base is diverse, ranging from large multinationals to countless small start-up companies on the leading edge of innovation. The leading economic sectors are in advanced manufacturing, information technology, knowledge creation, business and financial services, biotech and life sciences, energy, and the environment. The region also hosts Canada's Technology Triangle Inc (CTT), a not-for-profit, public-private regional economic development partnership that markets the competitive advantages of the Waterloo Region to the world and works to attract new businesses, investment, and talent to the region. The CTT's municipal partners are the cities of Cambridge, Kitchener, and Waterloo, and the townships of North Dumfries, Wellesley, Wilmot, and Woolwich. Other local jurisdictions in Southern Ontario are engaged in similar systematic policy intervention to support the private sector and promote economic development. For instance, the city of Hamilton has undertaken a range of business assistance programs and services aimed at promoting economic growth, job creation, and revitalization.[17] Some of these programs and services include assisting new start-up companies, corporate relocations, and the expansion and retention of existing businesses. The problems covered include site-selection assistance, information and research, and single-window coordination of the city's services that affect business, such as brownfield redevelopment, industrial-land development, and small-business creation.

Within the contexts described in sub-regions of Kitchener-Waterloo and Hamilton, the effectiveness of economic development policy intervention needs to be enhanced through multi-level governance arrangements in which central and local governments develop strong collaborative tools for synchronizing program activities. Given the complex process of transformation that industrialized economies are experiencing, the emphasis is on more collaborative mechanisms of selective public investment that target regional comparative advantages in the light of emerging international opportunities and threats.

As a further example of policy assertiveness in Southern Ontario's local jurisdictions, the Niagara region has tasked its Niagara Economic Development Corporation (NEDC) with a recently reviewed mandate to advance the economic prosperity of the region.[18] The Niagara region's challenges include slow population growth, an aging population, and a mass youth exodus; a lower than average number of post-secondary graduates; low relative earnings and high property taxes; and no interregional transportation network. Economics statistics (1996 and 2005) released by the NEDC highlight some of the weaknesses of the region. The region lost almost eight thousand manufacturing jobs between 1996 and 2005; the median income of was $23,400 in 2004, placing the region last on a list of eleven census metropolitan areas in Ontario; and employment growth was less than 1 per cent from 2000 to 2005, compared to an Ontario average of 17.5 per cent.

But it is not all dismal news. The region could draw from some strategic advantages: for example, it has a large number of tourism draws, with the Niagara brand known worldwide; the border location provides easy access to major US and Canadian markets; there are established (even if declining) manufacturing concentrations, particularly in auto parts and shipbuilding; and business costs are competitive with those of other locations in the Golden Horseshoe region. In the light of the region's weaknesses and potentials, the NEDC seeks to promote Niagara on a global scale and works in partnership with the region's twelve municipalities to provide services that encourage investment in and travel to the region, along with business support services to attract, maintain, and increase jobs in the region. Some of the key phrases featuring prominently and often in conversations held with the agency's officials include "fostering innovative partnerships" and "collaboration with businesses."[19]

Even the City of Toronto (often dubbed the industrial, financial, and commercial capital of Canada) is aggressively engaged in positioning itself for more active participation in the emergent global economy. The dynamic nature of the global economy is such that no matter how advanced a region's economic infrastructure, it must continue swimming alongside the tide of change or risk drowning." In this regard, the City of Toronto's Economic Development & Culture Division (EDC) has been mandated with facilitating a range of programs and services aimed at advancing Toronto's economic prosperity by working to improve the business climate within the city, diversifying the city's international portfolio (which includes a focus on emerging markets), anchoring and expanding strategic industry sectors through increased competition and collaboration, and enhancing and expanding Toronto's labour force.

A significant development in the region that reinforces the emergent policy assertiveness of municipalities and constitutes a critical part of the environmental context of FedDev's operations in Southern Ontario is the Ontario government's twenty-five year Growth Plan for the Greater Golden Horseshoe region (released in 2006) (Government of Ontario 2006). Under the government of Ontario's Places to Grow Act of 2005, which led to the creation of the Growth Plan for Northern Ontario, the Growth Plan for Golden Horseshoe has a number of aims to revitalize major cities and smaller communities so that they become vibrant and convenient centres of environmentally friendly growth and development. The Growth Plan also projects twenty-five centres (or cities) in the region as urban growth centres and economic generators. The significance of the Growth Plan is that it signals that the Ontario government acknowledges the need for active policy leadership to be vested within municipalities for defining the future of economic development in the region.[20] This development certainly serves as a catalyst for the policy ambitions of municipalities in the region, which have, to varying degrees, highly institutionalized policy engagements in economic development activities within their local jurisdictions.

What we observe from the few examples of sub-regions in Southern Ontario is that although municipalities and other sub-provincial jurisdictions are creatures of the provinces in Canada, in reality, they have been assuming greater policy responsibility and attendant policy autonomy and discretion, particularly over the governance of local economic development. Moreover, like the provincial government, all the sub-regions have their own divisions or agencies charged with actively promoting economic development. Further, they invariably emphasize collaborative models of policy governance with local private sector associations. Each city-region in Southern Ontario consists of a dense and self-conscious constellation of actors that share a common desire to influence the outcome of economic development policy. Rather than one fragile and docile high-need region within which FedDev is intervening, there is instead profound structural and institutional diversity in which many jurisdictions' actors are bound together by cognitive unity – aggressive adaptation to the dynamic forces of global economic change.

Understanding policy implementation in such a context requires an understanding of the character of the environment whose problems an agency like FedDev is mandated to resolve. The imperative of policy intervention in such environments is to establish strategic partnerships that can facilitate inter-jurisdictional and inter-organizational co-operation. Peter Evans' (1990) notion of "embedded autonomy" captures the paradox of agencies' need to be deeply immersed in and influenced by power relations within a given operating environment while still maintaining a degree of independence that allows accountability for its actions. Rather than delivering and directing, the legitimate role of FedDev is facilitating and empowering. Economic development policy intervention in this regard is neither primarily about public agencies like FedDev solely undertaking policy implementation nor about shifting such responsibilities completely to non-state actors. The emphasis is on building synergies for joint action with provincial, municipal, and non-state partners drawn especially from the private sector. Within such a context, governments act as partners and facilitators, providing support and frameworks that empower, rather than engaging in the direct delivery of service.

WHAT ARE THE IMPLICATIONS FOR FEDDEV?

The primary objective of this analysis is to explain how the external environment, often consisting of dynamic and complex institutional levels and loci within a political system, interacts with and impinges on the policy mandates and instruments of public agencies operating in multi-level governance systems. Insights drawn from implementation research and organization theory have been grappling with the need to analyze policy intervention by public agencies as a highly complex process in which public agencies engage other jurisdictions within the public sector as well as local non-governmental actors within a given political and geographical space. The process of policy implementation increasingly consists of complex inter-jurisdictional and state-society relations.

Against this backdrop, during the first year of its operation FedDev's focus was on establishing its organizational capacity for delivering a range of economic development programs that fell within its mandate.[21] During the first year, the agency seemed strangely silent on the need for building capacities for intergovernmental partnership with provincial and local jurisdictions, which would consist of investing in networks of existing economic development agencies in the region. The multi-actor implementation framework suggests, and FedNor's experience in Northern Ontario illustrates, that economic development policy intervention in a region such as Southern Ontario requires mechanisms of governance that transcend administrative boundaries and build cross-sectoral arrangements for coherent and effective regional policy. A federal agency like FedDev is thus expected to overcome administrative boundaries as well as to incorporate non-governmental actors in horizontal approaches to service delivery that would allow for institutional economies of scale, which in this context means sharing existing capacities and information as well as building a pool of knowledge for addressing structural challenges among a highly diverse and complex set of sub-regions within Southern Ontario. In its 2011–2012 Report on Plans and Priorities, FedDev has recognized the need to invest in the region through a balanced strategic portfolio leveraging various partnerships to position the agency as nimble and responsive to the needs of Southern Ontario (FedDev Report on Plans and Priorities 2011–2012).[22] This means not only delivering on its mandate through the suite of programming available, but also the institutionalization of collaborative mechanisms of policy delivery involving partners drawn from other tiers of government and outside the public sector.

In reality, FedDev is a tiny agency, compared to its provincial counterparts, with a small five-year budget of only about $1 billion. The Ontario Ministry of Economic Development and Innovations Ontario's Automotive Investment Strategy alone, just one among a suite of programs, is a $500 million commitment. Consequently, over the next few years FedDev's continued legitimacy and relevance in the region rests on developing and strengthening its working relationship with other agencies from other levels of government, in addition to its present focus on the private sector, universities and colleges, and non-profit organizations.[23]

The strategic choices of public agencies are based on environmental characteristics (Young-Hyman 2008). The marginal utility of FedDev's programs in the region is inextricably bound to, and influenced by, the institutional conditions within its operating environment.

FedDev's environmental imperatives necessitate an emphasis on investing in processes of mutual adjustment and developing shared norms with its provincial counterparts that increase incentives for joint policy action across institutional boundaries. The cases of the three older federal regional development agencies discussed in previous chapters illustrated that the adaptation of federal agencies to complex environmental and institutional forces of multi-level governance was shaped by the character of a particular political system. This means that FedDev will be better served by paying close attention to the political contingencies of Southern Ontario in terms of existing institutional capacity, organizational competences, competing agencies at the provincial and local levels, and the perspectives and demands of non-state actors in the region.

One of the distinctive features of FedDev that poses a potential constraint on its implementation strategies in the coming years is that whereas other regional development agencies, like ACOA and the WD, enjoy considerable departmental autonomy, FedDev is largely subsumed under the direct purview of Industry Canada (Government of Canada 2009c). FedDev shares this structural characteristic with FedNor, which means that although the agency has acknowledged the value of working with the private sector, community partners, and other organizations, including those from provincial and municipal jurisdictions, technically it lacks the policy discretion to allow it to sustain credible partnerships at the front lines.

The constraint that FedDev faces in fostering collaborative inter-jurisdictional and inter-organizational frameworks of policy intervention is that the agency is principally a program delivery organization, lacking authority to develop policies or deviate from those set within the framework of Industry Canada. Within organization theory, open-systems analysts would refer to FedDev's organizational link with Industry Canada as rendering the agency susceptible to a machine model or closed-systems view of policy implementation that de-emphasizes the complex relations in the broader political context within which agencies operate. FedNor's operational framework and mandate at birth was excessively mechanistic and unable to do justice to the realities of policy delivery in democratic environments or complex multi-level jurisdictions.

But as we learned from the adaptation of FedNor over the years, FedDev's model of policy delivery need not succumb to the top-down approach to economic development policy intervention. If FedNor was able to undertake some strategic adaptations by the late 1990s, FedDev could arguably do the same. If it does not, it risks the dissipation of its capacity and legitimacy to make effective policy penetration in the region. The window of opportunity is arguably widest when the agency is new and still building its organizational culture. Inasmuch as economic development in Southern Ontario is increasingly dictated by complex international and domestic forces, the capacity and legitimacy of FedDev seem to rest on adaptive capacities in the face constant change. Therefore, drawing from the lessons of the other federal economic development agencies, the immediate future of FedDev in Southern Ontario will be characterized by the pursuit of certainty and successful program outcomes under criteria of organizational rationality surrounded by complex interdependencies in its policy domains, as well as by the profound uncertainties posed by the heterogeneous and dynamic nature of its task environment. FedDev will face the paradox of pursuing its own organizational rationality (or predefined goals and instruments) in complex horizontal governance settings consisting of multiple actors, agents, and goals.

If it fails to pay attention to environmental contingencies during the critical years of organizational capacity building and strategy formation, after years of operation the agency's intervention will likely be plagued by intergovernmental rivalry (or the politics of visibility), duplication, and avoidable waste of resources. The culture of the agency may become less amenable to surrendering governance over opportunism and opportunistic behaviour as it becomes drawn into a preoccupation with seeking to maximize credit and visibility. Senior-level and even front-line officials that operate at the strategic interface of organizational boundaries may become inclined to view any level of surrender to joint policy action as interference, weakness or even failure.

CONCLUDING THOUGHTS

This discussion has argued that for a federal agency like FedDev, the most significant characteristic of delivering public policies and programs in the context of highly complex and dynamic policy environments such as that of Southern Ontario is the configuration of the institutions and the polity within which it is nested. The well-intentioned creation of a federal economic development agency for

Southern Ontario does not necessarily translate into greater governance capacity within the functions of the institutional structures of multi-level governance, especially in federal systems such as Canada. As Jeffrey Roy (2007) observes, the Canadian system tends to be out of balance, with a national framework of top-down direction, on the one hand, and bottom-up localized processes and energies, on the other, and with the former disproportionately outweighing the latter. Given the history of periodic intergovernmental tensions in federal or multi-level systems, the question becomes whether the confluence of forces (including the recent emergence of an economic crisis) that gave rise to FedDev's creation will maintain the agency as a relevant and capable player in the region well into the distant future.

The most crucial challenge, therefore, that FedDev may need to address is Canada's centralized public management infrastructure with its institutional tendency to make limited financial transfers to provinces at the cost of structurally impeding a stronger potential for localized responses. Older federal economic development agencies had to deal with this reality, and FedDev could learn from their experience. The experiences of ACOA, the WD, and FedNor suggest that the successful adaptation of federal economic development agencies to the imperatives of longer-term inter-jurisdictional and inter-organizational collaborative governance are critical determinants of policy intervention in complex multi-level systems. The implication for FedDev of the institutional frameworks of collaborative policy engagement seen in other regions in Canada is for it to focus its next few years of organizational capacity building on leveraging the potential strengths of multi-level governance while also navigating the political landmines.

A critical factor that explained the transformation of regional economic development in the other regions was the willingness and ability of the federal agencies to appreciate the imperatives of joint policy action. These agencies had to make difficult but necessary choices in order to enhance their policy engagement in a domain that was technically outside their constitutional jurisdiction. Their choices involved varying strategic adaptations that amounted to some measure of surrender of policy ownership. Moreover, they succumbed to democratizing arrangements whose technologies of decision making conflicted with the pyramidal federal reporting structure within which they were nested. Their surrender to joint policy action did not, however, mean absolute loss of autonomy, interference, weakness, or even failure. Furthermore, the process of pursuing collaborative joint policy action was not static but dynamic, transitory, and evolving. Not only was the process dictated by the specific character of actor constellations within their operating environments, but it was not permanently tied to one particular form. Organizational pragmatism, keen environmental scanning, and operational flexibility were critical variables of resilience and adaptability. Finally, the process also required the reciprocal responses of other agencies from other jurisdictions. These mutual adjustments among actors from several levels and loci in adapting the frameworks of their policy intervention in the region facilitated transitions to the more collaborative context of multi-actor and multi-level governance. Building capacity and legitimacy for effective policy intervention in multi-level systems, therefore, requires public agencies to identify the main actors within their field of operation and then to seek ways to coordinate the various bases of power. The engagement of FedDev in Southern Ontario requires a governance architecture that transcends and integrates the various levels of government as well as institutionalizes a framework of network governance.

9

Conclusion: Theoretical Implications and Practical Lessons

The problem of economic development is a generic challenge worldwide, even as resource-rich regions in developed and developing countries struggle to reach sustainable levels of growth (World Bank 2000). By the late 1980s, globalization, technological advancement, and other phenomena had created seismic structural changes that opened up new opportunities but also inflicted perplexing economic challenges, including those emerging for agriculture, forestry, mining, fishing and other sectors of the economy. Natural-resource-dependent regions are in the midst of economic and social change because of resource depletion, the substitution of synthetics for natural commodities, the substitution of capital for labour in production, the relocation of natural resource industries to low-cost jurisdictions in the developing world, and low real prices on global markets, which because of international trade agreements such as NAFTA and the WTO are no longer mitigated by subsidies and trade protection. The data confirm that the relative decline of the natural-resource-based economy in rural Canada has resulted from problems of sustaining employment in rural-based manufacturing, from increasing regional disparity, and from rural impoverishment that persists despite large income-equalization payments (Bollman 1992).

In Canada the issues for these regions' economic performance include the presence of declining sectors linked to older resource extraction industries, aging populations, the out-migration of the younger population, persistent poverty within First Nations communities, and the absence of coherent strategies to drive economic growth (Goldenberg 2008; Di Matteo 2006; Southcott 2006). On key socio-economic indicators such as the level of unemployment, average income, social welfare dependency, business productivity, and technical and business skills, certain regions of the country are performing worse than the national averages. But resource-dependent regions are not alone. These problems are long-term structural trends, and they continue to confront developed and developing regions alike (Bollman 1997). In particular, the recent global recession dating to 2007 has created considerable challenges even for regions once considered as major industrial and financial players in the world economy. Southern Ontario belongs to this group of regions, yet within the current context governments are faced with several options. First, do nothing. Second, create an agency (a ministry, a department, or the like), grant it resources to spend on the problem, and hope that the problem goes away. Third, divest responsibility to communities, give them some resources, ask them to provide annual reports to the public agency, and then hope they can figure out solutions to their problems. Finally, fourth, and often the most difficult but (as we have discussed in this book) also the most important option is to establish collaborative ventures consisting of inter-jurisdictional and inter-organizational partnerships.

The first option – to do nothing – is not without its proponents. As we discussed earlier, the neo-conservative resurgence of the late 1980s opposed most forms of policy intervention to address structural transformations in the economy. The market, like all natural orders, they argued, is an ecosystem undergoing constant change – the fittest species will survive and even prosper by migrating or adapting, and the degenerate or weaker ones will die or be eaten up by the strong. Making this extrapolation from nature has disturbing implications for our understanding of civilized societies and democratic politics, where citizens and taxpayers make legitimate claims on the institutions of the state to help address their socio-economic predicaments. The second option – to create an agency and task it with responsibility for the problem – has long been criticized as ineffective. For example, a conference of the Agricultural and Rural Restructuring Group (ARRG) held at Cambrose, Alberta, in 1991 concluded that narrow sectoral policies for agriculture, forestry, and other rural sectors no longer work to achieve rural economic and social objectives (Canadian Rural Development Institute 2004). This means that an agency created to fix the problems of a particular sector is confronted with profound complexity in its operating environment because the problems of a region are inter-sectoral and spatially defined. They must be addressed in more holistic ways.

The third option – to divest policy responsibility to communities – sounds appealing and has its own proponents (Goldenberg 2008). In a 1994 study titled "Towards a Whole Rural Policy for Canada" commissioned by the Parliamentary Joint Standing Committee and undertaken by the ARRG Research Network (CRRF 1994), the final report notes that transferring policy responsibility to communities may seem consistent with the view that development problems, opportunities, and constraints are idiosyncratic, complex, and community-specific. But more policy decentralization and localized responsibility for development, the report adds, should not presuppose the abdication of responsibility by public institutions. Often, communities lack the technical competencies that public agencies command. Moreover, the particularistic nature of local community perspectives may not do justice to the full scale of multi-layered complexity such as is taking place in the global economy. The problems of local communities are often nested within a wider region, which is nested within seismic perturbations at the national and global levels. Each of these levels of analysis, therefore, must be factored into the design of policy intervention if local regions are to adapt successfully and overcome their challenges of development over time.

This brings us to the fourth option – inter-jurisdictional and inter-organizational partnerships. These kinds of partnerships in multi-level systems involve public agencies from various levels of government and across departments sharing some interest or mandate in a particular region. The partnerships would also involve community actors, such as private sector and industry groups, civic organizations, and the like. The premise of this approach is that policy subsystems or environments are human systems relating to each other (MacNeil 1994; Rounds 1994). Navigating institutional boundaries to achieve joint policy action involves particular forms of collaborative governance aimed at softening and penetrating the jurisdictional rigidities of organizational boundaries – or "turf-bursting," as Leonard Apedaile (1992) put it – in order to achieve a good fit between policy intervention (characterized by inter-sectoral coherence) and systems complexity. The imperatives of systems complexity, therefore, imply the need to rethink the prevalent tendency to divide public policy intervention into sectoral parts (as governments are organized and prone to think and act), which never quite seem to come together for the people living with and through the problems of a particular region.

As we have seen, Canada has experimented with all four of these options. The discussion in chapter 4 traced the transformations in regional economic development policy in industrialized democracies back to its birth in the postwar optimism of development economists and public managers. We observed how in Canada the prominence of regional development as an area of policy concern by the late 1960s was a natural consequence of the rise of the postwar welfare state, with its emphasis on social equity and the redistribution of wealth. Thus, the spatial and regional ordering of society became an important policy concern in Canada, as it did in most industrialized nations. Addressing the structural weaknesses of slow-growth regions, therefore, led to a framework for policy development and program designs. Regional economic development became a testament to its controllers' belief that sufficient public and private investment could force slow-growth regions to catch up (Polese 1999). Another central premise was that national governments could fashion the spatial structure of the economy and, in turn, significantly affect the economic fortunes of lagging regions.

This book, however, has focused primarily on the institutional configuration of economic development policy intervention in Canada. Over the past five decades, Canada has created a plethora (or an alphabet soup) of economic development agencies, each tasked at various points with responsibility for "fixing" the problems facing particular regions. As we also noted in chapter 4, the present institutional infrastructure of regional economic development policy in Canada dates back to the major restructuring of 1987. With it came the creation of distinct regional development agencies for Western Canada, Atlantic Canada, and Northern Ontario, namely, the Western Economic Diversification Agency (WD), the Atlantic Canada Opportunities Agency (ACOA), and the Federal Economic Initiative for Northern Ontario (FedNor), respectively. The agency FORD-Q (later renamed CEDQ) was eventually created in 1991 for Quebec, and the Federal Economic Development Agency (FedDev) was established in 2009 for Southern Ontario.

The 1987 restructuring provided the institutional context and framework for the eventual transformation of regional economic development in Canada. Underlying this restructuring was the assumption that regional economic development policy intervention should be tailored to the distinct needs and priorities of each of the regions. The creation of federal agencies with policy autonomy and institutional discretion (especially in the case of ACOA and the WD) established an institutional space for the effective adaptive behaviours of the federal agencies as economic trends and political events in their operating environments forced a reconceptualization of their traditional models of policy intervention. How certain environmental perturbations ignited the avalanche of operational changes that have occurred within the agencies over the past two decades was the underlying narrative that structured the analysis.

The analysis used a theoretical framework of public policy governance called the multi-actor implementation framework to analyze transitions in the institutional infrastructure of regional economic development policy governance in Canada over the past two decades. This framework draws insights primarily from policy implementation research, governance theory, and inter-organizational theory to advance the discussion around policy intervention in complex and dynamic multi-level systems. Through the lens of the integrated multi-actor framework, two interrelated propositions were woven into the analysis of the four cases: first, that the political legitimacy and coordinating capacity of public agencies are indispensable elements of policy implementation and second, that policy implementation in multi-level governance systems can be seen as a complex mix of hierarchy and collaboration. These two propositions thus provide useful lenses for analyzing the institutional and policy adaptation of the four federal agencies to the changing political landscape of emergent complexity for multi-level governance in Canada. Moreover, they expand the lens of analysis beyond interjurisdictional challenges within the public sector to include an investigation into interactions between state and organized community and private sector interests.

In the early years (from 1987 to the mid-1990s) of the federal agencies' operations (with the exception of FedDev, which is still in its formative years), each insisted on putting their unique and visible stamp on the economic development of the provinces within their respective mandates. As far back as the late 1970s, however, provinces were beginning to build their administrative and institutional capacities, and by the early to mid-1990s, most provinces in Canada had developed systems capacities that could match the perceived encroachments of the federal government in their jurisdictional domain. The provinces became increasingly confident and eager to wrest their constitutional responsibilities, as they saw them, out of federal hands. In Northern Ontario, for instance, where FedNor was constrained by its close integration with Industry Canada, the result of this jurisdictional tension was costly: funded projects were characterized by fragmentation and duplication (Auditor General of Canada 2005).

Moreover, around the mid-1990s, as major global economic shifts occurred and the economic crisis in industrialized countries deepened, questions were raised in Canada and in other industrialized multi-level governance systems about the relevance and effectiveness of the engagement of central government agencies in various regions. In Canada we saw that various grassroots interests, including municipalities and organized labour, became more vocal in their criticism of the federal government, calling for a more comprehensive, integrated, and bottom-up approaches to regional development policy governance. Added to this wave of organized grassroots advocacy was a philosophical shift in thinking about economic development. The emergent discourse within Canada (as in other OECD countries) reflected the new paradigm of regional development in terms of policy rationale, strategy, and tools of program intervention.

Then, around the turn of the millennium, in the face of worsening economic performance for industrialized countries, the concept of the "new economy" gained a new fervour in Canada and other industrialized countries (OECD 2009). In regional development, the emergence of what became known as the "new regionalism" emphasized the pursuit of innovation policy through the creation of geographically concentrated knowledge clusters as the legitimate basis of government intervention in the modern economy. Innovation policy, my argument maintains, requires the geographical concentration of networks of knowledge production, dissemination, application, and commercialization, often at the sub-national level. In this regard, cities emerged as the most organic nodes for the institutional support systems that innovation clusters require. And as Daniel Drache (1999) observes, regional economies as highly localized complexes of economic activity began enjoying greater salience in the wake of global economic integration. Trans-national phenomena are thus providing the basis and opportunities for sub-national entities to increasingly project themselves as legitimate, capable, and sometimes well-resourced actors in their own right (Dyment 2001; Courchene 1999).

Although the Canadian Constitution dictates that municipalities are creatures of the provinces, most provincial governments are pragmatic about acknowledging and responding to the growing constellation of highly mobilized local jurisdictions and non-state actors. Moreover, some provinces see this as an opportunity to download policy responsibilities on to municipalities, sometimes without the appropriate resources to accompany the policy devolution (Sancton and Young 2009). Nevertheless, most municipal economic departments and their semi-autonomous economic development corporations have formulated ambitious strategic plans of their own. This phenomenon has coincided with the ideational wave in economic development that views municipalities as approximations of city-states in terms of the institutional requisites of their new role in the modern economy.

As we saw in the preceding chapters, major cities across Canada, along with local private sector groups, including the local chambers of commerce, raised concerns about the false juxtaposition of sectoral and spatial approaches to regional development in the country. Added to these trends was the rise in citizen participation and stakeholder involvement as local communities and regions, especially in New Brunswick, Manitoba, and Northern Ontario, sought closer control over their socio-economic destinies in the face of rapid and tectonic global economic restructuring. The sectoral approach, they maintained, rested on the premise that economic problems could be addressed by treating various sectors such as forestry, mining, or service industries in isolation from each other. The intrinsic interrelatedness of regional economic development, however, belied such an assumption. A spatial approach, in contrast, viewed regions as integrated entities requiring a concerted effort at the local level to tackle the complexities of economic development. Policy discussions thus emphasized more integrated and cross-sectoral approaches, with the aim of positioning regions as niches within the global economy. Businesses were thinking increasingly in terms of the "market of regions" in their investment calculations. Their argument was that domestic and international market pressures required a region-wide intersectoral framework for economic planning.

For federal agencies given a mandate to carry out a policy that falls within the purview of another jurisdiction, this phenomenon meant that the stage was set for considerable complexity in their operations. The multiplicity of policy actors within and outside the state thus compounded the complexity of multi-level governance. The combination of global economic restructuring, increasing grassroots activism, and the ideational shift toward the new regionalism meant that federal agencies had to reorganize themselves to effectively coordinate activities with other agencies or risk dissipation of their relevance in their operating environments. This requirement called attention to the willingness or ability of public agencies to reorganize their operations and, even, to structure features in ways that might involve sharing authority and power in highly networked multi-level systems. The flexibility that enhanced the successful adaptation of the federal regional development agencies can be seen as both a blessing and a curse. The blessings have already been elaborated – the ability to maintain the legitimacy and capacity for effective policy intervention in a dynamic and complex environment. The curse, however, is that the strategic adaptation of the agencies to the exigencies of their operating environments means they must often be all things to all stakeholders. Policy and operational coherence tends to become the casualty in such contexts.

Also, policy implementation in multi-level governance systems is a complex mix of hierarchy and collaboration. Federal agencies working within the context of specific provinces and regions have had to adapt to the shifts towards collaborative governance while seeking to preserve their organizational mandates and distinct identities as federal agencies. These tensions need to be constantly negotiated. At a broader level, the four cases illustrate how public policy governance in Canada and other complex multi-level systems is more than ever intertwined with the successful navigation of institutional boundaries between levels of government, as well as with non-state actors and community groups.

Three core principles can be extrapolated from the experience of the regional development agencies discussed in the book. First, these agencies recognized a clear and important reason for pursuing collaborative partnership with the emerging bases of power in their operating environments. Second, the benefits from collaboration were identified and appreciated not only by each of the federal agencies but also by a critical mass of actors from the provincial and municipal governments, as well by private sector and community groups. Third, it took a considerable amount of time – on average the span of a decade – for each of the federal agencies to make the strategic adaptations necessary in re-orienting their programs and forming joint ventures with the partners they deemed critical to their joint policy interventions.

CONCEPTUAL AND THEORETICAL IMPLICATIONS

As noted in the introductory chapter, in complex multi-level governance systems such as Canada, the United States, Australia, and the European Union, authority tends to be dispersed between orders of government (local, regional, provincial, national, and supranational), as well as across loci and sectors that include markets and civil society. While there is a growing appreciation for the imperatives of coordination across these multiple levels, currently not enough attention is given to how different political systems adapt their institutional and policy designs to effectively operate in the emergent complexity of multi-level governance systems. For instance in Canada, although the Constitution grants de jure responsibility for economic development policy to provincial governments, in practice this responsibility is shared between the federal government in Ottawa and its constituent units in the various provincial capitals (Simeon 2006).

Moreover, although municipalities are creatures of the provinces in Canada, in reality, they have been assuming greater policy responsibility and attendant policy autonomy and discretion, including the governance of local economic development (Siegel 2010; Sancton 2009). Finally, even though public agencies are granted the official mandate and responsibility for policy domains such as economic development, these mandates are increasingly shared with non-governmental organizations and active citizen groups (Kernaghan 2009). Each of these nodes of governance suggests a different and increasingly assertive manifestation of policy engagement. Understanding the nature and process of institutional and policy adaptation necessitated by the imperatives of the coordination of policy governance across these multiple levels and loci within the specific context of a given political system is absolutely integral.

It is also important at this point to revisit some of the questions addressed in the discussion of the four cases. What phenomena and mechanisms facilitate or deter the policy intervention of the federal agencies? What were the patterns of mutual adjustment among the constellation of actors in each of the regions? A succinct answer to theses questions is that the transformations that have taken place in regional economic development policy governance in Canada over the past two decades are a combination of systemic value changes and local contingencies. Systemic value change refers to the shifts in thinking about the economy, the appropriate instruments of public policy, and the institutional infrastructure of policy delivery. The local contingencies involve the actual constellation of policy actors drawn from various tiers of government, as well as private sector and other civic groups, and the resources of power they command. Policy intervention in complex multi-level governance systems, therefore, is a function of managing the multiple dependencies and actors with potentially competing or complementary resources, claims, and competences.

Past and present trends in the research and practice of public administration and public policy reflect both global trends and a country's political culture. As a reflection of current trends, the emergent themes in public administration research and practice are focusing on issues such as partnership, networks, collaboration, and horizontal management. What the multi-actor framework seeks to accomplish is to weave together insights from parallel but related disciplines that enrich our understanding of public management practice and research that views public servants as active policy agents. This book has drawn from and synthesizes several lenses of analysis. First, it pays attention to various levels of jurisdiction in joint policy action. Second, it recognizes the multiplicity of lenses of interpretation among agents, including the perceptions and values of non-governmental stakeholders. And third, it traces the various stages of evolving networks, noting the dynamic processes involved in collaborative policy actions. Synthesizing these various tools of analysis means rethinking collaborative governance contexts as learning networks. The effectiveness of policy implementation in such settings requires managers to make connections across organizations, bridge diverse cultures across levels of government and outside government, and share ideas, resources, and power with non-state actors. The present discussion, therefore, views collaborative governance arrangements as complex mechanisms of policy implementation operating within and across layers of government, as well as between the public and non-governmental sectors, and as constantly evolving over time.

Policy implementation research has been shaped by two broad concerns: administrative capacity, or the effectiveness of service delivery, and the legitimacy of the implementation process. Increasingly, however, scholars view the issues of legitimacy and capacity as inseparable in the world of practice (Exworthy and Powell 2004;

Hill and Hupe 2002). In joint policy action, the coordination of policy delivery, for instance, is not only a technical problem but also a political one, since public agencies have to synchronize their program instruments and delivery methods with those of agencies from other levels of government and of non-state actors and community groups. In this sense, joint policy action involves collaborative frameworks in which different agencies from various levels and loci are committed to working together over more than the short term with the aim of securing the delivery of benefits or added value that could not have been provided by any single agency acting alone, and it includes a formal articulation of a purpose and a plan to bind the partners together. Collaborative management provides opportunities for each partner to contribute to "something larger" (McSweeney 2011). Acting in this manner can open lines of communication, unite policy stakeholders in a common cause, create a better understanding of a given situation, and offer a realistic assessment of the collective strengths and weaknesses of actors within a policy domain, as well as pointing to opportunities for joint action.

The complexity of modern political and economic environments means policy implementation is better viewed as a process of navigating a course through the murky waters of inter-jurisdictional and inter-organizational politics, rather than simply as optimizing program output (O'Toole 2000; Pierre and Peters 2005). These new imperatives are not merely a passing fancy; they are becoming permanent features of the landscape of public policy. The effectiveness of policy implementation in these settings requires managers to be able to make connections across organizations, bridge diverse cultures across levels of government and outside government, and share ideas, resources, and power with non-state actors. The emphasis is on strategic partnerships that facilitate inter-jurisdictional and inter-organizational co-operation through which governments can solve social problems or commission innovations aimed at improving productivity and promoting economic development. While such network models of policy governance are becoming ubiquitous, the critical objective of research is both to appreciate the "politics" of these partnerships and to understand the requisites of the effective management of these inter-organizational relationships.

Inter-organizational and inter-jurisdictional collaborations are specific forms of partnerships designed to improve the governance of economic, social, and political transactions. Such collaborations involve some measure of surrender of jurisdictional authority by the partners, which often means surrendering governance over organizational opportunism. Moreover, they are democratizing arrangements whose technologies of decision making may conflict with the pyramidal structure of most public agencies. Inter-jurisdictional and inter-organizational collaborative ventures bring out the tensions between the ambitions of centralized, hierarchical, and multi-layered authority (such as exist in federal systems) and the imperatives of coherent and inter-sectoral policy engagement.

Another significant implication of this discussion is that collaborative joint policy actions are dynamic and transitory, rather than static and permanent. Policy intervention across organizational boundaries consists of economic, social, and political relations across community boundaries that need to be seen as living and dynamic, like the actors who make up the policy subsystem. Efforts to tie the inter-jurisdictional and inter-organizational linkages permanently to one particular form risks disabling leadership and reducing flexibility and effective adaptation and response to challenges and opportunities. This book, therefore, has demonstrated how each of the policy subsystems in all the cases studied has confronted broadly similar economic challenges and political transitions. It has also shown how the federal agencies responded in ways that were woven into the tapestry of the sub-systems within which they operate.

One of the primary tasks, therefore, in advancing the theoretical front lines of Canadian public administration research and practice will be to further understand and address the nature of the interaction between institutions, ideas, and agencies in public administration in all their complexity. Recognizing the resilience of institutions is still important, but future research must bring fresh insight into recurring themes by emphasizing the role of public servants as policy actors whose perceptions, ideas, and value frames are more important than the traditional literature on public administration has been willing to concede. I hold the conviction that the task confronting Canadian and international public administration scholarship is mapping the complex interdependences between public servants and their operating environments. This means that the rationalistic underpinnings of public administration as a process of planned change have been exaggerated. Public administration is increasingly about coping in uncertain and turbulent operating environments by finding an optimal fit between agencies' goals and environmental contingencies.

SOME LESSONS FOR PRACTITIONERS

This book concludes with some practical lessons that can be extrapolated for public managers and other policy stakeholders operating within complex, dynamic, and multi-layered policy environments. First, the experiences of the four regional development agencies indicate that public management is a process of proactive (or strategic) rather than reactive interaction with an agency's external environment. In particular, public managers face the difficult but necessary task of trying to understand and predict emerging events within their operating environments. Failing to take a proactive approach means risking legitimacy and being confronted with a weakened capacity for effective policy action in complex and dynamic policy subsystems.

A second lesson is that the policy initiatives and strategic choices of public agencies have secondary consequences, such as the reaction of other agencies. Despite the many virtues and advantages of collective action, partnerships of any nature and for whatever cause are not without difficulties. They can arise from factors such as ideational or cultural differences, personality differences, power contestation, opportunistic behaviour, and partner non-commitment or quasi-commitment. Consequently, in complex policy subsystems, directing and controlling policy delivery or implementation cannot be engineered with any degree of precision. For example, while instruments of public management such as strategic planning can provide useful road maps for laying out a vision of preferred action for an agency, these instruments need to be flexible, adaptive, and responsive to changing conditions and opportunities in complex and dynamic policy subsystems.

Third, and finally, public policy intervention in complex multi-level environments demands both the willingness and the ability of public managers to re-organize their agencies' cultures, operations, and, even, structural features in ways that frequently involve sharing authority and power, as well developing a learning culture. Although public policy intervention often operates under the official mandate of a public agency, relevant program initiatives are increasingly driven by target populations. Public policy intervention in complex environmental systems, therefore, involves expanding the range of interaction between public agencies and stakeholders. This goal opens lines of communication, brings together policy stakeholders, establishes a good understanding of a given problem or opportunity, provides a realistic assessment of the collective strengths and weaknesses of actors in the policy environment, and clarifies the potential benefits of joint action.

Collaborative governance is certainly not the easiest option for public policy engagement, but the other options, such as going it alone or divesting policy responsibilities to third parties like community groups, are not always feasible. In fact, the emergent imperatives of systems complexity and the increasing prevalence of "wicked problems" suggest the need to rethink the tendency of governments to dissect public policy intervention into sectoral parts as if most economic, social, or environmental problems respect such boundaries. As a senior policy official at one of the federal agencies said, "No one is able to do anything alone successfully anymore – things have become too complex and multi-faceted, and so they must be done in partnerships."

In the current age of increasing complexity and profoundly dynamic change, the practice of public administration in Canada and around the world is characterized by processes of mutual adjustment among public and non-governmental agencies bound by shared rules and norms that constrain behaviour, as well as provide incentives for collective policy action. This means that implicit assumptions of conventional public administration that view public servants as passive, "objective" cogs in a bureaucratic machine must be rejected. Public servants from various echelons of the civil service are active policy entrepreneurs, moral agents, conveyors of contestable value frames, and engaged citizens with subjective perceptions and vested interests in preferred policy outcomes. Public organizations, including ministries, departments, agencies, and corporations, leverage and even exploit shared rules and norms, rather than being mindlessly subject to the dictates of the institutions, as mainstream textbooks of public administration tend to suggest.

Finally, a key objective of this volume has been to answer some questions about public administration that reflect the complexities of the operating environment of policy implementation. Although public management is best understood as inextricably bound to, and influenced by, institutional conditions, it is equally, if not more, influenced by the nature of social interaction within a given operating environment. Public management scholarship and practice is best viewed through the lens of the dynamic interactions, iterations, and subjective value frames of policy actors within and outside the public sector, rather than through purely legalistic or technical assumptions about administrative structures and institutions. This entails paying greater attention to the enabling and relational skills for public managers as policy agents managing the many interdependencies that are a natural and necessary component of operating in highly politicized environments.

APPENDICES

APPENDIX ONE

ACOA Strategic Outcome and Program Activity Architecture for 2011–12, a Competitive Atlantic Canadian Economy

Program Activities	*Program Sub-activities*
Enterprise development	Innovation
	Entrepreneurship and business skills development
	International business development
	Financing continuum
Community development	Community mobilization
	Community-based business development
	Community investment
	Infrastructure programming
Policy, advocacy, and coordination	Policy
	Advocacy
	Coordination
Internal services	Governance and management support
	Resource management services
	Asset management services

Source: Courtesy of ACOA.

APPENDIX TWO

Western Economic Diversification Strategic Outcomes and Program Activity Architecture for 2011–12

Strategic Outcomes	*Program Activities*	*Sub-Program Activities*
The Western Canadian economy is developed and diversified.	Business development	Improve business productivity
		Market and trade development
		Industry collaboration
		Foreign direct investment
		Access to capital
	Innovation	Technology adoption and commercialization
		Technology linkages
		Technology research and development
		Community innovation
		Technology skills development
		Knowledge infrastructure
	Community economic development	Community planning
		Community development
		Community economic adjustment
		Community infrastructure
	Policy, advocacy, and coordination	Collaboration and coordination
		Research and analysis
		Advocacy
	Internal services	Governance and management support
		Resource management services
		Asset management services

Source: Courtesy of Western Economic Diversification Agency.

APPENDIX THREE

FedNor Strategic Outcomes and Program Activity Architecture for 2011–12 (Nested within Industry Canada Report on Plans and Priorities)

Program Activities

Business and Innovation Development (2011–12)
Program Sub-activities
- Business financing support
- Innovation and commercialization
- Enhanced enterprise productivity

Economic Regional Development and Infrastructure (2011–12)
Program Sub-activities
- Human capital and skills development
- Regional economic diversification
- Official Language Minority Communities Development Program

Community and Business Development (2010–11)
Program Sub-activities
- Northern Ontario Development Program
- Community Futures Program
- Official Languages Minority Communities Development Program

Policy and Advocacy

Internal Services

The strategic outcomes of the FedNor agency were economic diversification and growth, job creation, and sustainable, self-reliant communities in Northern Ontario.

Source: Courtesy of FedNor, Ontario.

APPENDIX FOUR

FedDev's Strategic Outcomes and Program Activity Architecture for 2011–12

Program Activities

Business and Innovation Development (2011–12)
Program Sub-activities
- Business financing support
- Innovation and commercialization
- Enhanced enterprise productivity

Economic Regional Development and Infrastructure (2011–12)
Program Sub-activities
- Human capital and skills development
- Regional economic diversification
- Official Language Minority Communities Development Program
- Brantford Greenwich-Mohawk Remediation Project
- Ontario Infrastructure Program Delivery

Community and Business Development (2010–11)
Program Sub-activities
- Southern Ontario Development Program
- Eastern Ontario Development Program
- Community Futures Program
- Official Languages Minority Communities Development Program
- Ontario Potable Water Program
- Brantford Greenwich-Mohawk Remediation Project
- Development projects for communities and businesses

Policy, Advocacy, and Coordination (2011–12)

Internal Services

The strategic outcome of the FedDev agency was a competitive and diversified economy in Southern Ontario.

Source: Courtesy of FedDev, Ontario.

Notes

CHAPTER TWO

1 "Politics" in this sense refers to the way different actors behave or interact as agents of policy implementation. Thus, the discussion focuses on those aspects of politics that constitute an intrinsic part of the dynamics of inter-organizational partnerships and policy implementation processes in multi-level governance systems, rather than dwelling on "high-level" personalities such as prime ministers, regional cabinet ministers, and premiers, or systemic phenomena such as political party competition. While a discussion of politics at this level of analysis might prove interesting, I am deeply convinced that such an undertaking may distract from the primary objective of this book.

CHAPTER THREE

1 The seminal works of William Stanley Jevons and Carl Menger were each originally published in 1871, and that of Leon Walras was first published in 1874.

2 Alfred Marshall's book titled *Principles of Economics* (1890) was one of the most influential economics textbooks in England well into the early years of the twentieth century. Marshall was, however, unique in his approach in the sense that he demonstrated a profound understanding of the spatial or regional dynamics of economic systems – structural characteristics that could be amenable to policy support or "correction." His ideas still continue to influence the works of scholars like Paul Krugman and Michael Porter, both of whose works link back to the regional part of Alfred Marshall's approach (but not to the broader neoclassical tradition).

CHAPTER FIVE

1 Interview with a policy development official at ACOA, Fredericton, New Brunswick.

2 Interview with a senior official at ACOA, Moncton, New Brunswick.

3 Interview with a senior official at ACOA, Moncton, New Brunswick.

4 Interview with a mid-level official in a provincial department, Business New Brunswick, Fredericton, New Brunswick.

5 Interview with a mid-level official at the New Brunswick Regional Development Corporation, a provincial agency located in Fredericton, New Brunswick.

6 See the following website for more details: http://www.moncton.ca/Assets/Government+English/Publications+English/EconomicDevelopment Strategy.pdf.

7 Interview with officials at the Economic Development Office of the City of Moncton.

8 Interview with a policy development official at ACOA, Fredericton, New Brunswick.

9 See the following website for more details on Saint John's Economic Development Service: http://www.saintjohn.ca/en/home/cityservices/developmentgrowth/economicdevelopment/default.aspx.

10 Interview with retired official at the New Brunswick Ministry of Local Government.

11 Interview with a Fredericton Chamber of Commerce official.

12 Ibid.

13 Interview with a senior-level policy official, Business New Brunswick, Fredericton, New Brunswick. The official presented a 1998 meeting of the New Brunswick Chamber of Commerce in which, he maintained, the discussion was focused on new ways that business firms can act as an association in proactively engaging the financial sector and leveraging new sources of capital for high-risk ventures.

14 Interview with a front-line (business support services) official at Business New Brunswick, Moncton.

15 Interview with a senior official at ACOA, Moncton, New Brunswick.

16 Interview with Policy officials at ACOA, Moncton, New Brunswick.

17 Interview with a recently retired senior official at ACOA, Moncton, New Brunswick.

18 Interviews with a Chamber of Commerce official in Moncton, as well as a front-line (support service) official in one of the Community Economic Development Agencies (CEDAS) located in Bathurst, New Brunswick.

19 Ibid.
20 Ibid.
21 Interview with a Policy Development official at ACOA, Fredericton, New Brunswick.
22 Ibid.

CHAPTER SIX

1 Interviews with senior officials at the Western Economic Diversification Agency and the Manitoba Ministry of Competitiveness and Trade, Winnipeg, Manitoba. Also, an interview with a mid-level official at Canada Business, Winnipeg, Manitoba.
2 Interview with a policy researcher at the Rural Development Institute in Brandon, Manitoba.
3 Ibid.
4 Interview with a mid-level official at Canada Business, Winnipeg, Manitoba. See also the Northern Development Strategy, a policy document of the Manitoba Ministry of Aboriginal and Northern Affairs.
5 Interview with an Aboriginal official at one of the province's Regional Development Corporations in Thompson, Manitoba.
6 See the following government website for more on the Plan, see http://news.gov.mb.ca/news/index.html?archive=&item=465.
7 The ministry's website can be located at http://www.gov.mb.ca/agriculture/.
8 Ibid.
9 Interviews with MAFRI officials in Winnipeg and Brandon, Manitoba.
10 Interviews with MAFRI officials. See also the conference website at http://www.capturingopportunities.ca/.
11 Interview with policy researchers at the Rural Development Institute, Brandon, Manitoba
12 Ibid.
13 See also the Manitoba Aboriginal and Northern Affairs Ministry website for access to and more details about the NDS: http://www.gov.mb.ca/ana/info/nds.html.
14 Interview with three front-line officials of the Regional Development Corporations and the Community Futures Development Corporations in Brandon, Manitoba.
15 Interview with a mid-level official at Canada Business, Winnipeg, Manitoba.
16 Ibid.

17 Interview with the president of the Manitoba Chamber of Commerce, Winnipeg.
18 Interview with a senior official at the Ministry of Innovation, Energy and Mines, Winnipeg, Manitoba.
19 Interview with a senior official at the Ministry of Innovation, Energy and Mines, Winnipeg, Manitoba.
20 See the following website for more details on the EDW's mandate: http://www.economicdevelopmentwinnipeg.com/.
21 Interview with an EDW official in Winnipeg.
22 Ibid.
23 Interview with an official at the City of Brandon's Economic Development office. See also the following website for more details: http://www.econdev.brandon.ca/.
24 Ibid.
25 Interview with an official at the City of Brandon's Economic Development office.
26 Interview with senior official at the Manitoba Chamber of Commerce.
27 Interview with senior policy official at the WD, Winnipeg.
28 Ibid.
29 Ibid.
30 Interview with a senior WD official
31 Interviews with senior officials at the WD, Manitoba.
32 Interviews with a City of Winnipeg official and an official of the provincial Ministry of Entrepreurship and Trade. See also the following website for details: http://www.yeswinnipeg.ca/.
33 Interview with a senior official at the Manitoba Chamber of Commerce.
34 Interview with policy officials at the WD.
35 Ibid.
36 Ibid.
37 Ibid.
38 Interviews with two senior officials at INAC and Agric-Canada, and also a mid-level official at INAC, Manitoba.
39 Interviews with RDI and MAFRI officials in Brandon.
40 Ibid.

CHAPTER SEVEN

1 Interview with a field official for the Ontario Ministry of Natural Resources, Thunder Bay, Ontario, 2009.
2 Interview with a retired mid-level program official at FedNor, Thunder Bay.

3 Ibid.
4 Interview with a senior official at FedNor, Thunder Bay, Northern Ontario.
5 Interview with a council member of the Northwestern Ontario Municipal Association (NOMA), Thunder Bay.
6 MNDM, as of September 2009, includes Forestry (MNDMF).
7 Interview with a mid-level FedNor official in Sudbury, Northern Ontario.
8 Interview with a middle-level official at the Northern Development Division of the Ministry of Northern Development and Mines (MNDM) in Thunder Bay.
9 Ibid.
10 Interviews with senior policy officials of the Ontario Ministry of Natural Resources (in Thunder Bay, Ontario) and the Ontario Ministry of Transportation (in Sudbury)
11 Interview with MNR senior policy official in Thunder Bay, Ontario, 2009.
12 Interview with a councillor-at-large in the Thunder Bay Municipality, 2009.
13 Interview with officials at the economic development offices of the Regional Municipality of Sudbury and the municipality of Thunder Bay, respectively.
14 Interview between the author and a representative of NAN.
15 Interview between the author and a FedNor official, Sudbury.
16 This document was put together in 2005 by a group of Northern Ontario Large Urban Mayors, the Northwestern Ontario Municipal Association, and the Federation of Northern Municipalities. http://www.city.greatersudbury.on.ca/content/div_mayor/documents/CreatingOurFuture_March29-05.pdf.
17 Northern Growth Strategy consultations were held between 2007 and 2011, with two major conferences held in 2009 and 2011, bringing together participants that included some key FedNor officials, municipalities, the private sector and other stakeholders in the region.
18 Interview with an official at the Greater Sudbury Chamber of Commerce.
19 Interview with a senior MNDM official in Sudbury.
20 Interview between the author and a FedNor official, Sudbury.
21 Ibid.
22 Interview with a senior level official at FedNor, Sudbury.

CHAPTER EIGHT

1 June 2010 conference organized by the University of Toronto Public Policy Institute. Also, in March 2011 the Institute of Public Administration of

Canada held a conference on regional economic development in which the president of FedDev was invited to serve as keynote speaker. At both conferences, some of the discussions involved debates about the relevance of creating a separate agency for Southern Ontario.

2 Interview with a mid-level program official at FedDev, Waterloo, Ontario.

3 Ibid.

4 Ibid.

5 Interview with a market researcher at DeGroote Business School located in McMaster University, Hamilton, Ontario.

6 Ibid.

7 For further details, see also the ministry's website at http://www.ontariocanada.com/ontcan/1medt/en/about_main_en.jsp.

8 Ibid.

9 Interview with two officials (one a senior policy researcher, and another a mid-level program officer) at the Ontario MEDT in Toronto.

10 For further details about the Ontario MRI, see the following website: http://www.mri.gov.on.ca/english/programs/default.asp.

11 Interview with a program officer at the Ontario MRI, Toronto.

12 Ibid.

13 Interview with a market researcher at DeGroote Business School, located in McMaster University, Hamilton, Ontario.

14 Just as the first draft of this book was completed in the fall of 2011, the Ontario government reorganized its ministries, which resulted in the merging of the MEDT and the MRI to become the MEDI. This is another illustration of the dynamic environment in which FedDev operates. It also illustrates the complexity of economic development and innovation policies in a turbulent global economy, as governments scramble to align the machineries of government with the imperatives of strategic policy governance in highly fluid and changing economic systems.

15 For further details on the Ontario MEDI's programs, see the following website: http://www.mri.gov.on.ca/english/programs/default.asp.

16 See City Region's website at http://www.regionofwaterloo.ca/en/doingbusiness/development.asp.

17 See city's website at: http://www.hamilton.ca/CityDepartments/PlanningEcDev/.

18 For more details, see the following website: http://www.niagaracanada.com/Home/About-Us/Key-Initiatives/Emerging-Clusters/.

19 Interviews with three officials within the Niagara Region (two NEDC officials and one St Catharines city councilor).

20 Interview with a policy development official the Ontario Ministry of Economic Development and Trade, Toronto.

21 Interview with a board member of FedDev, Toronto.

22 I believe that at this time of writing, it is still premature to engage in evaluative discussions about what FedDev has accomplished. The Reports on Plans and Priorities are lists of intended activities that, while useful for assessing the agency's strategic priorities and projections within the context of multi-level governance in complex environments, do not, however, provide a basis for performance evaluation of its programs. Moreover, unlike the older regional development agencies, which have published systematic reports on their performance, FedDev's reports (including official interviews) are mostly agency-generated anecdotal stories of the organization's investments in infrastructure, commercialization and science and technology in Southern Ontario. It would be unfair and unreliable to comment this early on the outcomes of these investments given the duration of time needed for economic cycles to reveal the outcomes of such projects.

23 The complexity of FedDev's operating environment is further underscored by the fact that just recently (in November 2011), the Ontario government announced the launch of a new fund for Southwestern Ontario, officially referred to as the Southwestern Ontario Development Fund (Government of Ontario 2011f). The fund would be modelled on the Eastern Ontario Development Fund (administered by the Ministry of Economic Development and Innovation), and would be designed to help local communities in the Southwestern Ontario region by addressing local economic development challenges in an environment of increasing global turbulence. The fund, which is projected to amount to about $20 million per year, will be geared not only to support the attraction and retention of employment and investment in Southwestern Ontario but also promote innovation and cluster development and collaboration in the regions.

Bibliography

Abele, Frances. 2006. *Policy Research in the North: A Discussion Paper*. Toronto, ON: Walter and Duncan Gordon Foundation.

ACOA Research Study. 1998. *The Wood Industry in Atlantic Canada: A Focus on Value-Added*. http://www.acoa-apeca.gc.ca/English/publications/ResearchStudies/Pages/home.aspx.

– 2002. *Rural Youth Migration: Exploring the Reality Behind the Myths*. Prepared by R.A. Malatest and Associates. http://www.acoa-apeca.gc.ca/English/publications/ResearchStudies/Pages/home.aspx.

– 2009. *The Atlantic Gateway Business Case*. Prepared by InterVISTAS Consulting Inc., in partnership with MariNova Consulting Ltd. and TranSystems Corporation. http://www.acoa-apeca.gc.ca/English/publications/ResearchStudies/Pages/AtlanticGatewayBusinessCase.aspx.

ACOA Sector-Focused Research. 2004a. *Accelerating Growth: Fostering Environmental Technology Innovation in Atlantic Canada: A Report for the Atlantic Environment Technology Advancement Network (AETAN)*. Prepared by ÆGIS Management Consulting Group (2004) Inc., in association with Lorne Ferguson Consulting. August 2004. http://www.acoa-apeca.gc.ca/English/publications/ResearchStudies/Pages/home.aspx.

– 2004b. *Atlantic Canada Fish & Seafood Tracking and Traceability Assessment*. Prepared by Ron Bulmer Consulting Inc. http://www.acoa-apeca.gc.ca/English/publications/ResearchStudies/Pages/home.aspx.

– 2005. *Fostering a Sustainable Salmon Farming Industry for Atlantic Canada*. http://www.acoa-apeca.gc.ca/English/publications/ResearchStudies/Pages/home.aspx.

– 2006. *The Ocean Technology Sector in Atlantic Canada*. Study conducted by the ACZISC Secretariat and Canmac Economics Ltd. http://

www.acoa-apeca.gc.ca/English/publications/ResearchStudies/Pages/home.aspx.

ACOA's Departmental Performance Report. 2000–01. Treasury Board of Canada Secretariat, 2000–2001. Departmental Performance Reports (DPR). http://www.tbs-sct.gc.ca/dpr-rmr/index-eng.asp.

– 2009–10. Treasury Board of Canada Secretariat, 2009–10. Departmental Performance Reports (DPR). http://www.tbs-sct.gc.ca/dpr-rmr/index-eng.asp.

– 2010–11. Treasury Board of Canada Secretariat, 2009–10. Departmental Performance Reports (DPR). http://www.tbs-sct.gc.ca/dpr-rmr/index-eng.asp.

ACOA's Fact Sheets & Brochures. 2009. http://www.acoa-apeca.gc.ca/English/publications/FactSheetsAndBrochures/Pages/home.aspx.

ACOA's Five-Year Report to Parliament. 2003–08. Parliamentary Reports.

ACOA's Policy Outreach Activities. 2001. "Adding Value to Wood Products in Atlantic Canada – A Stakeholder's View of the Issues University of New Brunswick," 28 February–1 March 2001. http://www.acoa-apeca.gc.ca/English/publications/ResearchStudies/Pages/home.aspx.

– 2003. "Submission to the Atlantic Energy Roundtable from Regulatory Issues Steering Committee and Industrial Opportunities Task Force," 31 October 2003. http://www.acoa-apeca.gc.ca/English/publications/ResearchStudies/Pages/home.aspx.

– 2004. "Aboriginal Voice – Atlantic Roundtable Summary of Proceedings Halifax, 21 September 2004," by Crossing Boundaries. http://www.acoa-apeca.gc.ca/English/publications/ResearchStudies/Pages/home.aspx.

– 2005. *Atlantica Growth Network: Transforming Vision into Reality*. http://www.acoa-apeca.gc.ca/English/publications/ResearchStudies/Pages/home.aspx.

ACOA's Report on Plans and Priorities. 2011–12. Treasury Board of Canada Secretariat, 2011–12. *Reports on Plans and Priorities*. http://www.tbs-sct.gc.ca/rpp/2011–2012/index-eng.asp.

Agranoff, Robert. 2007. *Managing within Networks: Adding Value to Public Administration*. Washington, DC: Georgetown University Press.

Agranoff, Robert, and Michael McGuire. 1998. "Multinetwork Management: Collaboration and the Hollow State in Local Economic Policy." *Journal of Public Administration Research and Theory*. J-PART 8(1): 67–91.

– 2003. *Collaborative Public Management: New Strategies for Local Governments*. Georgetown University Press.

Anderson, Frederick J. 1988. *Regional Economic Analysis: A Canadian Perspective*. Toronto: Harcourt Brace Jovanovich.

Anderson, George. 2010. *Fiscal Federalism: A Comparative Introduction*. Don Mills, ON: Oxford University Press.

Anselin, Luc, Attila Varga, and Zoltan Acs. 1997. "Local Geographic Spillovers between University Research and High Technology Innovations." *Journal of Urban Economics* 42:422–48.

Apedaile, Leonard P. 1992. *Working Harder, Getting More Efficient and Losing Prosperity: Arguments for New Rural Coalitions and Social Contracts, or On Getting the Problem Right*. Edmonton, AB: Department of Rural Economy, Faculty of Agriculture and Forestry, University of Alberta.

Atkinson, Michael M., and William D. Coleman. 1989. *The State, Business, and Industrial Change in Canada*. Toronto: University of Toronto Press.

Atlantic Canadian Universities Entrepreneurship Consortium. 2004. *Entrepreneurship in Atlantic Canadian University Environments Research (EUE)*. http://www.acoa-apeca.gc.ca/English/publications/ResearchStudies/Pages/home.aspx.

Atlantic Provinces Economic Council. 2001. *Atlantic Canada's Trade in the Post-FTA Era*. http://www.acoa-apeca.gc.ca/English/publications/ResearchStudies/Pages/home.aspx.

– 2002. *Foreign Direct Investment in Atlantic Canada*. http://www.acoa-apeca.gc.ca/English/publications/ResearchStudies/Pages/home.aspx.

– 2003. *Urbanization and the Aging Population: What's Ahead for Atlantic Canada?* http://www.acoa-apeca.gc.ca/English/publications/ResearchStudies/Pages/home.aspx.

– 2006. *The Changing Global Economy: The Implications and Opportunities for Transportation in Atlantic Canada*. http://www.acoa-apeca.gc.ca/English/publications/ResearchStudies/Pages/home.aspx.

Atwood, Evan, and Michael Trebilcock. 1996. *Public Accountability in an Age of Contracting Out*. Toronto: University of Toronto, Faculty of Law, Centre for the Study of State & Market.

Aucoin, Peter, and Herman Bakvis. 1984. "Organizational Differentiation and Integration: The Case of Regional Economic Development Policy in Canada." *Canadian Public Administration* 27(3): 348–71.

Aucoin, Peter. 1985. *Regional Responsiveness and the National Administrative State*. Toronto: University of Toronto Press.

Audit of the Federal Economic Development Initiative in Northern Ontario (FedNor): Northern Ontario Development Program (NODP).

Auditor General's Report 1995. OAG, *November Report of the Auditor General of Canada*. www.oag-bvg.gc.ca/internet/English/parl_oag_199511_e_1155.html.

Audretsch, David, and Maryann Feldman. 1996. "Innovative Clusters and the Industry Life Cycle." *Review of Industrial Organisation* 11:253–73.

Bakvis, Herman, and Grace SkogsTAD. 2002. *Canadian Federalism: Performance, Effectiveness and Legitimacy*. Don Mills, ON: Oxford University Press.

Bardach, Eugene. 1977. *The Implementation Game: What Happens after a Bill Becomes a Law*. Cambridge, MA: MIT Press.

Barnard, Chester I. 1953. *The Function of the Executive*. Cambridge, MA: Harvard University Press.

Barrett, Susan, and Colin Fudge. 1981. *Policy and Action: Essays on the Implementation of Public Policy*. London and New York: Methuen.

Bastian, Dietmar, and Ulrich Hilpert. 2003. *Regionalization of Globalised Innovation: Locations For Advanced Industrial Development and Disparities in Participation*. London: Taylor & Francis Ltd.

– 2007. "The Regionalization of Knowledge: The Territorial Basis of Development." In Philip Cooke and Dafnah Schwartz, eds., *Creative Regions: Technology, Culture and Knowledge Entrepreneurship*. Hoboken: Taylor & Francis.

Beaudin, Maurice, 2005. *The Agri-Food Industry in Atlantic Canada: Recognition and Development*. http://www.acoa-apeca.gc.ca/English/publications/ResearchStudies/Pages/home.aspx.

Beaumier, Guy. 1997. "Regional Development in Canada." *Current Issue Review*, 88–13E, Research Branch, Library of Parliament.

Benedetti, George J., and Rodolphe H. Lamarche. 1994. *Shock Waves: The Maritime Urban System in the New Economy*. [Moncton, NB]: Canadian Institute for Research on Regional Development.

Blake, Raymond. 2003. *Regional and Rural Development Strategies in Canada: The Search for Solutions*. Royal Commission on Renewing and Strengthening Our Place in Canada.

Bogason, Peter. 2000. *Public Policy and Local Governance: Institutions in Postmodern Society, New Horizons in Public Policy*. Cheltenham, England: E. Elgar.

Bollman, Ray D. 1992. *Rural and Small Town Canada*. Lewiston, NY: Thompson Educational Publishers.

– 1997. *A Stake in the North: Papers on Mining, Forestry, and Remote Tourism Employment*. Brandon, MB: Rural Development Institute, Brandon University.

Bollman, Ray, Roland Beshiri, and Verna Mitura. 2006. *Northern Ontario's Communities Economic Diversification, Specialization and Growth*. Agriculture and Rural Working Paper Series, Working Paper no. 82. Ottawa: Statistics Canada.

Bosch, Nuria, and Jose M. Durán. 2008. *Fiscal Federalism and Political Decentralization: Lessons from Spain, Germany and Canada*. Cheltenham, England: Edward Elgar.

Bourgon, Jocelyne. 2007. "Responsive, Responsible and Respected Government." *International Review of Administrative Sciences* 73 (1): 7–26.

Bourjeois, Yves, and Michel Trepanier. 2010. "Same Size, Same Social Characteristics, Same Performance? Comparative Study of Moncton and Trois-Rivieres." A presentation at the Innovation Systems Research Network 12th Annual Conference, 5–7 May 2010, Toronto, Ontario.

Bowen, Elinor. R. 1982. "The Pressman-Wildavsky Paradox: Four Addenda, or Why Models Based on Probability Theory Can Predict Implementation Success and Suggest Useful Tactical Advice for Implementers." *Journal of Public Policy* 2(1): 1–21.

Bradfield, Michael. 1988. *Regional Economic Analysis and Policies in Canada*. Toronto: McGraw-Hill Ryerson.

Bradford, Neil J. 2010. "Regional Economic Development Agencies in Canada: Lessons for Southern Ontario." Mowat Centre for Policy Innovation, School of Public Policy and Governance, University of Toronto.

Bradford, Neil J., and D. Wolfe. 2010. "Toward a Transformative Agenda for FedDev Ontario." Toronto, ON: Mowat Centre for Policy Innovation, School of Public Policy & Governance, University of Toronto.

Braibant, Guy. 2002 "The Past and Future of Public Administration." *International Review of Administrative Sciences* 68(3): 333–43.

Brenner, Y.S. 1966. *Theories of Economic Development and Growth*. New York: Praeger.

Brodkin, E.Z. 1990. "Implementation as Politics." In D.J. Palumbo and D.J. Calista, eds., *Implementation and the Policy Process: Opening up the Black Box*. New York: Greenwood Press.

Brooks, Stephen, and Lydia Miljan. 2003. *Public Policy in Canada: An Introduction*. Don Mills, ON: Oxford University Press.

Broome, André. 2007. "Seeing like the IMF: Institutional Change in Frontier Economies." PHD diss., Australian National University.

Brown, Kerry, John Burgess, Marion Festing, and Susanne Royer. 2010. *Value Adding Webs and Clusters Concepts and Cases*. Mering: Rainer Hampp Verlag.

Business Council of Manitoba. 2003. *Business Council of Manitoba, 2003–2004 Budget Recommendations.* http://www.businesscouncil.mb.ca/images/Publications/FiscalCompetitive/Task%20Force%20Report.pdf.

Butler, Michael, and Peter Allen. 2008. "Understanding Policy Implementation Processes as Self-Organizing Systems." *Public Management Review* 10(3): 421–40.

Canada. 1972. *Report to Parliament on the Administration of Development Incentives under the Regional Development Incentives Act and Section 10 of the Department of Regional Economic Expansion Act.* Ottawa: The Department.

Canada. Royal Commissions and Commissions of Inquiry. 1957. *Royal Commission on Canada's Economic Prospects: Final Report.*

Canada West Foundation. 2007. *Going for Gold Project.* http://cwf.ca/pdf-docs/publications/StateWest2010_Chapter_11.pdf.

– 2010; 2008; 2003. *State of the West.* http://www.wd.gc.ca/eng/56.asp.

Canadian Institute for Research on Regional Development. 2000. *Community Economic Development in Atlantic Canada: False Hope or Panacea?* http://www.acoa-apeca.gc.ca/English/publications/ResearchStudies/Pages/home.aspx.

– 2001. *Employment, Skills, and the Knowledge Economy in Atlantic Canada.* http://www.acoa-apeca.gc.ca/English/publications/ResearchStudies/Pages/home.aspx.

– 2002. *Peripheral Regions in the Knowledge-Based Economy.* http://www.acoa-apeca.gc.ca/English/publications/ResearchStudies/Pages/home.aspx.

– 2003a. *Atlantic Canada's Exports, with a Focus on SMEs and Rural Regions.* Canadian Institute for Research on Regional Development. Innovation in Atlantic Canada. ACOA Research Study, March 2003. http://www.acoa-apeca.gc.ca/English/publications/ResearchStudies/Pages/home.aspx#innovation.

– 2003b. *Innovation in Atlantic Canada.* ACOA Research Study, March 2003. http://www.acoa-apeca.gc.ca/English/publications/ResearchStudies/Pages/home.aspx#innovation.

Canadian Rural Development Institute. 2004. *Building for Success: Exploration of Rural Community and Rural Development.* By Greg Halseth and Regine Halseth. http://www2.brandonu.ca/organizations/rdi/publications.asp.

Careless, Anthony. 1977. *Initiative and Response: The Adaptation of Canadian Federalism to Regional Economic Development.* Canadian Public Administration Series. Montreal: McGill-Queen's University Press.

Checkel, Jeffrey T. 2005. *It's the Process Stupid! Process Tracing in the Study of European and International Politics.* Oslo: ARENA Working Papers.

City of Moncton. Department of Economic Development. 2007. *Accelerating Technology-Based Economic Growth and Entrepreneurship in Greater Moncton.* http://www.moncton.ca/Assets/Business+English/Accelerating+technology-based+economic+growth+and+entrepreneurship+in+Greater+Moncton+-+Implementation+Report+1+-+Applying+the+Benchmark.pdf.

City of Moncton. 2009. Economic Development Office. 2009. http://www.moncton.ca/Government/Departments/Economic_Development_Office.htm.

Colgan, Charles, and Stephen G. Tomblin. 2004. *Regionalism in a Global Society.* Peterborough, ON: Broadview Press.

College of the North Atlantic. 2005. *Roundtable on Improving Competitiveness and Productivity in Atlantic Canada: Final Report.* http://www.acoa-apeca.gc.ca/English/publications/ResearchStudies/Pages/home.aspx.

Conference Board of Canada. 2009. *Western Canada Productivity, Competitiveness, and Potential.* http://www.wd.gc.ca/eng/56.asp.

Conford, Alan. 2005. *Finding the Balance in Innovation and Commercialization.* Edited by Richard G. Lipsey. http://www.acoa-apeca.gc.ca/English/publications/ResearchStudies/Pages/home.aspx#innovation.

Conteh, Charles. 2009. "Institutional Legitimacy in State-Market Partnership: Singapore and Botswana." *Journal of Comparative Policy Analysis* 11(3): 369–83.

– 2011. "Policy Implementation in Multilevel Environments: Economic Development in Northern Ontario." *Canadian Public Administration* 54 (1): 121–142.

Cooke, Philip, and Dafnah Schwartz. 2007a. "Creative Regions: An Introduction." In Philip Cooke and Dafnah Schwartz, eds., *Creative Regions: Technology, Culture and Knowledge Entrepreneurship*. Hoboken: Taylor & Francis.

–, eds. 2007b. *Creative Regions: Technology, Culture and Knowledge Entrepreneurship*. London: Routledge.

Cooke, Philip, and K. Morgan. 1998. *The Associational Economy: Firms, Regions and Innovation.* New York: Oxford University Press.

Coulombe, Serge. 1999. *Economic Growth and Provincial Disparity: A New View of an Old Canadian Problem.* Toronto: C.D. Howe Institute.

Council of Canadian Academies. 2009. *Innovation and Business Strategy: Why Canada Falls Short.* www.scienceadvice.ca.

Courchene, Thomas J. 1999. *Responding to the NAFTA Challenge: Ontario as a North American Region State and Toronto as a Global City-Region.* http://www.irpp.org/newsroom/archive/1999/1025pape.pdf.

CRRF. 1994. *Development Strategies for Rural Canada: Evaluating Partnerships, Jobs, and Communities, Proceedings from the Fifth Annual ARRG Conference, 13–16 October 1993.* ARRG Working Papers Series No. 6. Wolfville, NS.

De Benedetti, George J., and Rodolphe H. Lamarche. 1994. *Shock Waves: The Maritime Urban System in the New Economy.* Moncton, NB: Canadian Institute for Research on Regional Development.

Denhardt, Janet V., and Robert B. Denhardt. 2003. *The New Public Service: Serving, Not Steering.* Armonk, NY: M.E. Sharpe.

Denhardt, Robert B. 2004. *Theories of Public Organization.* Belmont, CA: Thomson.

Desjardins, Pierre. 2002. *A Non-Homogeneous Periphery, Three Regions of New Brunswick: Madawaska, Gloucester and Kent-Westmorland.* Moncton: Canadian Institute for Research on Regional Development.

Desjardins, Pierre, A.R. Hobson, and Donald Savoie. 2000. *Trade, Equalization and Regional Disparities in Canada.* Canadian Institute for Research on Regional Development, University of Moncton. Moncton, NB.

– 2009. *Trade, Equalization, and Regional Disparities in Canada.* Canadian Institute for Research on Regional Development, University of Moncton. Moncton, NB.

Desjardins, Pierre-Marcel. 2005. *A Socio-Economic Profile of Atlantic Canada: Characteristics of Rural and Urban Regions, with Implications for Public Policy.* http://www.acoa-apeca.gc.ca/English/publications/ResearchStudies/Pages/home.aspx.

Di Matteo, Liveo. 2006. *Strategies for Developing a Broadly Based Regional Knowledge Economy in Northwestern Ontario.* A Report Prepared for the North Superior Training Board. Thunder Bay, ON: North Superior Training Board.

Doornbos, Martin R. 2006. *Global Forces and State Restructuring: Dynamics of State Formation and Collapse.* Basingstoke, England: Palgrave Macmillan.

Drache, Daniel. 1999. "Jobs and Investment Strategies in Canada: The Challenge for Policy-Makers." *Regional and Federal Studies* 9:38–80.

– 2006. "The Return of the Public Domain after the Triumph of Markets." In L. Budd, R. Paton, and J. Charlesworth, eds., *Making Policy Happen.* New York: Routledge.

Drummond-Hay, R., and D. Bamford. 2009. "A Case Study into Planning and Change Management within the UK National Health Service." *International Journal of Public Sector Management* 22(4): 324–37.

Dupre, J.S. 1985. "Reflections on the Workability of Executive Federalism." *Intergovernmental Relations* 63:1–32.

DuPuis, E.M., and S. Gillon. 2009. "Alternative Modes of Governance: Organic as CivqAic Engagement." *Agriculture and Human Values* 26(1–2): 43–56.

Dyment, D. 2001. "The Ontario Government as an International Actor." *Regional & Federal Studies* 11(1): 55–79.

Economic Council of Canada. 1977. *Living Together: A Study of Regional Disparities*. Ottawa: The Economic Council of Canada. Economic Development Winnipeg Inc. 2011. "Economic Overview." http://www.economicdevelopmentwinnipeg.com/winnipeg-economy/winnipeg-economy/economic-performance.

Elmore, Richard. 1981. "Backward Mapping: Implementation Research and Policy Decisions." *Political Science Quarterly* 94(4): 601–16.

Enright, M. 2003. "Regional Clusters: What We Know and What We Should Know." In J. Brocker, D. Dohse, and R. Soltwedel, eds., *Innovation Clusters and Interregional Competition*. Berlin: Springer-Verlag, 99–129.

Enterprise Saint John. 2010. *Mission, Vision, Values and Partners*. http://www.enterprisesj.com/mission_vision_and_values.

Evans, Peter B. 1990. *Embedded Autonomy: States and Industrial Transformation*. Princeton, NJ: Princeton University Press.

Exworthy, M., and M. Powell 2004. "Big Windows and Little Windows: Implementation in the 'Congested State.'" *Public Administration* 82(2): 263–81.

FedDev Ontario. 2009. *The Federal Economic Development Agency for Southern Ontario*. http://www.feddevontario.gc.ca/eic/site/723.nsf/eng/home.

FedDev's 2010–2011 Report on Plans and Priorities, http://www.feddevontario.gc.ca/eic/site/723.nsf/eng/h_00115.html.

FedDev's 2011–2012 Report on Plans and Priorities, http://www.feddevontario.gc.ca/eic/site/723.nsf/eng/h_00115.html.

FedNor. 2003. *Evaluation of the Community Futures Program in Ontario – Final Report 2003*. http://www.ic.gc.ca/eic/site/ic1.nsf/eng/h_02955.html?Open&c=16#itm16.

– 2004. *Northern Landscapes: Opportunities for Nature-Based Tourism in Northern Ontario 2004*. http://www.ic.gc.ca/eic/site/ic1.nsf/eng/h_02955.html?Open&c=16#itm16.
– 2006a. *Business Opportunities 2006*. http://www.ic.gc.ca/eic/site/ic1.nsf/eng/h_02955.html?Open&c=16#itm16.
– 2006b. *Summative Evaluation of the Northern Ontario Economic Development Fund (NODF)*, http://www.ic.gc.ca/eic/site/fednor-fednor.nsf/eng/h_fn01621.html.
– 2008. *The State of Exporting in Northern Ontario*. http://www.ic.gc.ca/eic/site/fednor-fednor.nsf/eng/h_fn01621.html.
– 2009. *Tourism in Northern Ontario: An Overview 2009*. http://www.ic.gc.ca/eic/site/ic1.nsf/eng/h_02955.html?Open&c=16#itm16.
– 2010. *Highlights of the 2010–2011 FedNor Business Plan*. http://www.ic.gc.ca/eic/site/fednor-fednor.nsf/eng/h_fn01621.html.
– 2011. *Marketing and Planning: Tourism Volume, Value and Characteristics in Northern Ontario 2011*. http://www.ic.gc.ca/eic/site/ic1.nsf/eng/h_02955.html?Open&c=16#itm16.
FedNor Action Plan. 2004–08. "Implementation of Section 41 of the Official Languages Act 2005." http://www.ic.gc.ca/eic/site/ic1.nsf/eng/h_02955.html?Open&c=16#itm16.
– 2008–13. "Implementation of Section 41 of Part VII of the Official Languages Act 2009." http://www.ic.gc.ca/eic/site/ic1.nsf/eng/h_02955.html?Open&c=16#itm16.
FedNor Business Plan. 2009–10. http://fednor.gc.ca/eic/site/fednor-fednor.nsf/eng/fn03584.html.
– 2010–11. "Highlights of the 2010–2011 FedNor Business Plan." http://fednor.gc.ca/eic/site/fednor-fednor.nsf/eng/fn03584.html.
Florida, Richard L. 1995. *The Rise of the Creative Class: And How It's Transforming Work, Leisure, Community and Everyday Life*. New York, NY: Basic Books.
Ford, J. Kevin, Neal Schmitt, Susan L. Schechtman, Brian M. Hults, and Mary L Doherty. 1989. "Process Tracing Methods: Contributions, Problems, and Neglected Research Questions." *Organizational Behavior and Human Decision Processes* 43 (1): 75–117.
Fredericton Chambers of Commerce. 1993. "Economic Development for New Brunswick: Attaining Self-Sufficiency by 2000." Brief Presented to Executive Council, Province of New Brunswick.
– 1994. "Surviving and Emerging in the New Economy." Brief Presented to Executive Council, Province of New Brunswick.

Fredrickson, H. George. 2007. "Whatever Happened to Public Administration? Governance, Governance, Everywhere." In Ewan Ferlie, Laurence E. Lynn, Jr, and Christopher Pollitt, eds., *The Oxford Handbook of Public Management*. Toronto: Oxford University Press.

Galbraith, John Kenneth. 1987. *Economics in Perspective: A Critical History*. Boston: Houghton Mifflin.

Gide, Charles, Charles Rist, and R. Richards. 1948. *A History of Economic Doctrines from the Time of the Physiocrats to the Present Day*. Boston: D.C. Heath.

Goggin, Malcolm L., Ann O. Bowman, James P. Lester, and Laurence J. O'Toole. 1990. *Implementation Theory and Practice: Toward a Third Generation*. Glenview, IL: Scott, Foresman/Little, Brown Higher Education.

Goldenberg, Mark. 2008. *Review of Rural and Regional Development Policies and Programs: A Research Project*. Ottawa: Canadian Policy Research Networks/Réseaux canadiens de recherche en politiques publiques.

Government of Canada. 1982. *Constitution Act of 1982*. http://www.solon.org/Constitutions/Canada/English/ca_1982.html.

– 1987a. *Government Organization Act, Atlantic Canada, 1987*. http://www.canlii.org/en/ca/laws/stat/rsc-1985-c-41-4th-supp/latest/rsc-1985-c-41-4th-supp.html.

– 1987b. *Western Economic Diversification Act 1987*. http://laws-lois.justice.gc.ca/eng/acts/w-6.8/page-1.html.

– 1995. *Auditor General's Report, 1995*. OAG 1995 November Report of the Auditor General of Canada. www.oag-bvg.gc.ca/internet/English/parl_oag_199511_e_1155.html.

– 2003. *Canada-Manitoba Economic Partnership Agreement, 2003*. http://www.wd.gc.ca/eng/82_4226.asp.

– 2009a. *Canada-Manitoba Economic Partnership Agreement, 2009*. http://www.wd.gc.ca/eng/82_4226.asp.

– 2009b. Federal Economic Development Initiative for Northern Ontario. http://fednor.gc.ca/eic/site/fednor-fednor.nsf/Intro.

– 2009c. The Federal Economic Development Agency for Southern Ontario (FedDev Ontario). http://www.feddevontario.gc.ca/eic/site/723.nsf/eng/home.

Government of Manitoba. 2003. *Manitoba's Action Strategy for Economic Growth*. http://www.gov.mb.ca/finance/budget07/economic_strategy/index.html?index.html.

– 2008. Ministry of Finance. Budget. "Opportunity and Stability: Moving Forward on Manitobans' Priorities. http://www.gov.mb.ca/finance/budget08/index.html.

– 2009. *Manitoba Innovation Framework*. http://www.gov.mb.ca/stem/innovation/index.html.

– 2011a. Manitoba Ministry of Entrepreneurship, Training and Trade. http://www.gov.mb.ca/ctt/invest/busfacts/overviews/ov_economic.html.

– 2011b. *Manitoba Agriculture, Food and Rural Initiatives: Financial Assistance and Funding Programs*. http://www.gov.mb.ca/agriculture/financial.html.

– 2011c. Ministry of Innovation, Energy and Mines. "Science, Innovation and Business Development." http://www.gov.mb.ca/iem/sibd/index.html.

– 2011d. Manitoba Aboriginal and Northern Affairs. "Northern Development Strategy (NDS)." *http://www.gov.mb.ca/ana/*.

Government of New Brunswick. 1989. *Standing Up to the Future: The Maritimes in the 1990s: A Report to the Council of Maritime Premiers*.

– 2002. *Greater Opportunity: New Brunswick's Prosperity Plan 2002–2012*. http://www.gnb.ca/0089/speeches-discours/2002–2012/framework-e.pdf.

– 2006. *Action Plan to Be Self-Sufficient in New Brunswick*. http://www.gnb.ca/2026/index-e.asp.

– 2009a. *Action Plan to Be Self-Sufficient in New Brunswick*. http://www.gnb.ca/2026/index-e.asp.

– 2009b. *International Trade Strategy 2009*. http://leg-horizon.gnb.ca/e-repository/monographs/30000000048173/30000000048173.pdf.

– 2010. Regional Development Corporation. *An Action Plan for Self-Sufficiency in Northern New Brunswick*. http://www2.gnb.ca/content/gnb/en/departments/regional_development/action_plan/an_action_plan_for_self-sufficiency_in_northern_new_brunswick.html.

– 2011. *The New Brunswick Economy: 2010 in Review*. http://www.sackvilletribunepost.com/Business/2011-06-02/article-2555003/The-New-Brunswick-economy-2010-in-Review-report-posted/1.

Government of Ontario. 1973. Ministry of Treasury, Economics and Intergovernmental Affairs. *Management of Growth*.

– 2005. *Grow North Act, 2005*.

– 2006. Growth Plan for the Greater Golden Horseshoe, 2006. https://www.placestogrow.ca/index.php?option=com_content&task=view&id=9&Itemid=14.

– 2009. Results Based Plan http://www.mndm.gov.on.ca/en/about-ministry/results-based-planning/results-based-plan-2009–2010.

– 2011a. Northern Development. http://www.mndm.gov.on.ca/en/northern-development.

– 2011b. About the Ministry. http://www.mndm.gov.on.ca/default_e.asp

– 2011c. Ontario Ministry of Economic Development and Trade (MEDT). *Programs and Services*. http://www.ontariocanada.com/ontcan/1medt/en/progserv_main_en.jsp.

– 2011d. Ontario Ministry of Research and Innovation (MRI). *Programs and Funding*. http://www.mri.gov.on.ca/english/programs/default.asp.

– 2011e. Ontario Ministry of Economic Development and Innovation (MEDI). *About the Ministry*. http://www.ontariocanada.com/ontcan/1medt/en/about_main_en.jsp.

– 2011f. Government of Ontario Newsroom. "McGuinty Government Announces New Development Fund to Help Local Communities," 28 November 2011.

Gow, Iain. 2009. "Government to Governance." In O.P. Dwivedi, T.A Mau, and B. Sheldrick, eds., *The Evolving Physiology of Government: Canadian Public Administration in Transition*. Ottawa: University of Ottawa Press 2009, 118–50.

Growth Plan for Northern Ontario. 2011. Ontario Ministry of Northern Development and Mines. https://www.placestogrow.ca/index.php?option=com_content&task=view&id=53&Itemid=65

Gupta, Monica D., H. Grandvoinnet, and Mattia Romani. 2004. "State-Community Synergies in Community-Driven Development." *Journal of Development Studies* 40:27–58.

Hale, Geoffrey E. 2009. *Uneasy Partnership: The Politics of Business and Government in Canada*. Toronto: University of Toronto Press.

Hall, Peter A. 1993. "Policy Paradigms, Social Learning, and the State: The Case of Economic Policymaking in Britain." *Comparative Politics* 25(3): 275–96.

Henry, John F. 2011. *The Making of Neoclassical Economics*. London: Routledge.

Hill, Michael J., and Paul L. Hupe. 2002. *Implementing Public Policy: Governance in Theory and Practice*. Thousand Oaks, CA: Sage.

– 2003. "The Multi-layer Problem in Implementation Research." *Public Management Review* 5:471–90.

Hirshman, A.O. 1965. *The Strategy of Economic Development*. New Haven, CT: Yale University Press.

Hirst, Paul Q. 1994. *Associative Democracy: New Forms of Economic and Social Governance*. Amherst: University of Massachusetts Press.

Hjern, Benny. 1982. "Implementation Research: The Link Gone Missing." *Journal of Public Policy* 2(3): 301–8.

Hjern, Benny, and Christopher Hull. 1987. *Helping Small Firms Grow: An Implementation Approach*. New York: Croom Helm, in association with Methuen.

Hodgetts, J.E., and D.C. Corbett. 1968. *Canadian Public Administration*. Toronto: Macmillan of Canada.

Hogwood, B.W., and L.A. Gunn. 1984. *Policy Analysis for the Real World*. New York: Oxford University Press.

Holbrook, Adam, and David A. Wolfe. 2000. "Introduction: Innovation Studies in a Regional Perspective." In J. Adam Holbrook and David A.Wolfe, eds., *Innovation, Institutions and Territory: Regional Innovation Systems in Canada*. Kingston: School of Policy Studies, Queen's University, 1–15.

– 2002. *Knowledge, Clusters, and Regional Innovation: Economic Development in Canada*. Montreal: McGill-Queen's University Press.

Hooks, J., and N. Palakshappa. 2009. "Co-operation and Collaboration: The Case of the De-regulated New Zealand Electricity Industry." *International Journal of Public Sector Management* 22 (4): 292–309.

Hoque, Z. 2005. "Securing Institutional Legitimacy or Organizational Effectiveness? A Case Examining the Impact of Public Sector Reform Initiatives in an Australian Local Authority." *International Journal of Public Sector Management* 18 (4): 367–82.

Holst, Brian. 2011. "Innovation with Industry Partners." ThinkNorth II Summit, Organized by the Ministry of Northern Development, Mines, and Forestry (MNDMF), Sudbury and Thunder Bay, Ontario. June 2011.

Howitt, Peter. 2007. *Innovation, Competition and Growth: A Schumpeterian Perspective on Canada's Economy.* Toronto: C.D. Howe Institute. http://www.cdhowe.org/pdf/commentary_246.pdf.

Howlett, Michael, and Michael Ramesh. 2003. *Studying Public Policy: Policy Cycles and Policy Subsystems*. Toronto: Oxford University Press.

Hull, C.J., and Benny Hjern. 1987. *Helping Small Firms Grow: An Implementation Approach*. New York: Croom Helm, in association with Methuen.

Hutchison, T.W. 1981. *The Politics and Philosophy of Economics: Marxians, Keynesians, and Austrians*. New York: New York University Press.

Hysing, E. 2009. "From Government to Governance? A Comparison of Environmental Governing in Swedish Forestry and Transport." *Governance* 22 (4): 647–72.

Industry Canada. 1987. http://www.ic.gc.ca/eic/site/ic1.nsf/eng/00132.html#fednor. See also http://www.parl.gc.ca/Content/LOP/ResearchPublications/2011-05-e.htm.

– *Performance Report for the Period Ending March 31, 1997*. http://www.ic.gc.ca/eic/site/ic1.nsf/eng/h_00226.html.

– *Performance Report 1998–1999*. http://www.ic.gc.ca/eic/site/ic1.nsf/eng/h_00226.html.

– 2000. *Technology Partnerships Canada: Investing In Our Future, Annual Report 2000–2001*. http://www.ic.gc.ca/eic/site/ic1.nsf/eng/h_02955.html?Open&c=18#itm18.

– 2002. *Government Response to the Tenth Report of the Standing Committee on Industry, Science and Technology*. http://www.ic.gc.ca/eic/site/ic1.nsf/eng/h_02955.html?Open&c=12#itm12.

– 2005. *Technology Partnerships Canada 2004–2005: Year in Review – Building Canada's Future*. http://www.ic.gc.ca/eic/site/ic1.nsf/eng/h_02955.html?Open&c=18#itm18.

– 2007. *Mobilizing Science and Technology to Canada's Advantage*. http://www.ic.gc.ca/eic/site/ic1.nsf/eng/h_00231.html.

– 2008a. *State of the Nation 2008 – Canada's Science, Technology and Innovation System* . http://www.ic.gc.ca/eic/site/ic1.nsf/eng/h_02955.html?Open&c=12#itm12.

– 2008b. http://www.ic.gc.ca/eic/site/ic1.nsf/eng/h_00226.html.

– 2008c. "Mid-Term Evaluation of the Northern Ontario Development Program (NODP) Final Report," http://www.ic.gc.ca/eic/site/ae-ve.nsf/eng/02859.html.

– 2009a. *Supporting Culture and Innovation: Report on the Provisions and Operation of the Copyright Act 20*. http://www.ic.gc.ca/eic/site/ic1.nsf/eng/h_02955.html?Open&c=12#itm12.

– 2009b. *Work That Matters*. http://www.ic.gc.ca/eic/site/ic1.nsf/eng/04525.html.

– *Performance Reports*. 2009–2010. http://www.ic.gc.ca/eic/site/ic1.nsf/eng/h_00226.html.

– Report on Plans and Priorities. 1998–1999. http://www.ic.gc.ca/eic/site/ic1.nsf/eng/h_00227.html.

– Report on Plans and Priorities. 2009–10. *Industry Canada Three-Year Plan for Transfer Payment Programs*. http://www.ic.gc.ca/eic/site/ic1.nsf/eng/h_00227.html.

– Report on Plans and Priorities. 2010–11. http://www.ic.gc.ca/eic/site/ic1.nsf/eng/h_00227.html.

– Business Plan. 2010–2011. http://www.ic.gc.ca/eic/site/ic1.nsf/eng/h_04341.html.

Information Tools for Marketing and Planning – Tourism Volume, Value and Characteristics in Northern Ontario: Canadian and International Travel Surveys (2002). 2005 http://www.ic.gc.ca/eic/site/ic1.nsf/eng/h_02955.html?Open&c=16#itm16.

Information Tools: Marketing and Planning – Tourism Volume, Value and Characteristics in Northern Ontario 2009. http://www.ic.gc.ca/eic/site/ic1.nsf/eng/h_02955.html?Open&c=16#itm16.

Innis, Harold Adams. 1956. *Essays in Canadian Economic History*. Toronto: University of Toronto Press.

Jevons, William Stanley. 1970. *The Theory of Political Economy*. Harmondsworth: Penguin.

Jreisat, J.E. 2002. *Comparative Public Administration and Policy*. Oxford: Westview.

Keast, Robyn, Myrna P. Mandell, Kerry Brown, and Geoffrey Woolcock. 2004. "Network Structures: Working Differently and Changing Expectations." *Public Administration Review* 64 (3): 363–71.

Kernaghan, Kenneth. 2005. "CAPAM Symposium on Networked Government." *International Review of Administrative Sciences* 71 (3): 445–6.

– "Moving towards Integrated Public Governance: Improving Service Delivery through Community Engagement." *International Review of Administrative Sciences* 75 (2): 239–54.

Kernaghan, Kenneth, D.B. Marson, and Sanford Borins. 2000. *The New Public Organization*. Toronto: Institute of Public Administration of Canada.

Kettl, Donald F. 1990. "The Perils – and Prospects – of Public Administration." *Public Administration Review* 50(4): 411–19.

– 2000. "Public Administration at the Millennium: The State of the Field." *Journal of Public Administration Research and Theory* 10 (1): 7–34.

Kickert, W.J.M. 1993. "Steering at a Distance: A New Paradigm of Public Governance in Dutch Higher Education." *Governance* 8 (1): 135.

– 1997. *Managing Complex Networks: Strategies for the Public Sector*. London: Sage.

King, J. E. 2002. *A History of post-Keynesian Economics since 1936*. Cheltenham, England: E. Elgar.

Klijn, E.-H. 1996. "Analyzing and Managing Policy Processes in Complex Networks: A Theoretical Examination of the Concept Policy Network and Its Problems." *Administration & Society* 28(1): 90.

– 2008. "Complexity Theory and Public Administration: What's New?" *Public Management Review* 10(3): 299–317.

Klijn, E.-H., and G. Teisman. 2008. "Complexity Theory and Public Management." *Public Management Review* 10 (3): 287–97.

Kooiman, J. 2000. "Societal Governance: Levels, Models and Orders of Social-Political Interaction." In J. Pierre, ed., *Debating Governance*. New York: Oxford University Press.

– 2003. *Governing as Governance*. Thousand Oaks, CA: Sage.

– 2006. *Governing as Governance*. London: Sage.

Koppenjan, Johannes Franciscus Maria, and Erik-Hans Klijn. 2004. *Managing Uncertainties in Networks: A Network Approach to Problem Solving and Decision Making*. London: Routledge.

Kosonen, K. 2007. "On Strengthening the Knowledge Base of Knowledge-Intensive SMEs in Less Favoured Regions in Finland." In P. Cooke and D. Schwartz, eds., *Creative Regions: Technology, Culture and Knowledge Entrepreneurship*. Hoboken: Taylor & Francis.

Krasnick, Mark R. 1986. *Perspectives on the Canadian Economic Union*. Toronto: University of Toronto Press.

Krasnick, M., and Royal Commission on the Economic Union and Development Prospects for Canada. 1986. *Fiscal Federalism*. Toronto: University of Toronto Press.

Krugman, Paul R. 1990. *Increasing Returns and Economic Geography*. Cambridge, MA: National Bureau of Economic Research.

– 1991. "Increasing Returns and Economic Geography." *Journal of Political Economy*. 99 (3): 483–99.

– 1994. *Urban Concentration: The Role of Increasing Returns and Transport Costs*. Washington: World Bank.

Krugman, Paul R., and Anthony Venables. 1993. "Integration, Specialization, and Adjustment." Cambridge, MA: National Bureau of Economic Research.

Kurz, Heinz-Dieter. 2011. *Innovation, Knowledge and Growth: Adam Smith, Schumpeter and the Moderns*. New York: Routledge.

Leiva, Fernando Ignacio. 2008. *Latin American Neostructuralism the Contradictions of Post-Neoliberal Development*. Minneapolis: University of Minnesota Press. http://public.eblib.com/EBLPublic/PublicView.do?ptiID=433186.

Lewis, B.L., J. Boulahanis, E. Matheny. 2009. "Joined-up Governance: Mandated Collaboration in US Homeless Services." *International Journal of Public Sector Management* 22 (5): 392–9.

Lewis, Jenny, Mark Considine, and Damon Alexander. 2011. *Networks, Innovation and Public Policy: Politicians, Bureaucrats and the Pathways to Change inside Government*. Basingstoke, England: Palgrave Macmillan.

Liddle, J. 2009. "The Northern Way: A Pan-Regional Associational Network." *International Journal of Public Sector Management* 22 (3): 192–202.

Linder, S.H., and B.G. Peters. 1987. "A Design Perspective on Policy Implementation: The Fallacies of Misplaced Prescription. *Policy Studies Review* 6 (3). 459–75.

Lindquist, Evert. 2006. "Organizing for Policy Implementation: The Emergence and Role of Implementation Units in Policy Design and Oversight." *Journal of Comparative Policy Analysis: Research and Practice* 8 (4): 311–24.

– 2009. "Public Administration Research and Organization Theory: Recovering Alternative Perspectives on Public Service Institutions." In O.P. Dwivedi, B.M. Sheldrick, T.A Mau, and J.E. Hodgetts, eds., *The Evolving Physiology of Government: Canadian Public Administration in Transition*. Ottawa: University of Ottawa Press.

Loorbach, Derk A. 2007. *Transition Management: New Mode of Governance for Sustainable Development*. Utrecht, the Netherlands : International Books.

Loxley, John, and Jim Silver. 2007. "Community Economic Development: An Introduction." In John Loxley, Jim Silver, and Kathleen Sexsmith, eds., *Doing Community Economic Development*. Halifax, NS: Fernwood.

Lucas, R. 1988. "On the Mechanics of Economic Development." *Journal of Monetary Economics* 22, 3–42.

Mackenzie, Michael, Byron Sheldrick, and Jim Silver. 2010. *State Policies to Enhance the New Economy: A Comparative Perspective*. http://www.policy.ca/policy-directory/Detailed/State-Policies-to-Enhance-the-New-Economy_-A-Comparative-Perspective-750.html.

MacNeil, Teresa. 1994. "Building Multi-Community Rural development Partnerships." In *Development Strategies for Rural Canada: Evaluating Partnerships, Jobs, and Communities, Proceedings from the Fifth Annual ARRG Conference, 13–16 October 1993*. Wolfville, NS: ARRG Working Papers Series No. 6.

Mair, Douglas, and Anne Miller. 1991. *A Modern Guide to Economic Thought: An Introduction to Comparative Schools of Thought in Economics*. Aldershot, England: E. Elgar.

Mandell, Myrna, and Robin Keast. 2008. "Evaluating the Effectiveness of Interorganizational Relations through Networks." *Public Management Review* 10 (6): 715–31.

Manitoba Innovation Framework. 2003. http://www.manitoba.ca/iem/innovation/infotech.html.

– 2009. http://www.gov.mb.ca/stem/innovation/index.html.

Maritimes Union Study. 1989. *Standing Up to the Future: The Maritimes in the 1990s*. A Report to the Council of Maritime Premiers.

Marx, Karl, and Friedrich Engels. 1848. *The Communist Manifesto*. New York: Washington Square Press (reprinted 1967).

– 1867. *Capital*. Chicago: Encyclopaedia Britannica (reprinted 1952).

Matland, R.E. 1995. "Synthesizing the Implementation Literature: The Ambiguity-Conflict Model of Policy Implementation." *Journal of Public Administration Research and Theory*: J-PART 5 (2): 145–74.

Mawson, J. 2007. "Regional Governance in England: Past Experience, Future Directions?" *International Journal of Public Sector Management* 20 (6): 548–66.

Mazmanian, D.A., and P.A. Sabatier. 1981. "Effective Policy Implementation." Lexington, MA: Lexington Books.

McGee, Harley. 1995. *Getting It Right: Regional Development in Canada*. Montreal: McGill-Queen's University Press.

McGillivray, Brett. 2007. *Canada : A Nation of Regions*. Don Mills, ON: Oxford University Press. Canadian Institute for Research on Regional Development. 2003. *Innovation in Atlantic Canada*. ACOA Research Study, March 2003. http://www.acoa-apeca.gc.ca/English/publications/ResearchStudies/Pages/home.aspx#innovation.

McMillan, Charles. 2006. *Embracing the Future the Atlantic Gateway and Canada's Trade Corridor*. A study prepared for the Asia Pacific Foundation of Canada, sponsored by the Atlantic Canada Opportunities Agency and CN Rail. Moncton, NB: Atlantic Canada Opportunities Agency.

McNiven, J.D., and J.E. Plumstead. 1998. *Comparative Perspective on Regional Development*. Prepared for the Atlantic Canada Opportunities Agency.

McSweeney, Erik. 2011. " Regional Economic Planning: What the Research Has Revealed. " ThinkNorth II Summit, Organized by the Ministry of Northern Development, Mines, and Forestry (MNDMF). Sudbury and Thunder Bay, Ontario. June 2011

Meier, Gerald M. 1994. *From Classical Economics to Development Economics*. London: Macmillan.

Melvin, James R. 1987. "Regional Inequalities in Canada: Underlying Causes and Policy Implications." *Canadian Public Policy* 13 (3): 304–17.

Menger, Carl. 1950. *Principles of Economics: First, General Part*. Glencoe, IL: Free Press.

Merton, Robert. 1949. *Social Theory and Social Structure*. New York: Free Press.

Ministry of Finance (Canada). 2006. *Advantage Canada: Building a Strong Economy for Canadians*. Ottawa.

Mintz, J. M., and M. Smart. 2003. *Brooking No Favorites: A New Approach to Regional Development in Atlantic Canada*. Toronto: C.D. Howe Institute.

Mintzberg, Henry. 1996. *Managing Government Governing Management*. Boston, MA: Harvard Business Review.

Mitchell, Wesley C. 1967. *Types of Economic Theory: From Mercantilism to Institutionalism*. New York: A.M. Kelley.

MNDMF. 2010. *Annual Report*. http://www.mndmf.gov.on.ca/about/annual_report_e.asp.

Nelles, H.V. 2005. *The Politics of Development: Forests, Mines and Hydro-electric Power in Ontario, 1849–1941*. Montreal: McGill-Queen's University Press.

New Brunswick Regional Development Corporation. 2010. Regional Development Corporation. An Action Plan for Self-Sufficiency in Northern New Brunswick. http://www2.gnb.ca/content/gnb/en/departments/regional_development/action_plan/an_action_plan_for_self-sufficiency_in_northern_new_brunswick.html.

Newman, J. 2006. "Joined-Up Government: The Politics of Partnership." In L. Budd, R. Paton, and J. Charlesworth, eds., *Making Policy Happen*. New York: Routledge.

Nishnawbe Aski Nation. 2009. http://www.nan.on.ca/.

Nonaka, Ikujirô, and Hirotaka Takeuchi. 1995. *The Knowledge-Creating Company: How Japanese Companies Create the Dynamics of Innovation*. New York: Oxford University Press.

Norrie, K.H., and Doug Owram. 1996. *A History of the Canadian Economy*. Toronto: Harcourt Brace Canada.

North, Douglas C., Y.S. Brenner, J.D. Gould, and A.J. Youngson. 1975. "Review of *A Short History of Economic Progress*." *Journal of Economic History* 35 (4): 844–6.

Northeastern Ontario Chambers of Commerce. 2009. http://www.nocc.ca/.

Northern Ontario Growth Plan. 2011. https://www.placestogrow.ca/index.php?option=com_content&task=view&id=53&Itemid=65.

Northwestern Ontario Association of Chambers of Commerce. 2009. http://www.noacc.ca/.

Northwestern Ontario Municipal Association. 2000. "Strategic Goals." http://www.noma.on.ca/article/mission-vision-core-values-and-guiding-principles-155.asp.

– 2007. Enhancing the Economy of Northwestern Ontario. www.noma.on.ca/pdf/Enhancing%20the%20Economy%20of%20NWO%20%20Jan.

OECD. 1997. *Regional Competitiveness and Skills*. Paris: OECD.

– 2007a. *Linking Regions and Central Governments: Contracts for Regional Development*. Paris: OECD.

– 2007b. *Higher Education and Regions: Globally Competitive, Locally Engaged*. http://www.acoa-apeca.gc.ca/English/publications/ResearchStudies/Pages/home.aspx.

– 2009. "Investing for Growth: Building Innovation Regions." Meeting of the Territorial Development Policy Committee. http://www.oecd.org/ document/27/0,3343,en_2649_33735_33711480_1_1_1_1,00.html.

Ontario's Ministry of Economic Development and Trade (MEDT). 2011. http://www.ontariocanada.com/ontcan/1medt/en/about_main_en.jsp.

Ontario Ministry of Research and Innovation. 2011. http://www.mri.gov.on.ca/english/programs/default.asp.

Osborne, Stephen. 2010. "Delivering Public Services: Time for a New Theory." *Public Management Review* 12 (1): 1–10.

O'Toole, Laurence J., Jr. 1986. "Policy Recommendations for Multi-Actor Implementation: An Assessment of the Field." *Journal of Public Policy* 6(2): 181–210.

– 1997. Treating Networks Seriously: Practical and Research-Based Agendas in Public Administration. *Public Administration Review* 57(1): 45–52.

– 2000. "Research on Policy Implementation: Assessment and Prospects." *Journal of Public Administration Research and Theory* 10(2): 263.

– 2007. "Inter-organizational relations in implementation." In *Handbook of Public Administration*, edited by B. Guy Peters and Jon Pierre. Thousand Oaks, CA: Sage Publications.

O'Toole, L.J., Jr, and K.J. Meier. 1999. "Modelling the Impact of Public Management: Implications of Structural Context." *Journal of Public Administration Research and Theory* 9(4): 505–26.

Pal, L.A. 2006. *Beyond Policy Analysis: Public Issue Management in Turbulent Times*. Scarborough, ON: ITP Nelson.

Palumbo, Dennis James, D.J. Calista, and Policy Studies Organization, eds. 1990. *Implementation and the Policy Process: Opening Up the Black Box*. New York: Greenwood Press.

Parsons, Craig. 2007. *How to Map Arguments in Political Science*. Oxford: Oxford University Press.

Peet, Richard, and Elaine R. Hartwick. 2009. *Theories of Development: Contentions, Arguments, Alternatives*. New York: Guilford Press.

Perroux, François. 1961. *L'Économie du XXe siècle*. Paris: Presses universitaires de France.

Peters, B. Guy. 2001. *The Future of Governing : Four Emerging Models*. Lawrence: University Press of Kansas.

Peters, B. Guy, and Pierre, Jon. 2000. *Governance, Politics, and the State*. New York: St Martin's Press.

– 2003. *Handbook of Public Administration*. London: Sage Publications.

Petras, J.F., and H. Veltmeyer. 2003. *Cardoso's Brazil: A Land for Sale*. Lanham, MD: Rowman & Littlefield.

Pierre, Jon. 2000. *Debating Governance*. New York: Oxford University Press.

Pierre, Jon, and B. Guy Peters 2005. *Governing Complex Societies: Trajectories and Scenarios*. New York: Palgrave Macmillan.

Polese, Mario. 1999. *From Regional Development to Local Development: On The Life, Death and Rebirth of Regional Science as a Policy Relevant Science*. http://dev.hil.unb.ca/Texts/CJRS/bin/get.cgi?directory=Autumn99/&filename=Polese.htm.

Policy Research Initiative. 2006. *The Emergence of Cross-Border Regions between Canada and the United States: Roundtable Synthesis Report, May 2006*. http://www.acoa-apeca.gc.ca/English/publications/Research-Studies/Pages/home.aspx.

Pollitt, Christopher. 2007. "Towards a New Public Administration Theory." *International Review of Administrative Sciences* 73 (1): 37–41.

Porter, Michael E. 1990. *The Competitive Advantage of Nations*. New York: Free Press.

– 1998a. "Clusters and Competition: New Agenda for Companies, Governments, and Institutions" In Michael Porter, ed., *On Competition*. Boston, MA: Harvard Businesss School Publication.

– 1998b. *On Competition*. Boston: Harvard Business School Press.

– 2000. "Location, Competition, and Economic Development: Local Clusters in a Global Economy." *Economic Development Quarterly* 14 (1): 15–34.

– 2001. "Regions and the New Economics of Competition." In A.J. Scott, ed., *Global City-Regions: Trends, Theory, Policy*. Oxford: Oxford University Press, 139–57.

Pressman, Jeffrey, and Aaron Wildavsky. 1973. *Implementation: How Great Expectations in Washington Are Dashed in Oakland; or, Why It's Amazing That Federal Programs Work At All, This Being a Saga of the Economic Development Administration as Told by Two Sympathetic Observers Who Seek to Build Morals on a Foundation of Ruined Hopes*. Berkeley: University of California Press.

Public Policy Forum. 2007. *Improving Canada's Business Environment and Competitiveness*. http://www.ppforum.ca/publications/improving-canadas-business-environment-and-competitiveness.

Report of the Auditor General. 1995. *OAG 1995 November Report of the Auditor General of Canada*. www.oag-bvg.gc.ca/internet/English/parl_oag_199511_e_1155.html.

Rhodes, Rod A.W. 2000. "Governance and Public Administration." In Jon Pierre, ed., *Debating Governance*. Oxford and New York: Oxford University Press.

Romer, Paul M. 1986. "Increasing Returns and Long-Run Growth." *The Journal of Political Economy* 94 (5): 1002–37.

Rosehart Report. 2007. *Northwestern Ontario Preparing for Change*. www.mndm.gov.on.ca/nordev/documents/noef/REPORT_FEB2008.

Rosenbaum, Allan. 2006. "IASIA Symposium on Government Reform in an Era of Governance: Introduction." *International Review of Administrative Sciences* 72 (1): 9–10.

Rothstein, Bo. 2007. "Political Legitimacy for Public Administration." In Guy Peters and Jon Pierre, eds., *Handbook of Public Administration*. Thousand Oaks, CA: Sage Publications.

Rounds, Richard. 1994. "Policy Directions for Future Rural Development." Development Strategies for Rural Canada: Evaluating Partnerships, Jobs, and Communities, Proceedings from the Fifth Annual ARRG Conference, 13–16 October 1993, Wolfville, Nova Scotia. ARRG Working Papers Series No. 6.

Roy, Jeffrey. 2007. *Business and Government in Canada*. Ottawa: University of Ottawa Press.

Ruff, Norman J., Peter Aucoin, and Herman Bakvis. 1989. "Review of *The Centralization-Decentralization Conundrum: Organization and*

Management in the Canadian Government." Canadian Journal of Political Science / Revue Canadienne de Science Politique 22 (2): 404–5.

Rural Development Institute. 2005. *Immigration and Rural Canada: Research and Practice.* http://www.acoa-apeca.gc.ca/English/publications/ResearchStudies/Pages/home.aspx.

Sabatier, Paul A. 1986. "Top-down and Bottom-up Approaches to Implementation Research: A Critical Analysis and Suggested Synthesis." *Journal of Public Policy* 6(1): 21–48.

Sabatier, Paul A., and H.C. Jenkins-Smith. 1993. *Policy Change and Learning: An Advocacy Coalition Approach. Theoretical Lenses on Public Policy.* Boulder, CO: Westview Press.

Sabatier, Paul and Daniel Mazmanian. 1981. *Implementation and Public Policy.* Lanham, MD: University Press of America.

Sagini, M.M. 2007. *Strategic Planning and Management in Public Organizations: Behavior in Organizations.* Lanham, MD: University Press of America.

Sancton, Andrew. 2009. "Introduction." In Andrew Sancton and Robert Young, eds., *Foundations of Governance: Municipal Government in Canada's Provinces.* Toronto: University of Toronto Press.

Sancton, Andrew, and Robert Andrew Young. 2009. *Foundations of Governance: Municipal Government in Canada's Provinces.* Toronto: University of Toronto Press.

Savoie, Donald. 1981. *Federal-Provincial Collaboration: The Canada-New Brunswick General Development Agreement.* Montreal: McGill-Queen's University Press.

– 1986. *Regional Economic Development: Canada's Search for Solutions.* Toronto: University of Toronto Press.

– 1990. *The Politics of Public Spending in Canada.* Toronto: University of Toronto Press.

– 1992. *Regional Economic Development: Canada's Search for Solutions.* Toronto: University of Toronto Press.

– 1997. *Rethinking Canada's Regional Development Policy: An Atlantic Perspective.* Moncton, NB: Canadian Institute for Research on Regional Development/Institut canadien de recherche sur le developpement.

– 2001. *Pulling against Gravity: Economic Development in New Brunswick during the McKenna Years.* Montreal: Institute for Research on Public Policy.

– 2003. "Reviewing Canada's Regional Development Efforts." In *Royal Commission on Renewing and Strengthening Our Place in Canada*, St John's, NL.

– Scharpf, Fritz W. 1993. *Games in Hierarchies and Networks: Analytical and Empirical Approaches to the Study of Governance Institutions.* Boulder, CO: Westview Press.

Schofield, J. 2004. "A Model of Learned Implementation." *Public Administration* 82(2): 283–308.

Schulte-Mecklenbeck, Michael, Anton Kühberger, and Rob Ranyard. 2011. "A Handbook of Process Tracing Methods for Decision Research: A Critical Review and User's Guide." New York: Psychology Press.

Schumpeter, Joseph A. 1947. "The Creative Response in Economic History." *Journal of Economic History* 7 (2): 149–59.

Science Council of Canada. 1967. *Annual Report: Science Council of Canada.* Ottawa: Science Council of Canada.

– 1978. *Annual Report: Science Council of Canada.* Ottawa: Science Council of Canada.

Scott, Allen J. 2001a. *Global City-Regions: Trends, Theory, Policy.* Cambridge, UK: Oxford University Press.

– 2001b. "Industrial Revitalization in the ABC Municipalities, Sao Paulo: Diagnostic Analysis and Strategic Recommendations for a New Economy and a New Regionalism." *Regional Development Studies* 7:1–32.

Scott, Allen, and Michael Storper. 2003. "Regions, Globalization, Development." *Regional Studies* 6–7.

Segsworth, Robert. 2009. "How's It Going? Results Measurement and Economic Development in Northern Ontario, 1981–2006." Presented at a Workshop on Economic Development Policy in Northern Ontario, hosted at Laurentian University from 29–30 October 2009.

Selznick, Philip. 1984. *Leadership in Administration: A Sociological Interpretation.* Berkeley, CA: University of California Press.

Seok Eun Kim, and Gee Weon Chang. 2009. "An Empirical Analysis of Innovativeness in Government: Findings and Implications." *International Review of Administrative Sciences* 75(2): 293–310.

Siegel, David. 2010. "The Leadership Role of the Municipal Chief Administrative Officer." *Canadian Public Administration* 53 (2): 139–61.

Simeon, Richard, and Ian Robinson. 1990. State, Society, and the Development of Canadian Federalism. Toronto: University of Toronto Press.

Simeon, Richard. 2006. *Federal-Provincial Diplomacy: The Making of Recent Policy in Canada, with a New Preface and Postscript. Studies in the Structure of Power, Decision Making in Canada.* Toronto: University of Toronto Press.

Sinclair, T.A.P. 2001. "Implementation Theory and Practice: Uncovering Policy and Administration Linkages in the 1990s." *International Journal of Public Administration* 24, 77–94.

Skelcher, C., and H. Sullivan. 2008. "Theory-Driven Approaches to Analysing Collaborative Performance." *Public Management Review* 10 (6): 751–71.

Skousen, Mark. 2007. *The Big Three in Economics: Adam Smith, Karl Marx, and John Maynard Keynes*. Armonk, NY: M.E. Sharpe.

Smith, Adam, Edwin Cannan, and Max Lerner. 1937. *An Inquiry into the Nature and Causes of the Wealth of Nations*. New York: The Modern library.

Southcott, Chris. 2006. *The North in Numbers : A Demographic Analysis of Social and Economic Change in Northern Ontario*. Thunder Bay, ON: Lakehead University, Centre for Northern Studies.

Southcott, Chris, and Stephen McBride. 2003. *Provincial Hinterland: Social Inequality in Northwestern Ontario*. Halifax, NS: Fernwood.

Sproule-Jones, Mark. 2000. "Horizontal Management: Implementing Programs across Interdependent Organizations." *Canadian Public Administration* 43: 92–109.

Steiner, M., ed. 1998. *Clusters and Regional Specialisation*. London: Pion.

Stiglitz, Joseph. 2002. *Globalization and its Discontents*. London: Allen Lane/Penguin.

– 2006. *Stability with Growth: Macroeconomics, Liberalization and Development*. Oxford: Oxford University Press.

Stirati, Antonella. 1994. *The Theory of Wages in Classical Economics: A Study of Adam Smith, David Ricardo, and Their Contemporaries*. Aldershot, England: E. Elgar.

Stoker, Gary. 1998. "Governance as Theory: Five Propositions." *International Social Science Journal* 50 (1): 17–28.

– 2000. "Urban Political Science and the Challenge of Urban Governance." In J. Pierre, ed., *Debating Governance*. New York: Oxford University Press.

Stoker, R.P. 1991. *Reluctant Partners: Implementing Federal Policy*. Pittsburgh, PA: University of Pittsburgh Press.

"Strategic Outcomes for ACOA." 2009. http://www.tbs-sct.gc.ca/ppg-cpr/dep-min2-eng.aspx?Dt=9.

"Strategic Outcomes for WD." 2009. http://www.tbs-sct.gc.ca/ppg-cpr/dep-min2-eng.aspx?Dt=9.

"Strategies Used by WD to Advance Government-Wide Initiatives, such as Sustainable Development and Official Languages." http://www.wd.gc.ca/eng/15.asp

Sun, Laixiang. 1997. *Emergence of Unorthodox Ownership and Governance Structures in East Asia: An Alternative Transition Path*. Helsinki: UNU World Institute for Development Economics Research (UNU/WIDER).

Sustainable Development Technology Canada. 2010. *Cleantech Growth and Go-to-Market Report*.

Taylor, Frederick Winslow. 1967. *Scientific Management Comprising Shop Management: The Principles of Scientific Management*. New York: Harper.

Teisman, Geert, and Erik-Hans Klijn. 2008. "Complexity Theory and Public Management." *Public Management Review* 10 (3): 287–97.

Teisman, Geert, Arwin Buuren, and Lasse Gerrits. 2009. "An Introduction to Understanding and Managing Complex Process Systems." In Geert Teisman, Arwin Buuren, and Lasse Gerrits, eds., *Managing Complex Governance Systems*. Routledge Critical Studies in Public Management, 3. London: Routledge.

The First Atlantic Regional Research Money Conference. 2005. *Growing Technology Business in Atlantic Canada: Moncton, New Brunswick, 6 October 2005*. Conference Proceedings, Research Money Inc. http://www.acoa-apeca.gc.ca/English/publications/ResearchStudies/Pages/home.aspx.

Thompson, James D. 1967. *Organizations in Action: Social Science Bases of Administrative Theory*. New York: McGraw-Hill.

Timonen, Virpi. 2003. *Restructuring the Welfare State: Globalisation and Social Policy Reform in Finland and Sweden*. Cheltenham, UK: Edward Elgar.

Todaro, Michael P. 2001. *Economic Development*. New York: Longman.

Tompkins, Jonathan. 2005. *Organization Theory and Public Management*. Australia: Thomson Wadsworth.

Treasury Board Secretariat. 2009–10. *ACOA's Departmental Performance Reports*. http://www.tbs-sct.gc.ca/dpr-rmr/index-eng.asp.

Treib, O., H. Bahr, and G. Falkner. 2007. "Modes of Governance: Towards a Conceptual Clarification." *Journal of European Public Policy* 14 (1): 1–20.

Tubin, D., and M. Levin-Rozalis. 2008. "Interorganizational Cooperation: The Structural Aspect of Nurturing Trust." *International Journal of Public Sector Management* 21 (7): 704–22.

Van Meter, D.S., and C.E. Van Horn. 1975. "The Policy Implementation Process: A Conceptual Framework." *Administration & Society* 6(4): 445–88.

Walras, Léon. 1954. *Elements of Pure Economics; or, The Theory of Social Wealth*. London: Published for the American Economic Association and the Royal Economic Association and the Royal Economic Society by Allen and Unwin.

Wamsley, Gary, and Mayer Zald. 1973. *The Political Economy of Public Organizations: A Critique and Approach to the Study of Public Administration*. Lexington, MA: Lexington Books.

Watkins, Thayer. 2010. *The Economic History and Regional Economic Policy of Canada*. http://www.sjsu.edu/faculty/watkins/canada.htm.

WD's Audit of Regional Operations: Manitoba Region. 2010. http://www.wd.gc.ca/eng/60.asp.

WD's Corporate Business Plan. 2010. http://www.wd.gc.ca/eng/59.asp.

WD's Departmental Performance Reports. 2004–05. Treasury Board of Canada Secretariat, 2004–5 – Departmental Performance Reports (DPR). http://www.tbs-sct.gc.ca/dpr-rmr/index-eng.asp.

– 2009–10. Treasury Board of Canada Secretariat, 2009–10: Departmental Performance Reports (DPR). http://www.tbs-sct.gc.ca/dpr-rmr/index-eng.asp.

WD's Departmental Strategy. 2009. http://www.wd.gc.ca/eng/15.asp.

WD's Report on Plans and Priorities. 2011–12. Treasury Board of Canada Secretariat, 2011–12: Reports on Plans and Priorities. http://www.tbs-sct.gc.ca/rpp/2011–2012/index-eng.asp.

WD's Research and Market Studies. 2007. *Impact Study of WD's Investments in Western Canada's Life Sciences Cluster*. Source: Price Waterhouse Coopers LLP (September 2007). http://www.wd.gc.ca/eng/56.asp.

– 2008. *Strategic Investments: Western Canadian Attitudes about Government and the Economy*. http://www.wd.gc.ca/eng/56.asp.

– 2009a. *Innovation: Impact Assessment of the Technology Adoption and Commercialization and Knowledge Infrastructure Sub-Activities of the Innovation Component of the Western Diversification Program*. http://www.wd.gc.ca/eng/56.asp.

– 2009b. *Efficient Cities: The Interrelationship between Effective Rapid Transit Systems and the Optimal Utilization of Land Use Entitlements*. http://www.wd.gc.ca/eng/56.asp.

– 2010. *Tomorrow's Gateways: Value Capture Strategies in Key Sectors and Potential for Foreign Direct Investment in Western Canada*. IE Market Research Corporation. http://www.wd.gc.ca/eng/56.asp.

WD's Research and Market Studies. *Reaching Out: Exploring SME Exporting Opportunities and Challenges.* http://www.wd.gc.ca/eng/56.asp.

– *Western Canada – Where the Spirit of Innovation Meets a World of Opportunity.* http://www.wd.gc.ca/eng/56.asp.

WD's Western Canadian Fact Sheets. 2011. http://www.wd.gc.ca/eng/58.asp.

Weber, Max. 1964. *The Theory of Social and Economic Organization.* London: The Free Press of Glencoe.

Webster, Douglas. 2002 "Regional Development Planning." *The Canadian Encyclopedia.* http://www.thecanadianencyclopedia.com/index.cfm?PgNm=TCE&Params=A1ARTA0006746.

Western Centre for Economic Research. 2004. *A Primer on Western Canadian Entrepreneurship.* http://www.wd.gc.ca/eng/56.asp.

– 2006. *Revisiting Portraits of Small Business Growth and Employment in Western Canada* http://www.wd.gc.ca/eng/56.asp.

White, Paul, S. Levine, and G.J. Vlasak. 1973. "Exchange as a Conceptual Framework for Understanding Inter-organizational Relationships: Applications to Nonprofit Organizations." In A.R. Negandhi, ed., *Modern Organizational Theory: Contextual, Environmental, and Sociocultural Variables.* Kent, OH: Kent State University Press.

Wilkins, Joy. 2011. "Preparing for the Future: Labour Market and Population Planning." ThinkNorth II Summit, Organized by the Ministry of Northern Development, Mines, and Forestry (MNDMF). Sudbury and Thunder Bay, Ontario. June 2011.

Williamson, O. E., and S.E. Masten. 1995. *Theory and Concepts.* Vol. 1 of *Transaction Cost Economics.* The International Library of Critical Writings in Economics, 54. Aldershot, England: Edward Elgar.

Winter, Soren. 1990. "Integrating Implementation Research." In D.J. Palumbo and D.J. Calista, eds., *Implementation and the Policy Process: Opening Up the Black Box.* New York: Greenwood Press.

– 2007. "Implementation Perspectives: Status and Reconsideration." In B.G. Peters and J. Pierre, eds., *Handbook of Public Administration.* Thousand Oaks, CA: Sage Publications.

World Bank. 2000. *World Development Report 2000.* Washington, DC: World Bank.

2009. *World Development Report 2009: Reshaping Economic Geography.* Washington, DC: World Bank.

Young-Hyman, Trevor. 2008. "The Potential for Effective Regional Development Agencies in Turkey: A Comparative Analysis." *Regional & Federal Studies* 18(4): 375–402.

Index